STO

5·15·78

The Energy Connections: Between Energy and the Economy

The Energy Connections: Between Energy and the Economy

Sidney Sonenblum

Ballinger Publishing Company • Cambridge, Massachusetts
A Subsidiary of Harper & Row, Publishers, Inc.

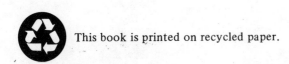

Copyright © 1978 by Ballinger Publishing Company. All rights reserved. No part of this publication may be reproduced, stored in a retrieval system, or transmitted in any form or by any means, electronic mechanical photocopy, recording or otherwise, without the prior written consent of the publisher.

International Standard Book Number: 0-88410-076-6

Library of Congress Catalog Card Number: 78-15374

Printed in the United States of America

Library of Congress Cataloging in Publication Data

Sonenblum, Sidney, 1924-
  The energy connections.

  1. Energy policy—United States. 2. United States—Economic policy—1971-
3. Energy consumption. 4. Economic development. I. Title.
HD9502.U52S62   330.9'73'092   78-15374
ISBN 0-88410-076-6

To Barbara and Michael and Yonosan

Contents

List of Figures

List of Empirical Highlights

List of Appendix Tables

Preface

The question of how energy relates to economic growth goes to the core of the formulation of the energy policy of the United States. It is in many ways a highly technical issue. But it is not the sole province of the technicians. I have tried, in this small, nontechnical volume, to describe the major perspectives on economic growth and the role of energy in that growth. It is out of these perspectives that national energy policy will eventually emerge.

The title to this volume has been adapted from an article by Sam Schurr and Joel Darmstadter. I am grateful to them not only for the title but also because their written works are an invaluable guide to the subject matter covered in this book.

Part of the research undertaken for this report was supported by the California State Energy Commission while I was research Professor at the University of California, Los Angeles.

More significant support was provided by my wife, Barbara Biggs, throughout the evolution and completion of this book.

The Energy Connections: Between Energy and the Economy

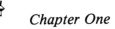 *Chapter One*

Policy Characteristics of the Energy Connection

If the current energy debate were only about energy it is unlikely that passions would run so high. But the debate is also about economic growth—its impact on society and how energy helps such growth to speed up or slow down. These added issues raise the specters of deprivation in living standards and destruction of the environment, and force us to examine our ideas about the nature of the good society.

Although it is now cloaked in the crisis language of the seventies, this debate is not new and its history provides some of the rationale for current energy policy. Out of this debate has emerged a number of conflicting views relating to the desirability of economic growth, the relationship between economic growth and energy use, the effects of energy usage in limiting or expanding the opportunities for growth, and whether there is some sense in which energy is being wasted—and if so, how?

Analyses provide no clear-cut answers to the questions raised by these issues. However, people have strong and disparate feelings about them, and it is these feelings, at least as much as their analytic base, that have become the crucible in which energy policy is being forged.

High levels of employment, growing standards of living, and reduction of poverty have generally been viewed as desirable and, for the past three decades, considered to be dependent upon an adequate rate of growth in economic activity. Until recently, although a central objective of economic policy has been to maintain or speed up the rate of national economic growth, the link between such growth and the supply or consumption of energy has not evoked major concern.

During the last decade, however, both the desirability and the feasibility of sustained economic growth have been called into question. These doubts have been encouraged by the accumulation of evidence that industrial societies have only a limited capacity to adapt the physical environment to their own purposes or to control the relationship between the physical and economic processes.

Energy is an important component of this new challenge to economic growth because it is perceived as increasingly difficult to obtain, its availability is unequally distributed, and its production and use are environmentally destructive. Because of these physical characteristics of the energy resource, some observers have argued that increased energy consumption will have such undesirable environmental and social consequences that maintaining historical rates of economic growth is an unsuitable objective for any humane society. Furthermore, it is claimed, increased energy consumption will make the conditions for obtaining adequate supplies so stringent that sustained economic growth is not even a feasible objective for a mature society.

The recent revival of interest in the damaging effects of economic growth serves as a reminder that there always have been those who have questioned its desirability as well as those who have advocated its pursuit. These competing views of economic growth have, in turn, evoked a dual image of energy. The Dr. Jekyl—or enabling—image pictures energy as the servant of civilization nobly working to release people from drudgery, while selflessly providing increasing levels of material well-being. The Mr. Hyde—or disabling—image is that of energy as a saboteur of civilization, pandering to the baser instincts of people while destroying the environment and consuming the patrimony of future generations.

Both the enabling and disabling images highlight the dependence of economic growth on increasing energy use. The enabling school of thought points out that the expanded use of energy is essential to the progress of civilization because "the process of economic development is in effect the process of utilizing more energy to increase the productivity and efficiency of human labor and in fact one of the best indications of the wealth of the human population is the amount of energy it consumes per person" [61, p. 71]. On the other side, the disabling school of thought fears that continued tapping of energy resources will cause the demise of civilization since "the same ingenious contrivances that extend our view, that speed our travel and multiply our strength in beneficial pursuits, are equally potent to destroy" [75, p. 51].

Taken one step further, the disabling image pictures some threshold range of energy consumption that, if exceeded, will result in social and physical deterioration. The increasing rate of per capita energy consumption, coupled with world population growth, has now brought the threshold level much closer in time so that the disabling consequences of energy use represent a real and not merely theoretical threat. This belief in the imminence of reaching some threshold level of energy consumption is based on the view that the economic process is anchored to the world's energy base, and this base is subject to necessary physical constraints. These constraints are that energy use degrades the environment and reduces the available energy stock, thereby lowering the amount of energy still remaining to do work. From this physical viewpoint energy usage transforms low entropy into high entropy; that is, energy usage—which converts valuable natural resources (low entropy) into waste (high entropy)—is ultimately disabling.

But the "waste" produced through energy usage includes not only environmental degradation but also those goods and services that contribute to the enjoyment of life. The very purpose of the economic process is to create "waste" through the provision of goods and services. Thus, for the economist—whether or not the economist perceives the economic process as having its roots in the energy base—the key issues are posed in terms of the enabling consequences of energy usage. These raise the questions of how and to what extent the use of energy limits or promotes economic growth. Physicists and economists agree that potentially there are two kinds of limits—both of which occur because energy resources are transformed into "waste." The first is the limit relating to the availability of energy resources; the second is the limit imposed because energy consumption is environmentally destructive. There may be differences in judgment about how and at what speed these limits affect the economic process, but there is no debate about their economic and physical reality.

The other half of the picture is that energy usage may have a unique role in promoting economic growth. For example, it is one means by which mineral resource scarcities can be averted, since it is through the use of energy that lower-yield minerals can be obtained; it may be the key to overcoming food and fiber scarcities, since it is through energy and chemicals that the productivity of agricultural land is improved; and it is instrumental in overcoming the scarcities of other consumer goods, since it contributes to overall productivity improvements through the substitution of capital for labor. Thus it is for these very specific reasons that energy is especially important to economic growth—namely, its role as a substitute for minerals, agricultural land, and labor, all of which are perceived as being in scarce supply [7].

But what about energy resources themselves? Aren't they also in scarce supply? The typical physicist might respond to this question by saying that low-entropy resources are the ultimate scarcity since they are nonrenewable and essential to the economic process. However, for the typical economist there is no ultimate scarcity, there are only relative scarcities, in different degrees for specific items. A particular resource may be relatively scarce because there is only a finite amount available. The disabling consequences of imposing increasing demands on such a scarcity were dramatized by Malthus, for example, in his dismal forecasts of subsistence living standards resulting from combining limited agricultural land with a growing population. Or, a particular resource may be relatively scarce because it is exhaustible. The disabling consequences of "running out" were dramatized by Jevons in his prediction of the end of the industrial revolution as a result of the physical limits of coal deposits in England. Or, a particular resource may be relatively scarce because increasing its supply can be achieved only by diminishing its quality. Ricardo dramatized the disabling consequences of such scarcities in terms of the increasing costs they produced for a growing economy.

But even though particular resources of specified quality may become increasingly scarce, the notion that such a resource constraint must limit economic growth by no means necessarily follows. Substitutes, it is claimed, will be found for these specific scarcities. Such substitutes may come at higher costs, bringing with them diminishing returns, and the diminishing returns may be so severe that a substantial constraint on economic growth would be established. Yet this need not be the result if technological change and a properly functioning price system make possible less costly substitutes. The latter is indeed what seems to have happened in the past, and, until recently, the conventional judgment has been that it would continue to happen in the future.

These high hopes are based to a large extent on a theoretical view of economic processes that expects forces to be set in motion to respond effectively to scarcities of any particular resource. In this view the exhaustible characteristic of fossil fuels does not raise any special problems for economic theory. Like any other capital asset, the present value of an exhaustible resource is theoretically based on expectation of the future income that it will provide. Therefore, given the right assumptions, the market will first bring in the low-cost producers, only drawing in the high-cost producers when the former are depleted. As a consequence it is socially efficient not only to use low-cost deposits but to use them up, as well [89]. Even though the quantity of an exhaustible resource can only decrease over time it should be used up in accordance with the market processes.

This conventional theoretical view has become increasingly unacceptable to many, particularly those concerned with formulating energy policy. For only in theoretical models are estimates of future earnings of assets readily and accurately available. Estimating the future earnings of exhaustible resources is especially difficult, and relying on such estimates for energy policy is especially hazardous. It is only in theoretical models, furthermore, that substitutes are always available for scarce resources. There is nothing in the facts of the physical universe to guarantee the existence of such substitutes.

There are those who believe that exhaustible resources do have a special social significance and should not be used up heedlessly, even if they are low in cost: "Nonrenewable goods must be used only if they are indispensable, and then only with the greatest care and the most meticulous concern for conservation" [23, p. 237]. And there are those who believe that energy usage is perversely related to social efficiency. To them, energy use is not a measure of progress but of destruction: "The level of energy consumption is probably the best index of the amount of damage that an individual or a society is doing to the environment. Indeed, energy use is central to nearly every kind of environmental impact from human activities" [32, p. 40]. Environmental degradation lowers the quality of living for present as well as future generations by polluting the environment and reducing the places of natural beauty available for solitude and recreation. What substitutes can technology make available for these amenities?

The ecologically-minded and the resource scarcity-minded end up in the same place. If they belong to the disabling school of thought, then growth should be limited because of impending ecological disaster, or it will be limited by pending resource scarcities. If they belong to the enabling school of thought, technological and social innovations will enable growth to continue without disaster.

The extremism sometimes associated with the current energy debate occurs when only one or the other of these images is being projected. More sober discussions accept the potential reality of both while debating the relative importance of each. Current policy in the United States seems to embrace both images and to focus on creating incentives designed to conserve energy in those uses that are destructive, while expanding the energy base for productive uses.

Although this requires an overall policy that includes both energy conservation and energy expansion incentives, the specific mix will be influenced greatly by whether or not economic growth is perceived as being significantly and substantially dependent on increased energy usage.[1] If the link between economic growth and energy consumption is significant and substantial, it can be labeled an *alpha connection*; if it is not, then it can be called a *beta connection*. Whether history supports an alpha or a beta connection is a matter of dispute; which of these connections applies to the future is still more a matter of conjecture. Those who favor an alpha connection generally perceive energy as if it were a causeway in the channel for economic growth; those who lean toward a beta connection see energy as a source of growth.

Perceived as a source of growth (the beta-connection view), energy is counted as just one among a number of growth determinants; and these other determinants are considered to be quantitatively more important to growth. Irrespective of what happens to energy, these other determinants—including such factors as more capital, higher quality labor, advances in knowledge, economies of scale, and improved management—will continue to raise the level of economic activity. Furthermore, the economic structure is such that these other factors will easily substitute for the energy input when reduced availability of energy makes this necessary. From this view, even if the conditions for obtaining energy became increasingly unfavorable, economic growth would not stop or even slow down significantly. Conversely, favorable conditions of energy supply would not be heralded as a primary cause of the nation's economic growth.

When perceived as a causeway for growth (the alpha-connection view), energy makes it possible for investment to be productive, technology to advance, and labor efficiency to improve. Energy, therefore, is credited with the contributions to growth made by these other factors. Since energy is unique in this respect, substitutes for energy are not readily available. From this view energy usage would need to increase—the causeway would need to be widened—if total output in the economy is to grow. Conversely, if the energy causeway gets clogged, growth becomes extremely difficult to achieve.[2]

---

1. A significant and substantial link indicates that the feedback from energy usage to the overall economy is important; a reduction in energy use, for instance, will lead to a nontrivial decline in the total output of the economy.

2. Using less metaphorical and more technical terminology, the alpha connection implies that energy's share in the total value of output is high, or that the elasticity of substitution for energy is small. The beta connection implies a small value share and a high elasticity of substitution. It is generally agreed that the

Views as to whether there is an alpha or a beta connection generally are supported with reference to the long-term historical record of energy consumption. They generally are based, however, on particular standards of what "truly" constitutes economic growth and on particular paradigms of how the growth process "really works."

The historical record indicates that there is an interaction between energy and the economy in which economic growth has promoted increased energy consumption, while energy consumption has, in turn, influenced the pace and consumption of economic growth. For most of this century, policy has been focused on the first part of this connection, and the dominating concern has been whether energy resources would be adequate to meet the requirements imposed by a growing economy. Only recently, as increasingly unfavorable conditions surround the supply of energy, has it become important to consider the second part of the connection, which raises the issue of whether the increasing use of energy limits economic growth or fosters it.

Whether energy is considered to be growth-limiting or growth-inducing may depend on how the growth process itself is being perceived. There are four important channels for growth as it relates to energy. In one channel economic growth is reached through "recovery"—that is, filling the gap between actual and potential output of an economy by putting unemployed resources to work. In a second channel economic growth is achieved through "expansion"—that is, raising the economy's long-run capacity to produce. In a third channel economic growth means "development"—that is, fundamentally transforming the economic structure through changes in technology, trade patterns, working conditions, and methods of resource allocation. In a fourth channel economic growth means "progress"—that is, introducing processes which assure that changes in the nation's product contribute to the ultimate aims of society and human welfare.

The statistical record suggests that the energy connection is different in each of these channels for economic growth. The growth-limiting impact of rising energy costs is most striking from the perspective of the economic recovery paradigm. Studies have shown that the sudden rise in import prices of oil meant a loss in real income for energy consumers in the United States, which led to a

value share of energy has been small but is becoming larger, and that the elasticity of substitution is substantial but not unlimited. Therefore, whether it is an alpha or a beta connection that more accurately describes the future, depends on the size of the energy price increases and energy's elasticity of substitution.

reduced demand for other goods and services, creating multiplier effects that further reduced economic activity. At the same time, income leaked out to oil-producing countries without returning to the United States through the usual channels of trade and finance, so that the higher energy costs and resulting negative balance of payments were inflationary.

The depressing impact on economic recovery resulting because of the reversal from favorable to unfavorable conditions of energy supply was clear and substantial. But the question arises as to whether such effects are permanent, since the economy will seek out mechanisms for adjustment. What is in doubt is whether the conditions of energy supply are of sufficient importance to the economy over the long run as to effect technology or other inputs so that economic capacity, economic development, or economic prog-ress will be significantly affected.

An important economic-growth paradigm—that is, the neoclassical or pure theory of growth—deals with this kind of issue by identifying the forces that lead an economy to settle into some long-term equilibrium. Eventually, under the pure theory assumptions, the economy must reach a steady state in which output changes at some constant, natural rate that is determined not by energy but by growth in the labor supply and by technological change. In this view—which focuses on labor and capital as the critical determi-nants—energy is of little importance in promoting growth. However, energy is perceived as helping to set limits to growth in two particular variants of the steady state: the stationary and doomsday states.

The stationary state is a no-growth situation reached in the absence of technological progress and population increase. The difficulties associated with obtaining energy and the environmental degradation caused by its consumption, it is argued, must eventually lead to a stationary state. In this paradigm energy plays the growth-limiting role that had been assigned to land exhaustion and degradation by classical economic theory. In its modern guise, however, a moral dimension is often added to these views, namely, that achieving a steady state cannot be left to chance and should be reached quickly and deliberately in order to protect future genera-tions from morally unjustified levels of poverty and social stress.

The doomsday state is predicated on the view that society has almost reached the point of no return. The destructive consequences of the extent and methods of energy consumption, either standing alone or coupled with other aspects of pollution, population growth, resource depletion, and urban crowding, are irreversible. Traditional mechanisms for adjustment, such as a functioning price system, technological advance, and finding substitutes for scarce resources, are not expected to be strong enough to prevent these consequences, and society, if it is not to commit suicide, must find acceptable means for adjusting to lower levels of material welfare.

In contrast to the image of a steady state is the more turbulent image of economic development, which involves shifts in resources among producing sectors or regions, and changes in the organization of the work process. Favorable conditions of energy supply generally are perceived as facilitating both these productivity-improving processes, and therefore as contributing to economic growth. Conversely, unfavorable conditions will reduce the opportunities for resource shifts and work process changes, and this will, in turn, slow down the pace of economic growth.

Over the long term, economic development has been accompanied by the shift of the workforce out of agriculture into industry and services, the concentration of productive resources in urban and suburban places, and the continuing application of resources to the dynamic or innovative sectors of the economy. Energy usage is perceived as having contributed to each of these: by raising productivity in the industrial sector and consequently attracting resources to manufacturing, as well as releasing resources for use in services production; by increasing the mobility of people and goods, which—through the expansion of the locational opportunities of households and firms—contributes to the urbanization process; and facilitating the allocation of more resources to innovative activities by creating new knowledge and disseminating advanced technology through the direct use of energy in those dynamic sectors that are high-energy consumers.

The form in which energy is provided, as well as its quantity, has influenced economic development. As new fuel forms have replaced older forms—as coal has replaced wood and then yielded to liquid fuels, and as the direct consumption of raw energy has been encroached upon by converted energy through electric power—they have made possible the transitions from a mechanized to an industrialized to a service-oriented organization of production, and from a goods to a nongoods structure of consumption. This has involved changes in the work process inside the factory, on the farm, and in offices, and these changes have raised productivity; changes in the transportation system have influenced the location of communities and the spatial configuration of economic activity; and changes in the goods available to consumers have affected the living styles of all U.S. families.

Economic capacity growth and economic development generally imply more production or more consumption. However, for many people, more production and more consumption do not mean economic progress. One set of challenges to establishing economic growth as a desirable social objective is based on the techniques adopted for quantifying economic activity. Ordinarily, these techniques seek to provide an overall measure of economic performance whose changes over time can be monitored. No matter which measure of performance is adopted (for example, variants of gross national product, national income, or household consumption), it is an artifact dependent on arbitrary statistical assumptions. This means that it excludes from the measure of economic performance some socially valuable activities while setting a positive value on other activities that are really a cost to present and future societies. Measures of economic performance, therefore, do not and cannot measure "well-being" or "fulfillment" in a deeper sense. This leads some critics to conclude that measures of economic performance are not only misleading but contribute to society's acceptance of false standards that confuse material consumption with human welfare. On the other side, economic factors are surely an important component of well-being, and statistical studies tend to confirm that even if there is not a one-to-one relationship, increased consumption moves in the same direction as economic progress.

Some observers believe that it is essential to expand the sources of energy supply in order to achieve the goals of economic progress, which requires simultaneously increasing living standards, avoiding environmental degradation, and providing for future generations. Others believe that this would be possible with a wise use of energy; anything other than a wise use is considered a waste of energy that can no longer be tolerated.

Behind these beliefs are more fundamental perceptions as to whether there is an alpha or beta connection between economic growth and energy consumption; whether economic growth is desirable or undesirable; and whether energy use is enabling or disabling. How these perceptions are combined will heavily influence whether the emphasis of energy policy will be on expanding energy supply, on shifting to new energy forms, or on conserving the use of energy.

A policy that creates incentives to expand the supply of fossil and nuclear fuels can be identified as an "alpha expansion" policy. It will be advocated by those who perceive economic growth as being desirable and dependent on proven energy resources whose use is not considered to be disabling.

A policy that creates incentives for developing and adopting nondisabling sources of energy can be labeled as a "beta expansion" policy. Its advocates perceive economic growth as desirable, although not dependent on such disabling energy sources as fossil and nuclear fuels.

A policy that seeks to reduce the pace of economic growth by lowering energy consumption is called an "alpha conservation" policy. This is because its advocates believe that although economic growth is dependent on energy usage, growth is not desirable and energy use is disabling.

Finally, a policy that pursues incentives to adopt energy-saving habits and technologies is a "beta conservation" policy. Its advocates perceive economic growth as desirable, although not dependent on energy sources, so that energy conservation represents the most cost-effective means of achieving the economic growth objectives.

For most of this century the United States has obtained its energy under relatively favorable conditions. Energy prices in the United States have been relatively low as compared with other industrialized countries; energy costs generally have been a small share of a family's budget or a firm's expenses; the energy consumer generally has not been required to pay the full costs associated with its production and use, either because of regulated prices or because the market price fails to cover pollution costs; and energy costs and prices have increased over time at a slower rate than the general price level. As a consequence the price incentives have been against adopting techniques of production or consumption habits that would use less energy if this meant having to use more labor, capital, and energy-conserving materials, or having less access to leisure, household appliances, and convenient forms of transportation.

These favorable price conditions have undoubtedly contributed to the rise in per capita energy usage and the increased quantity of energy required by workers and by machines. To some observers such increases are corroborating evidence that there has been a profligate use of energy in the past. In spite of this increased energy usage, however, there has been a long-term decline in the ratio of the quantity of energy consumed per dollar of national output. In part, it is claimed, this decline can be traced back to the increased energy consumption that has encouraged productivity advances, a consumption shift to services, and improvements in thermal efficiency. So the fact of more energy consumption need not mean wasteful energy consumption, and certainly not so in the context of economic measures of efficiency.

If energy prices increase and alpha conservation policies are adopted, economic growth will be deliberately slowed down. Under beta conservation policies it is the energy requirements needed to maintain growth that will be reduced. If energy prices rise while expansion policies are adopted, countervailing forces to the depletion of presently available energy supplies will be established and change the structure of the energy base, particularly under beta expansion conditions. Although there will be some quick effects on energy supply and consumption resulting from such market-policy forces, their full impact will be felt only after new technologies are developed, energy-using equipment and appliances are replaced, and new habits of consumption are adopted.

Whether energy consumers and producers will respond in sufficient and timely fashion to provide for the wise use of energy in the future is as much a matter of dispute as is the meaning of the term wise. In the following chapters I do not resolve these disputes. But by evaluating relevant data and reflecting on the various perceptions regarding the relationship between energy and economic growth, I hope to identify some of the reasons for and the ramifications of the various positions that are in current vogue.

Chapter Two

Disabling Characteristics of the Energy Connection

It has been said that "energy is the basic natural resource" because "without energy man would be at the mercy of his environment" [16, p. v]. Yet in the conventional economic approach, energy is perceived as only one among a number of other important inputs to the production process, all of which are needed to provide the goods and services that society desires. The conditions under which the energy is obtained and the uses to which it is put are all considered to influence the relationship between energy and economic growth. In this conventional view, it is not energy but the ability of humanity to adapt the physical environment to its own purposes that is perceived as controlling the relationship between the physical and economic processes.

The extent to which humanity can control its environment is constrained by three characteristics of energy resources: (1) their availability is limited; (2) their location is unequally distributed; and (3) their conversion is polluting. So humanity's success in controlling its environment is secured at a price, and the uneasiness about the costs associated with energy scarcity, energy pollution, and energy location has, more than anything else, raised challenges to the conventional economic view and created doubts about the actual and desirable relation between energy and economic growth.

ENERGY SCARCITY

For millions of years nature has considerately been storing up sunshine in the form of fossil fuels. Because of this, vast quantities of energy were available to be used when industrial development imposed its demands. As a consequence, for the past two hundred years much more energy has been extracted from that energy stock than has been put back, and the differential is becoming ever larger. This energy-stock depletion has a fairly specific meaning in physical terms, but its meaning is more ambiguous in economic terms.

One way to account for energy-stock depletion in economic terms is by imagining "user cost" to be a component of the total cost of an extracted resource. User cost represents the cost to the owner of depleting the resource stock; it could be thought of as the amount by which the present value of the resource is reduced when a unit of resource is extracted.

But the magnitude of user cost is not easy to determine, since it depends on expected prices of the resource in the distant future. The competitive market, which has inadequate mechanisms for dealing in future transactions, cannot guarantee the "correct" user cost. To the extent that owners of the resource attach a higher value to the user cost than do consumers, there is likely to be concern expressed about rising energy prices and their effects on economic growth or living standards. When owners are exporting countries and consumers are importing countries, the concern focuses on import dependency and its consequences for political and economic developments.

Ultimately, society responds to stock depletion by lowering the rate of consumption or increasing the effective energy stock. The former can be accomplished through energy conservation and more efficient use of energy, and the latter by shifting from extractive to nonextractive sources of energy—that is, reducing energy dependency on fossil fuels. The effective stock of fossil fuels can also be increased by new discoveries and more effective extraction technologies. Successful implementation of such strategies would not only raise energy availability over the long term but would also have more immediate effects on lowering user costs, which in turn could moderate the rising costs of energy and reduce import dependencies.

This view of energy as a capital stock is essentially an optimistic view, since it holds out the prospect for restoring a long-term balance between the energy stock and the demands being imposed on it. There is another view, however, which indicates that no matter how much stock depletion is resisted, or in what fashion, there is a cost that cannot be overcome: the cost associated with the physical consequences of energy conversion.

In this view, human ingenuity cannot change the fundamental physical condition that energy conversion decreases the stock of low entropy, which then becomes unavailable for other purposes at other times.[1] This physical condition, it is claimed, forces humanity's economic struggle to center on environmental low entropy. This continuous tapping of low entropy is "the most important long-run element of mankind's fate" [23 p. 42].

As part of this struggle, invention and technology are employed to obtain progressively more of economic value from the low entropy that is used up. And indeed it is the case that although society is increasing the pace of its total consumption of low entropy, it is even more rapidly increasing the return of valuable goods and services that are being obtained from the low entropy.

From this perspective, economic value is determined by the low entropy that is used up. There is no way that humanity can engage in a trade with nature that exchanges money for low entropy. Therefore, pecuniary measures of value, such as market prices or GNP, do not adequately represent the using up of low entropy by the economic processes.

This concern with sustaining the flow of low entropy into the economic system makes it desirable to take account of the energy consumed to provide energy. This can be done by substracting from the total energy output that amount of energy inputs required to provide the energy output. This differential has come to be called *net energy*. Net-energy analyses are being recommended as a supplement to the more conventional economic analyses because they provide a more realistic account of the energy reserves available for the further production and distribution of goods and services. From a policy perspective, net energy analysis draws attention to the potential for reducing energy consumption by lowering the amount of the energy resource left in the ground during the extraction operation or dispersed in nonretrievable form during the processing operation, and lowering the amount of the energy resource and other fuels or

---

1. Entropy is a physical concept that can be defined precisely only in technical terms. Without seeking technical accuracy, the meaning of entropy might be understood in simple terms by relating it to the combustion process. Before a piece of coal is burned there is energy in the coal available to do work. As the coal is burned, this work is done and the energy is no longer available in the piece of coal. But this energy is not lost—it is merely dissipated from the coal into the larger system. The consequence of this dissipation is that the energy is no longer capable of performing mechanical work. Entropy, then, is an index of the availability of energy to do work. Low entropy refers to a structure in which most of the energy is still available to do work; high entropy refers to a structure in which the energy is not available to do work. Thus, it is low entropy, not energy, that is valuable in the sense of performing work; it is low entropy, not energy, that is used up in the process of energy conversion; it is low entropy, not energy, that is in short supply in the world [75, p. 18].

electricity that are used to support these operations. By substracting the energy it takes to produce energy, net energy accounting shows that some energy-production technologies that may be relatively cheap in dollar terms are relatively costly in energy terms.

Another kind of question is, How much total energy does a particular consumer good or service actually require? Each consumer good or service directly requires some energy usage in its production and distribution; in addition, that same consumer good indirectly uses up the energy needed to provide the other inputs that are required for its production. Input-output techniques are particularly well suited to such analyses, since the indirect as well as the direct energy requirements for producing a particular item can be traced through an interindustry transactions matrix. It has been shown that a number of commodities that directly require relatively small amounts of energy for their production actually need significant amounts of total energy inputs because much of the energy content of materials and equipment is burned up in their production and distribution [55].

What the energy-accounting techniques have in common is their focus on energy itself—all economic processes are described in terms of their energy content. In this way the overall energy implications of particular courses of action can be spelled out, and the desirability of adopting particular energy-saving measures can be investigated. The danger in energy accounting is that the focus on saving energy can become an obsession. While it is desirable to use energy efficiently, it is also important to give other inputs the same attention. Focusing on the efficiency of a single input does not embody overall social or economic efficiency, which requires consideration of the "totality of inputs and their costs rather than the physical amounts of one input (where costs can always be reduced by increasing other costs)" [51, p. 11].

Based on its preliminary studies, the U.S. Energy Research and Development Administration (ERDA) finds no reason to be concerned about the imminence of zero or negative net energy consequences from the technologies in use. They find that, with the exception of some very low-grade energy resources, there are no energy-production technologies that use up more energy than they provide. Most of the technologies return from 4 to 10 times the energy they expend for energy production. So energy inputs come to 10-25 percent of energy output. However, for some conventional fuel systems the requirements may be as low as 5 percent, while for some of the newer systems (such as oil from shale used to produce electricity), the energy requirement may be 40 percent of the energy output, or even higher. Nuclear electric power returns about 4 times the energy input it requires [100, p. 99].

Odum and his colleagues have calculated similar net energy yield ratios—that is, the ratio of total energy output to the direct and indirect energy inputs needed to produce it.[2] But they are less sanguine than ERDA about the implications. What they stress is that high-yield sources are limited in their quantity and not widespread in their location. Furthermore, potentially new energy sources such as nuclear and solar power have relatively low net-yield ratios due to their low quality and energy-intensive investment requirements. It is their conclusion that the U.S. will continue to be dependent on the energy sources that are now in the range of a 4-to-10 yield ratio. As the energy quality of these sources falls off, the yield ratios will necessarily decline and the costs of producing energy will increase. The prognosis becomes clear that "as the net energy of fuels to the U.S. goes down, so will the activities that can be sustained" [95, p. 269].

It is then argued that if these physical conditions exist, there can be little long-run value in trying to increase the available stock of energy. The appropriate strategy, rather, should be to lower the consumption of energy. But there is no consensus about what the consequences will be of such a lowering in energy consumption.

In one view what is implied by a lowering of energy usage is that although increased energy consumption will be required to provide the growing service demands of the population, this will be offset by gains made in the efficiency of energy consumed in industrial, transportation, and agricultural activities. Zero energy growth is possible even as economic growth is sustained: "We can thus continue to increase per capita GNP for many decades after zero

---

2. The yield ratios they have calculated are as follows:

Type	Yield Ratio
Geothermal power (volcanic region)	57.4
Hydroelectric power	19.0
Tidal power (20-ft tide)	13.7
Western coal and 1,000 mi transport	10.6
Alaska oil	6.3
Gulf of Mexico oil	6.0
Near East oil by exchange, 1975	5.7
Oil in exchange for grain, 1975	4.4
Nuclear fission power	2.7
Low energy agriculture	2.1
Low energy forestry	1.5
Nuclear fission with an accident	1.4
Wind powered electricity (10 mi/h)	0.3

Source: 95, p. 261.

energy growth is achieved—although, of course, in time the limits of increased productivity must be reached" [35, p. 94].

Other energy conservation advocates hold a different view. They see the physical and environmental constraints to be so severe that survival can be assured and desirable goals achieved only by profound changes in lifestyles that will make it possible to set a ceiling to energy consumption. For example, dispersed suburbs will be less feasible, capital-intensive production less profitable, production techniques less energy consuming, and distances between living and working shortened. "Given time for the reactions to occur, the future becomes not an extension of the past, but a new set of dynamic factors being shaped to conform to the new energy situation" [95, p. 81].

Several major strategies are available to society, either through the operation of the market, or through the formulation of energy policy: to increase the availability of extractive or nonextractive energy resources and to constrain the demand for energy through improvements in efficiency or through changes in lifestyle. Whether these strategies are deemed desirable and feasible depends on the views one has of the interactions between economic and physical processes. Since these views differ, advocacy of particular strategies also differs.

As a hedge against uncertainty, public policy seeks to pursue a "proper mix" of strategies. But the resort to a mix of strategies should not obscure the fact that there are real and important differences about what the mix should be. And these differences exist only partly because information is differentially available or interpreted; primarily the differences exist because special interests are at stake, and conflicting views about what threatens the national interest lead to different judgment about the proper strategy mix.

Those who favor an emphasis on increasing the supply of fossil fuel and nuclear-based energy—the alpha expansionists—seem to be primarily concerned about the economic and political risks of an energy shortage. The concern here is that to err on the side of providing more energy-producing capacity than is needed will only mean some income losses to energy companies; but to err on the side of too little capacity will threaten the nation's survival. To the alpha expansionists it is imprudent to adopt policies that flirt with energy shortages, because "the risk of being wrong is simply too great to take" [67, p. 9].

Those who argue for the development of technologies needed to provide energy from renewable or inexhaustible sources—the beta expansionists—seem mainly worried that the nation will not be ready, when the time comes, to move out of the oil and gas-based economy. Thus, while conservation may buy some time, the real problem of adequate supply must eventually be faced and the basis for this must be currently prepared: "The fundamental issue that lies before us is not the simple one so commonly identified as the increase of energy for consumption by a greedy nation. Rather it is the question of whether this nation will be ready with new, practical economical sources of energy to replace oil and gas when their availability begins to decline" [35, p. 354].

The claims of those who emphasize energy conservation in the strategy mix—the beta conservationists—are that conservation is cost-effective, both in environmental and economic terms, and that it extends the time available for new technologies to be developed. The argument put forth by this group is that it generally costs less to save a barrel of oil (or its equivalent) than it does to develop a new barrel of supply. Furthermore, a barrel of oil saved means that pollutants will not be emitted as a result of energy extraction and transportation, the environment will not be degraded as a result of fossil-fuel consumption, and there will be a lessened need for disposal of waste heat and other materials. As a result, intolerable environmental degradation and fuel depletion will be postponed, permitting more time to develop technologies that use inexhaustible and nonpolluting energy sources.

The advocates of changing lifestyles—the alpha conservationists—tend to believe that only through such changes will we be able to achieve a level of frugal energy consumption that is compatible with the realities of energy supply and environmental safety. No longer can society encourage industrial production; it must be restricted. No longer can society be profligate in its energy consumption; it must adopt frugal attitudes and living styles. Furthermore, according to this view, changing lifestyles are not only essential but are probably also desirable in that they will permit redirection of society's goals into more fulfilling channels: "Instead of pursuing ever higher levels of Gross National Product, our society might in the future choose to adopt such goals as ensuring that every person's biological and psychological needs were adequately fulfilled; maximizing all opportunities for personal growth and self-fulfillment; improving our educational, medical, and other public service systems; making jobs more personally rewarding and satisfying; eliminating all vestiges of racial, ethnic, or sexual discrimination; creating livable and enjoyable communities; or expanding political democracy to include maximum possible citizen involvement. All such alternative national goals would be significantly less energy demanding than our present goal of industrial productivity" [71, p. 4].

A mix of strategies, rather than focusing on a single one, is necessary, because they have different time dimensions in which their impact can be felt. Significant effects in the near term (that is, over the coming decade), can be achieved from both energy conservation and a heightened capacity to provide energy. It has been recently estimated [100] that the adoption of available techniques could permit industry to reduce its energy consumption by 15 percent of what it might be in 1985; energy conservation in commercial buildings and housing could reach 10 percent of the 1985 demands by this sector; and the transportation and electric utility sectors could reduce their energy consumption by up to 5 percent of their 1985 energy needs. In addition, enhanced fossil fuel recovery techniques, expanded use of coal, and increased nuclear power capacity could help lower the nation's oil import dependency over the coming decade. It is unlikely, however, that any combination of available strategies could reduce import dependency to near zero.

In the mid-term—between 1985 to 2000—development of synthetic fuels, goethermal deposits, and solar energy, along with conservation through more efficient utilization of waste heat, will be added to the near-term techniques adopted to save energy and increase its supply. Only over the long term—after the year 2000—can there be a realistic expectation of significant amount of energy supplies from the inexhaustible fuel resources.

In evaluating the desirability of pursuing a particular course of energy conservation or capacity expansion, it is useful to know over what time horizon its impact will be felt, by how much it will increase (or save) energy supply, what its net energy yield will be, and what its environmental effects will be. There is considerable uncertainty about the consequences of many of the most discussed and viable proposed techniques. Yet experimentation with and even commitment to specific techniques must be made in spite of these uncertainties. Figure 2-1 lists some of the important programmatic components of an energy strategy and provides some judgments about the potential consequences for each component.

ENERGY POLLUTION

Not only a large part of the general public but also some observers with a long perspective on history believe that the current energy situation is a minor crisis. It is believed that energy scarcities cannot by themselves cause a major change in societal trends. But how energy is provided and how much there is does not occur "by itself." Rather, it is influenced by other social goals, and it affects their achievement.

	Impact Horizon	Resulting Expansion in Energy Supply	Net Energy Yield Ratio	Environmental Effects from Entire Energy Cycle	
				Polluting	Serious Accident
Increased Efficiency in Energy Uses					
Conservation in Buildings	Near term and beyond	High	Very high	Low	Low
Conservation in Consumer Products	Near term and beyond	High	Very high	Low	Low
Conservation in Industry	Near term and beyond	High	Very high	Low	Low
Conservation in Transportation	Near term and beyond	High	Very high	Low	Low
Waste Heat Utilization	Mid-term and beyond	Moderate	Very high	Low	Low
Efficiency in Electricity Conversion	Long term	?	?	Low	Low (?)
Efficiency in Power Transmission	Long term	?	?	Low	Low (?)
Preserve and Expand Domestic Resources					
Coal Use for Power	Near term and beyond	Very high	High	High	High
Conventional Nuclear Reactors	Near term and beyond	Very high	Low	Low	?
Enhanced Oil & Gas Recovery	Near term and beyond	Very high	High	Moderate	High
Hydroelectric	Near term and beyond	Low	High	Low	Low
Breeder Reactors	Mid-term and beyond	High (?)	High	?	?
Develop Synthetic Fuels					
From Coal	Mid-term and beyond	Very high	Moderate	High	High
From Oil Shale	Mid-term and beyond	High (?)	Low	High	High
From Hydrogen	Long term	?	?	Low	?
Expand Underutilized Sources					
Geothermal	Mid-term and beyond	Moderate	High	Moderate	Low
Solar Heating & Cooling	Mid-term and beyond	Moderate	High (?)	?	?
Waste Materials	Near term and beyond	Moderate	Low (?)	Low	Low
Electric Transportation	Long term	?	?	?	?
Develop Inexhaustible Sources					
Fusion	Long term	High (?)	?	Low	Low
Fuel Cells	Long term	High	?	Low (?)	Low
Wind	Long-term	Moderate (?)	Low	Low	?
Tidal	Long term	Low	High	?	?
Biomass	Long term	?	?	?	?

Figure 2-1. Strategies for Energy Conservation and Supply

It is futile to expect that a mix of energy strategies can be found that will have no effect on the broader environment. The effects are likely to be both significant and extensive, because their "environmental and social costs cover a wide spectrum of concerns and each policy or action produces a different mix of impacts and costs" [49, p. 553].

Production and use of energy means that residuals (effluents, heat, and possibly radiation) are vented into the air, water, and land. These emmissions have direct major consequences for health, property values, and the location of production activities. They may disrupt the natural processes as well. Since these natural processes in turn provide services that add to well-being (food production, recreation, and the like), there will be further indirect consequences resulting from pollution. Accidents are a particularly important source of damage to health, property values, and natural processes.

There are other environmental transformations that can result from energy conversion, the most important of which are physical and visual damage to the landscape and noise escalation. As a consequence, natural processes are altered. while the value of property and the location of industry and residence are also influenced.

In more innocent days when economic growth was deemed as primarily beneficial, with few associated costs, it was customary to relate energy directly to growth. In the 1950s a comprehensive national study could conclude: "As in the past the combination of increased energy and improved technology today provides the main promise of further economic growth within the physical limitations of natural resources" [79, p. 103]. Now that pollution is perceived as a significant cost, the net social impact of energy conversion is much more in doubt: "Tte production and use of energy resources, lie at the center of the source of pollution, and it is difficult to enumerate all their crimes" [87, p. 118].

It is not by accident that widespread concern about pollution is of relatively recent vintage. For perceptible and threatening pollution is itself a relatively new phenomenon resulting primarily from recent changes in human productive activities. For example, following World War II, detergents, plastics, synthetic pesticides, herbicides, and manmade radio isotopes emerged as the result of new productive technologies and scientific achievements. "Thus the chief reason for the sharp increase in environmental stress in the United States is the sweeping transformation in production technology in the postwar period. *Productive activities with intense environmental impacts have displaced activities with less serious environmental impacts; the growth pattern has been counter-ecological"* [87, p. 63].

The effects of adding pollution to the energy-growth equation are depicted in Figure 2-2. At the same time that growing energy production and use contribute to economic growth, they add to pollution directly and indirectly because secondary polluting effects result from expanded production and consumption of goods and services. In the extreme view, the fundamental dilemma of this equation is that increasing energy conversion threatens biological survival and assures our socioeconomic future, while lowering energy conversion compels the opposite trade-off. In less stark terms, the ecologists see "the arresting of growth as a necessary, though not sufficient, condition for saving the ecosystem. The economist sees growth as a necessary, though not sufficient, condition for social progress and stability" [87, p. 4].

Even if it is unnecessary to choose between biological and social survival, most people now believe that pollution's costs as well as the benefits of growth should be included in any formula relating energy to a net social utility. Once pollution costs are included, the level and mix of goods and services comprising the net social utility will be

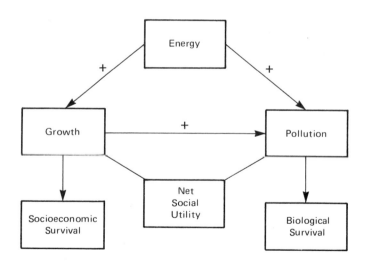

Figure 2-2. The Energy-Growth-Pollution Equation

different than if pollution costs are not counted. How much they are different and whether different is perceived as better will depend, at least in part, on who is made to bear the costs of pollution or its abatement and what causes the pollution damage.

In principle, with given technologies, prices, and lifestyles, there is some optimally efficient amount and mix of energy, in the sense that the costs of pollution and the benefits of growth are equal at the margin. A properly functioning market that includes the valuation of all pollution costs would, presumably, arrive at such an efficient quantity of energy usage. However, when polluting costs are not included, there is a tendency for firms and consumers to overuse polluting sources such as energy. The problem is not that the price system doesn't work when polluting resources are used; the problem is that "it works with marvelous efficiency in the wrong direction" [49, p. 615].

The concern over environmental pollution can be traced back to the thirteenth century when the burning of soft coal in London polluted the air. It was not until the 1960s that the serious and widespread threat to well-being resulting from pollution was recognized. However, in one of the few cases of economic theory accurately anticipating an economic problem, Pigou had elaborately analyzed the pollution issue as early as the 1930s. The analysis says that some economic behavior escapes the pricing and allocation mechanisms of the market. As a consequence, there are spillovers or externalities, which are beyond the control of the people who suffer from them. The conventional recommended response to this situation is for government to impose pollution taxes or to regulate standards for environmental protection. Imposing pollution taxes would, to the extent possible, "internalize the externalities." Since everyone would then be compelled to pay the full costs of one's own consumption, resources would be allocated efficiently. Regulation would treat environmental protection as a product that polluters are compelled to provide so that efficient resource allocation would result.

Taxation is likely to have effects very different from regulation on both the rate of overall economic growth and the incidence of who bears the cost. It is also claimed that particular industries in specific places would be disproportionately affected, causing intolerable levels of unemployment in those places and in turn preventing the economy from reaching its full growth potential. Yet for some people it is precisely such growth retardation that is the bitter medicine that needs to be prescribed over the long run.

Methods of dealing with pollution that go beyond reliance on the market include imposing residuals charges, establishing quality and emissions standards, regulating specific production processes, and controlling the quantity and distribution of the energy supply and other goods and services.

In the longer run, the net social utility can be raised by changing the relationship between energy, growth, and pollution. The polluting effects of energy can be reduced by shifting to less polluting fuels, lowering the dependence of growth on energy usage by taking advantage of conservation opportunities, and mitigating the effects of economic growth on pollution by changing the product mix of consumption.

Changes such as these—working in the opposite direction—have been the major cause of increasing pollution over the last three decades; that is, the stepped-up adoption of energy-using technologies has upped the pace of environmental pollution. To reverse the process—to bring about new relations between energy, growth and pollution—would seem to require the adoption of different technologies applied to energy supply, pollution abatement, and conservation. But even apart from the dispute about whether new technologies are available and whether their technical implications are known, there are dissents to the view that technology is a viable method for resolving the conflict between growth and pollution. At the extreme is the view that it is already too late for technology to forestall such effects as global climatic disaster. More moderate is the view that there is inherently a conflict between economic growth and environmental preservation, so all that technology can do is reduce the tension but not eliminate the conflict.

New technologies use equipment, which raises another dilemma— can pollution be lowered without substantial increases in energy uses? Such increases would be required, it is claimed, because pollution-control technologies are themselves energy intensive. Thus, attempts to control pollution may involve adding to production processes the control equipment that requires still more energy consumption and fuel burning. Although such a self-defeating process is a possibility, the evidence does not indicate that the energy penalty for achieving environmental standards is very high. The available estimates suggest that the additional energy needed for pollution control would come to about 2 percent of the nation's total energy use, with most of the penalty resulting from air pollution controls over automobiles and power plants [102, p. 328].

The new technologies will also require great amounts of money and resources for investment and operating purposes, which might mean having to divert these resources from other social needs, including health care, education, welfare, recreation, and job training. If this occurs, then the poor would be bearing a disproportionate share of the costs of overcoming energy pollution and scarcity. And even beyond this redistribution effect, there is some doubt that the people of the United States are willing to pay the pollution bill by meeting fewer social needs.

It is because of this that economic growth becomes an attractive alternative to diverting resources to energy-related purposes. But such growth, it is claimed, depends to some extent on increased energy usage. For it is only in a high energy-using society that productivity can increase by so much that both a rising living standard and environmental improvements can be achieved and kept in appropriate relation to each other.

Most people would support the objective of pursuing environmentally acceptable energy technologies. And most informed observers would agree that there is no technology available to meet everyone's standards regarding an acceptable resolution of the dilemma that energy raises living standards through enhancing prosperity while undermining prosperity through its environmental impacts. Such a consensus, however, does little to resolve the conflict or reduce the acrimony between those who support and those who oppose a particular regulation, facility, or process. Part of the reason is that people in different circumstances will value differently the relationship between a unit of prosperity and a unit of environmental improvement. They also place a different value on a unit of environmental deterioration where they live compared to a similar unit somewhere else. Perhaps most important, they give a different value to a unit of prosperity now compared with a unit of environmental improvement later. Short-term public interest, which favors economic prosperity, is not the same as the long-term interest that pushes for environmental survival.

In a democracy, citizens are often asked to support or oppose a particular environmental regulation or the construction of a specific power plant. Rarely are such decisions based on the determined consequences of the particular choice. Rather, they are based on feelings, vague but still powerful, about whether alpha expansion is a greater or lesser risk to society than conservation or development of alternative energy sources.

The alpha expansionist feeling is that "in a highly industrial society such as ours the continuity of energy supply is a priority that clearly exceeds, on a short-term basis, the priority of gradual improvement in our total environment or the gradual development of alternative energy resources" [2, p. 75]. The beta expansion and conservation feeling is that "the situation that civilization has reached the predicament where large-scale environment disruptions are not only possible but perhaps likely, without having developed the knowledge to understand the possibilities in detail or to cope with them, gives reason to slow greatly the growth in energy consumption. Only such a slowdown can buy the time needed to obtain more knowledge of the threats and to develop and deploy more benign technologies" [49, p. 579].

Adequate information would help greatly in judging these alternative views, but information is lacking about what standards and practices are environmentally unacceptable and what technologies are associated with maintaining an acceptable environment. The effects of this on making informed choices is compounded by the difficulties involved in trying to make comparisons among impacts that are inherently not comparable. These noncomparabilities occur primarily because there is a multitude of types of environmental damage resulting from particular technologies; because the distribution of effluents and their natural dilution effects vary over space and time; and because the level and costs of specific environmental residuals are measured in varying degrees of probability.

The kinds of environmental information that could be particularly useful would interrelate the origin, characteristics, and consequences of the environmental impact: the origin of the impact—the stage of activity in the energy supply and consumption cycle (exploration, harvesting, concentration, refining, transportation, conversion, storage, end use, and waste management); the characteristic of the impact—what is changed in the environment (are effluents released, accidents caused, aesthetics reduced, and so on); and the consequences of the impact—the damages, or sometimes benefits, produced by what is done to the environment (particularly in terms of what is done to health and to the economic and natural processes).

The following sections discuss some of what is known about energy-related environmental impacts. Figure 2-3 identifies the most significant characteristics and consequences of the environmental impacts and summarizes the relationship between the two categories.

Air Pollution

The principal causes of energy-related air pollution are mobile sources (particularly motor vehicles), stationary fuel combustion (including power plants), solid waste disposal, and industrial processes. Air pollution occurs at virtually all the stages in energy systems. Perhaps most serious is the air pollution that can and does occur at the extraction stage (for coal and uranium); in transporta-

Characteristic of Impact	Consequences of Impact: Health: Death	Health: Disease and Injury	Health: Genetic	Economic Processes: Property Value	Economic Processes: Location of Households	Economic Processes: Location of Industry	Natural Processes: Air	Natural Processes: Water	Natural Processes: Land
Pollution									
Effluent (gaseous, liquid, solid)		Major		Major	Major	Major	Major	Major	Major
Heat		Major				Major	Major	Major	Major
Land, visual, noise transformation		Major		Major	Major			Major	Major
Accidents	Major	Major	Major	Major			Major	Major	Major
Radiation		Major	Major						

Figure 2-3. Pollution Impacts

tion (for oil, gas, and possibly uranium); in refining (for oil); in conversion (for coal, oil, and nuclear energy); at the end-use stage (for oil); and at the waste-management stage (for coal and nuclear energy).

The total wastes that we put into the air approach one pound of material per person per day [102, p. 309]. This is an average; in some places it comes to much more and regularly reaches levels injurious to health, property, and the natural processes.

Whether air pollution raises the mortality rate is not clear. Statistical analyses comparing different areas suggest that it does, something like a 50 percent rise in air pollution raise mortality by 4.5 percent [49, p. 609]. However, the statistical analyses may be methodologically suspect, and it is difficult to demonstrate in a laboratory the relation between death and acute air pollution. It does seem to be the case, however, that death related to air pollution is most common among aged and infirm persons with a low life expectancy rather than among otherwise healthy individuals.

The more common and perhaps more serious situation is the urban resident's exposure to nonfatal but significant concentrations of various air pollutants. Major illnesses resulting from such exposure are chronic respiratory disease, aggravated heart-lung ailments, and children's respiratory disease. Important nonurban diseases associated with air pollution are pneumoconiosis (black lung disease) in coal miners, and silicosis and lung cancer in uranium miners.

Plants and animals are also damaged by air pollution. For example, photosynthesis can be retarded by pollutants; crops and animals can be harmed by phosphate reductions; and plants can be affected by sulfur and nitrogen oxides, by ozone, and by various hydrocarbons. Routine effluents of energy conversion can also severely damage property.

Water Pollution

Water quality and requirements are affected by virtually every stage of energy conversion. For example, sulfuric acid seeping from coal mines into streams and lakes occurs at the extraction stage and oil spills occur during transportation. Residuals are released in the refining stage and coolant is required at the conversion stage. However, energy-related effects, while important, are not the major reasons for water pollution, which is heavily affected by recreation and urban waste.

The costs of water treatment increase rapidly as more water quality must be achieved. The percentage of these costs associated with energy-related pollution are estimated to be a small but still important share of the total costs of water pollution control. A large part of these energy-related costs would derive from thermal discharges, which are a major concern of those worried about the potential increase in power generation. In order to extract energy from fossil fuels, the power plant must dispose of its waste heat, which it usually does by transferring heat to the cooler waters of oceans, lakes, and rivers. Enormous quantities of cooling water are required—perhaps two-fifths of the water used in the United States is required for cooling electric power plants [19, vol. 3, p. 2].

What are the major effects of energy-related water pollution? It is likely to affect human health through hydrocarbons from oil spills entering the food supply, and from acidic water, which produces heart problems. Poor water quality results in corrosion of industrial and domestic water-using equipment. Water pollution cuts down fish catches and seems to affect fish reproduction, as well as reducing water-based recreation services. Perhaps the most important consequence is the loss in water supply at a time when there are expectations of worldwide drought.

Land Pollution

The most visible aspects of energy-related land pollution are the ravages of strip mining, the accumulation of processed wastes from underground mining, subsidence of rock strata overlying abandoned coal mines, and the unsightliness of energy production and transportation facilities.

Ground subsidence resulting from underground coal mining and extraction of oil, natural gas, and geothermal steam primarily endangers residencies and other structures. It does not affect agriculture, which can be carried on after the ground has subsided. Strip mining, open-pit mining of coal, uranium, tar sands, and oil shale, and motion of spoil banks all affect agricultural and recreational pursuits. Evaporative losses of hydro-dam reservoirs cause downstream salinity and affect agriculture. Oil derricks, offshore platforms, transmission towers, refineries, and port facilities mar the beauty of regions, affecting recreational opportunities and lowering property values.

Other energy-related land-polluting concerns are disposal of waste (including, particularly, radioactive wastes and sledge from scrubbing), the loss of recreational areas, and the foreclosed opportunities for land used up in energy production and transportation. In addition, "cheap energy" is often cited as causing the extensive land-use requirements of suburbanized settlement patterns and a transportation system dependent on highways. Finally, the transporting of Alaskan oil across land opens up the potential for damage from pipeline leaks, destruction of terrain and wildlife, and despoliation of the Alaskan tundra.

Accidents

The possibility of accidents exists at almost every stage of the energy cycle; the potential of serious harm to health, the natural processes, and property values is a matter of grave concern. Deaths and injuries from accidents are a known hazard of mining, particularly serious for deep coal mining but also occurring in surface mining and oil and gas extraction. Transportation of fuels is an even more serious cause of accidents. The greater distance the fuel is transported, the greater the number of accidents that will occur.

Major oil spills in ports and on the high seas are a spectacular cause of damage to aquatic life and to property value, as well as a cause of disease and injury. But quantitatively more important than the spectacular accidental spill is the day-to-day routine seepage from tankers and other commercial vessels. In addition, there is the pollution from ostensibly minor incidents such as pipeline breaks, spent lubricants, incompletely burned fuels, and storage seepage.

Oil and gas pipeline transport over land damages health and wildlife, mainly by seepage but also through occasional explosions. Fires and explosions at extraction sites are not frequent but do occur often enough to cause serious losses of property and life, as well as injury.

Positive discharge of radioactive materials from nuclear power plants and from the transportation and storage of nuclear materials also present a health hazard. However, there is not yet agreement as to how much damage actually results from such seepage and with what stringency emissions standards should be imposed.

Perhaps of greatest concern to the public is the unpredictable catastrophe—the nuclear disaster, the LNG explosion, the collapsed hydrodam. Considerable thought and resources go into the prevention of such accidents. The probability of their occurring is low, but it is not zero. Many observers believe that there are no possible precautions that will guarantee against nuclear theft, sabotage, meltdowns, or explosions. Even one such event can cause intolerable loss of life and property, with potentially irreversible genetic and environmental effects. What scales can weigh such consequences and tell us what risks are acceptable or what alternatives might be even more costly?

Long-Term Pollution

The possibility of long-term, irreversible global damage is a major threat, not because the probability of its occuring is high, but because the consequences are so severe. These threats relate most significantly to food production, climatic effects, and chemical damage. Perhaps the greatest potential for energy-related long-term damage is in the area of food production. A productive agriculture depends on the control of crop pests through natural enemies, the maintenance of soil fertility through natural nutrient cycles, and the persistence of an area's climatic conditions. Similarly, production of protein in the sea depends on maintaining the appropriate chemical and structural characteristics of nearshore waters and the integrity of estuarine habitats. All this is threatened by energy production and conversion.

The climatic effects of waste heat resulting from unrestrained combustion of fossil fuels represent another danger of catastrophic potential, but uncertain probability. Global climate may be changed by the carbon dioxide and particulate matter released from the combustion of fossil fuels. Local climates can be permanently influenced by increased humidity associated with hydroelectric reservoirs and cooling towers, by power plant heat discharge, and by the low-grade heat generated through energy use.

Long-term ecological damage can also result from the uncontrolled introduction of toxic materials into the air, water, and land. Chemical balance of surface waters can be influenced by fossil fuel combustion or salt and acid runoff from mining operations. Chemical damage can also take place by disposal of brines from oil drilling, exploitation of steam and geothermal resources, storage of materials from scrubbing operations, tanker operations, refinery discharges, and atmospheric fallout from automobile emissions.

Most of the foreseeable environmental damage tends to be localized in scope. Sometimes the damage is permanent, and sometimes it can be reversed. Its costs and the consequences or recovery from it are likely to be high, raising issues of whether the benefits are worth the costs, how the costs should be distributed, and what kinds of trade-offs are preferable. These are familiar decisions that society confronts in many areas. Although localized environmental damage may provoke a response that goes beyond "business as usual," it does seem possible that "business not radically different from usual" can carry on.

The situation is quite different, however, when global environmental damage is at stake. For in such situations there may be, in the ecologist's term, no "resiliency"—no possibility for the system to restore itself in an ecologically viable fashion. In such a case, the business-as-usual attitude or even business-not-too-far-from-usual may be totally unacceptable.

ENERGY LOCATION

The United States is endowed with considerable quantities of fossil fuel resources. From 1850 through World War II, the nation has actually produced at least as much energy as it has consumed, and usually slightly more. This was true not only for energy requirements in the aggregate but separately for wood, coal, oil, and gas as well. But beginning in 1947 the nation's demand for oil began to exceed its production, and the shortfall has become larger ever since. This has not been the case for other fuels, particularly coal, which has consistently been produced in sufficient quantities for some to be exported.

In the mid-1970s the United States imported one-fifth of its energy demands. A decade ago this figure was one-tenth, and two decades ago it was one-fifteenth. Although the import increase is substantial, it does not seem at first glance to be alarming that one-fifth of the nation's total energy requirement is provided by imports.

What is alarming is that imports are concentrated in a particular fuel source—two-fifths of the nation's demand for crude oil and petroleum products are currently being imported, and the share is rising. In the early 1970s, imports were only one-quarter, and a decade ago they were only one-fifth of oil consumption in the United States. In 1970 the United States spent $15 per person for imported oil ($3 billion in the aggregate); by the mid-1970s the country was spending nine times as much for imported oil. Since oil now supplies almost half the nation's energy needs and has been doing so for almost two decades, there could be a severe shock to the nation's economy if imports were drastically reduced. The 1973/74 oil embargo demonstrated that the United States is not indifferent to severe oil-supply disruptions or price increases.

Both demand and supply factors have contributed to the increasing trend in import dependency. On the supply side the availability of inexpensive imported oil made it an attractive buy compared to other fuels. It also discouraged expansion of domestic production, which peaked in 1970, and even then was only one-third above the production rate sustained in the late fifties. Our disinclination to increase domestic capacity in the pre-embargo period applied particularly to the production of petroleum products, which in the early seventies comprised about two-thirds of oil imports compared with about one-third of crude oil, whereas in the late fifties the proportions were reversed. Also, the declining real price of oil imports in the pre-embargo period discouraged domestic exploration, contributing to severe reductions in the quantity of oil drilling and reduced levels of proven oil reserves.

On the demand side the favorable price situation was only one cause of accelerated oil imports. In addition, oil began rapidly to replace coal as a power plant fuel, partly for environmental reasons. Another cause of growth in oil consumption was the increasing demand for motor vehicle travel combined with reduced mileage per gallon, which resulted from power-consuming accessories on cars and heavier car weights.

After the embargo, oil prices increased, with a moderately dampening effect on oil consumption and imports. On the supply side the Federal Energy Administrator (FEA) reports that drilling activity has increased, federal leasing on the outer continental shelf has been stepped up, processes to increase crude oil recovery have been stimulated, and the decline in domestic oil production has slowed down [101]. The major effect of the embargo, however, has been to raise questions about the future and the consequences of continued import dependency.

In the absence of significant policy changes, continued reliance on oil imports seems highly likely. With no major domestic policy changes, the United States might be importing half its total energy requirements in 1985, and three-fifths in 1990 [95, p. 14]. Recent estimates by the FEA [101, p. xxvii] suggest that, without policy changes, oil imports could double by 1985; with gradual deregulation of oil and gas prices, the FEA indicates that the level of oil imports could remain stable. If the nation adopted a maximum effort to increase domestic supply and cut demand, oil imports could be reduced to one-fifth their current level by 1985. However, after 1985 imports would begin to rise again as domestic reserves are depleted.

It is not only reliance on oil imports, but increasing dependence on Middle East imports, that is of concern. Before the embargo, about four-fifths of U.S. oil imports came from Caribbean and Canadian sources. However, according to ERDA, imports from Canada are expected to be phased out, while those from Venezuela are not likely to increase. Coupled with the fact that other countries are also heavily dependent on imported oil, all of this raises "the prospect of increasingly stiff terms for imported energy even without political upheavals in the Middle East" [25, p. 30]. The increasingly stiff terms of imported energy refer to import price increases, actual supply disruptions, and uncertainty about the availability and price of imports. These have both domestic and international consequences.

Before the 1960s most observers were relatively unconcerned about the possibility of import price increases. But with the reality of the Middle East crises in 1957, 1967, and 1973 and the advantage of hindsight, rising import prices are now perceived as a threat to the world and the U.S. economy. In the United States the immediate effect of higher import prices is to raise industry and household costs, and therefore lower as well as redistribute the real GNP. But the growth potential of the U.S. economy is high and the dollar value of imported energy is a small share of the GNP. So from one perspective, rising costs of oil imports would not seem to portend catastrophic consequences: "A higher oil import bill . . . is not a trivial blow to our real income as a nation but it is not a catastrophe *per se* in a country whose output grows 4 percent average per year and fluctuates cyclically from zero, or negative growth, to 8 or 9 percent per year" [2, p. 188].

But this perspective views the effects of higher import prices to result primarily from the changed conditions of oil supply. The repercussions of overall demand for goods and services appear more important: "The oil crisis has slowed the U.S. economy from the standpoint of demand rather than supply" [37, p. 88]. The specific demand effects of the 1973/74 oil price increases were to lower household consumption of goods and services in general, but particularly of automobiles; to raise interest rates due to an increased demand for money; and to hike wages due to higher consumer prices. These events produced further repercussions throughout the economy with the result that real GNP was reduced, unemployment was increased, and inflation was stimulated.

Recent estimates indicate that as a result of the fourfold increases in imported oil prices since 1973, the United States lost about $60 billion of GNP and over 2.5 million jobs in 1977 alone. And if the effects are cumulated from 1974 through 1976, the oil price increases cost almost $200 billion of GNP and 5 million jobs [12, p. 45]. These losses have already occurred. Whether they continue depends on how the United States responds. To the extent that higher import prices produce some desirable energy savings and perhaps improved allocation and management of domestic resources, these GNP costs could diminish over time.

Although proper resource management might reduce the GNP losses due to import price increases, the losses are not likely to be eliminated. The economic reality is that equipment is run by energy, and higher oil prices make it less attractive for industry to purchase energy-using equipment. Since capital intensity is perceived as a major cause of productivity improvements, the growth rate in GNP will be permanently lower as long as higher oil prices are maintained, because "the new combination of labor, capital, energy, and materials is less productive than it was before OPEC emerged" [12, p. 46].

It may be that the effects of actual or feared oil supply disruptions are even more important than those of rising oil prices. The complex economies that characterize major industrial countries are sensitive to sudden nonavailability of key inputs; their consequences quickly ripple through the entire economy. In this case the concern is that shortages of fuel will cause cutbacks in industrial production, which will lead to increased unemployment as well as bottlenecks adding to inflation.[3]

In addition, it needs to be pointed out that the uncertainty itself about a more severe import embargo or a more rapid price increase produces some social costs, even if these events never materialize. The purchase of energy-conserving industrial equipment, smaller cars, energy storage facilities, and mass transit facilities are to some extent motivated by the fear of supply disruptions and rising energy costs, rather than the possible benefits they might provide. Perhaps the most serious social costs of such uncertainties are that expansion and research programs of the domestic energy industry are hampered by the fear of price undercutting by the exporting countries.

Dependence on an unreliable supply of oil is also perceived as a threat to the national security: "The nation's entire capacity to act in a crisis may become restricted by its dependence on energy sources over which it has no control" [87, p. 93]. Barring a nuclear conflict, oil is needed to run the machines of war—land vehicles, ships, and aircraft. In addition, we require oil to build these machines and to maintain a smoothly operating economy for ourselves and our allies in time of war. Under current supply trends, Western Hemisphere oil would be inadequate to sustain full-scale nonnuclear warfare, and military requirements for ourselves and our allies would be hard to satisfy without access to Middle Eastern oil.

Reduced dependence on oil imports is perceived by many as

---

3. The evidence on this issue is mixed. Fears of industrial and commercial shutdown for a lack of essential fuels were not realized directly as a result of the 1973/74 oil embargo. However, the severe winter of 1977 apparently strained the natural gas supply sufficiently to cause temporary shutdowns of industrial plants and closures of public facilities in the Midwest and eastern parts of the country. But, in the even more severe winter of 1978, fuel shortages were not widespread.

essential to lowering the nation's vulnerability to energy blackmail. However, dependence works in both directions, since the oil exporting countries need U.S. goods and services, particularly food products, to advance their own economic and social progress.

So reliance on domestic energy supplies to promote national security may result in a lower rate of economic progress than would occur by increasing international oil trade. From a U.S. standpoint, whether the import dependency risk is worth taking will be predicated, to some extent, on the strength of the OPEC cartel and on the foreign-policy objectives of the OAPEC countries, both of which at the moment are highly uncertain.

There are many uncertainties about the consequences of changing trends in international oil trade. U.S. oil imports are now about a quarter of all imports. Would further increases in oil imports so deteriorate the U.S. balance of payments that a restrictive monetary policy would need to be adopted? And what would happen to international financial flows as a consequence of increased U.S. imports? Will the oil-exporting countries spend on imports as much as they are earning from their exports? Most of the oil exporters appear to have sufficient defense and economic development needs to assure their expanded purchase of imports from increased oil earnings. However, others are accumulating net petro-dollars. Is this accumulation likely to give them a sufficient stake in international economic order so that they will exercise constraint in their export pricing and supply policies? How will the accumulated funds be invested, and where? If they are invested in the United States, is that good or bad? In other words, will they add to needed growth of manufacturing and other facilities, or will they increase our vulnerability to these countries? If U.S. oil imports expand, will it reduce the availability of supplies to Western Europe, Japan, and the less-developed countries? Or would it perhaps contribute to rising world oil prices to the particular detriment of the less-developed countries, which can least afford it? But perhaps rising oil prices could be matched by price increases for other kinds of natural resources, which would generally be welcomed by the less-developed countries. Would competition for fuels become a disruptive influence among friends and weaken new alliances, or would it trigger a new era of international cooperation in economic and energy policies?

A fundamental consideration in the development of new international arrangements is the relation between the worldwide distribution of energy resources and the position of poor nations vis-à-vis the rich. The developed nations have about one-third of the world's population, and use four-fifths of the world's energy. The United

States, with 6 percent of the world's population, consumes a third of the world's energy. The average American consumes 200 times the energy needed for survival [64]. It is disparities such as these that make it dangerous to think of the world in homogeneous terms. The world consists of haves and have-nots, and energy shortages may exacerbate these differentials. It is, indeed, even possible that new haves and have-nots will be created along fuel availability lines. At the least, there is a potential for conflict that necessarily engages the attention of nations.

If present trends continue, the disparity between rich and poor nations will increase. While the energy-producing countries will be able to rapidly improve their economic and political bargaining posture, the position of most of the poorer countries will deteriorate in relative, if not in absolute, terms. For the less-developed countries even more than for the industrialized ones, what the rising costs of energy have meant so far is lower living standards, higher inflation, increased debt, reduced growth, and a slower rate of industrialization. Furthermore, there has been a growing skepticism about the ability or willingness of the developed nations to find adequate solutions to the poorer countries' economic problems.

Present trends may only be temporary, however, and views about what is desirable or feasible for the future are varied and conflicting. One popular scenario is that even though developed nations are richer because they are energy-intensive, the high productivity of the rich provides an opportunity for raising living standards throughout the world. In this view, if energy is made available to the developed countries, the poor nations will be able to obtain a faster rate of growth through trade than if they were to use that energy in domestic production. So some people would favor the continued high use of energy by developed countries in order to advance the lot of the poor.

An alternative to this view is that the energy consumption of the rich represents a barrier to economic growth of the poor. This line of reasoning highlights concern that the more the rich consume, the less is left for the poor; the big losers in the energy shortage are not the developed countries but the less-developed countries, which will not now have the opportunity to make the big leap forward in their economic development—for economic development depends on low-cost oil for fertilizer, irrigation, transportation, and industrialization. Further, the developed countries not only use up the oil, but also, because they can afford it, contribute to rising oil prices that hurt the poor substantially more than the rich. Such a situation is neither sustainable nor tolerable.

While faster growth for poor nations is possible, it may not be desirable, since economic growth may not increase the quality of life or make it easier to achieve distributional equity among nations. Rather, it may only hasten the day that environmental disaster and intolerable social strains will descend on the poor nations.

Views about the impact of new technologies also vary. In one opinion, new sources of energy will be developed. However, these are likely to be high-cost sources, ill suited to the needs of the less developed nations, which can best use oil as their basic fuel. But oil is also needed by the developed nations in order to get through the transition period required to develop new energy sources. Since the developed nations are in a more favorable position to afford the oil, the disparities between rich and poor are likely to increase. [62].

In an alternative view, the energy technologies now most appropriate to poor nations require little capital and infrastructure, and are those on which the richer countries are likely to rely in the long run. Therefore, the poor countries should speed up intensive economic development in nonenergy areas so that long-run disparities between the rich and poor can be reduced. In the meantime, "interim means should be urgently sought to assist those poor countries whose importation of energy-intensive technologies (especially in agriculture) has made them dependent on energy which due to others' extravagance, they can no longer afford" [59, p. 127].

Chapter Three

Sources of Economic Growth

PRODUCTION FUNCTIONS AND GROWTH ACCOUNTING

According to the neoclassical model, economic growth occurs because the supply of labor and capital expands and the productivity of these factors increases over time. In this view, the economy is visualized as some vast input to output relationship, where the quantity of output is dependent upon the amount of inputs and how they are combined in the production process. This relatively simple production-function view of the economy has provided an extraordinarily rich basis for theoretical analyses and empirical investigation of the determinants of economic growth.

In the traditional production function, labor and capital are the major factors of production. If it is assumed that perfect competition prevails, that there are constant returns to scale, and that there is no technological progress, the growth in output will equal the weighted sum of the growth in the labor and capital inputs, the weights being represented by the shares of total income received by labor and capital. When this kind of production function is applied to actual data describing changes over time or differences among countries, it is discovered that only part of the changed quantity of output can be accounted for by changes in the weighted sum of the inputs. That is, some of the observed change in output is "left over" in the sense that it is not explained by the change in the inputs. It seems natural to think of what is left over as a measure of productivity improvement in the combination of production-factor inputs. Since this measure does not distinguish labor productivity from capital productivity, it has come to be called total factor productivity.

Improvements in total factor productivity are in part attributable to technological progress. In most production-function analyses, technological progress is assumed to be exogenous—that is, brought about by some process independent of economic forces. In addition to the effects of exogenous technological progress, the measured magnitude and stability of the total factor productivity depends on the form in which the production function is specified,[1] on the way that labor and capital are measured,[2] and on the importance of variables other than labor and capital that happen to be left out of the production function.[3]

Apart from the errors of measurement and specification of form, the determinants of total factor productivity can be grouped into two sets of characteristics: (1) the technical characteristics of the production process; and (2) the movement of the relative prices for the factors of production. The technical characteristics refer to a number of issues: whether the application of better production techniques will reduce the cost of all factors of production; whether new techniques lead to a greater saving in one input than in another; the difficulties or ease of exchanging factors of production in the course of the production process; the economies or diseconomies that arise in the course of changes in the scale of the economy's operation; and, finally, whether the returns to scale are evenly distributed among all factors of production.

Relative price movements influence factor productivity through

1. For example, the total factor productivity might be lower if the form of the (Cobb-Douglas) production function described above was replaced by a more general (CES) production function that does not assume constant returns to scale. This is because in such a function the effects on output growth resulting from increasing returns to scale would not be implicit in the factor productivity, but would be incorporated with the effects of the factor inputs.

2. If the measured quantity of labor and capital does not properly take into account changes in the quality of these inputs, the magnitude of the factor productivity would incorporate these quality effects. Quality alterations in the labor input are transmitted through changed characteristics of the work force, such as skills, educational achievements, age levels, and ethnic mix. Quality changes in the capital input are sometimes considered to be "embodied" in the capital stock. For example, the most recent vintage capital goods would be expected to incorporate the latest designs, so that a capital stock with a high proportion of "new" equipment would be of high quality.

3. There might be some inputs to production—such as energy consumption—that should be identified separately in the production function because they have an important effect on output growth. When these factors are not named specifically, their effects are also implicitly included with the factor productivity.

their effects on the relation between capital and labor. For example, if there is a relative increase in wage rates, there would be, if possible, a substitution of capital for labor, and technological innovations would seek to concentrate on labor-saving devices. The impact of relative price changes will depend on the possibilities of substitution between capital and labor; if the substitution possibilities are good, the change in relative prices will have substantial effects on the factor productivity. But if there are few substitution possibilities between labor and capital, even major relative price changes will have little effect.

By using the aggregate production function, economic growth can be quantitatively related to changes in the quantity of the factors of production, changes in the quality of these factors, exogenously determined technological progress, technical characteristics of the production process, and relative price movements among the production factors. Thus the production function can be used to estimate the parameters of the growth equation, which indicate the effect that each of these forces have had on past growth. These parameters, then, along with assumptions about expected labor and capital changes, can predict future levels of economic activity.

A related approach to quantifying the various sources of economic growth has come to be known as growth accounting. In growth accounting, the observed rate of growth in output between two dates is separated into component growth rates indicating the contribution to overall growth made by specific determinants. Although the logic of the production function can identify the determinants, the production function is not used to estimate their quantitative impact on growth.

The estimating procedure in growth accounting depends on measuring the growth trends in total output and in each of the determinants of output.[4] Comparing growth rates over a particular time span quantifies how much the change in each determinant contributed to the change in total output. The contribution to total output growth of each determinant depends on its relative importance in fostering growth and on the magnitude of its change. At the

---

4. A growth index for total factor input can be obtained by computing a growth index for the labor, land, and capital components of input, and then weighting each by its share of national income. But the growth index for total factor productivity cannot be obtained through this "adding up" process, since not all of the individual components of productivity can be independently derived. Therefore, the total factor productivity index is obtained as a residual through dividing the index of total output by the index of total input. The next step is to calculate the growth rate in total output, and those for the total input and the total factor productivity indexes. The growth rate in total output is then allocated between the total input and the total factor productivity in proportion to the growth rates of the two indexes.

extremes a determinant of theoretical importance to fostering output growth will have little impact on actual growth if it remains relatively stable over the time span. Similarly, a theoretically unimportant determinant may actually have a large impact on growth if it changes significantly over the time span.

The many specific determinants of growth can be consolidated into two broad groups: the total factor input group, including labor and capital inputs, and the total factor productivity group. An analysis of the growth rate and its allocation in 24 countries, roughly over the decade of the fifties, showed that the total factor productivity accounted for between one-third to one-half of the total growth in output, with contributions of total factor productivity to growth tending to be smaller in developing countries than in industrialized nations [71]. Labor tends to represent between one-half and two-thirds of the total factor input, which accounts for the remaining total output growth. Generally, if there are proportionately high contributions from the capital input and total factor productivity, total output will be growing at a relatively rapid pace.

Among European countries the most important sources of growth, over the decade of the fifties, were the increased capital stock and the advances in knowledge [27]. Together these sources tend to account for about half the growth in each country, even though the growth rate over the period varied among countries from 3 to 7 percent per year. In the United States, total factor input contributed more to growth than did total factor productivity; the reverse was the case for the European countries. The greater contribution of total factor inputs in the United States was caused primarily by the increased education per worker and, to a somewhat lesser extent, by rising employment. Improved resource allocation contributed much more to growth in the European countries than in the United States.

In spite of such differences it is the similarities among countries that deserves emphasis. Denison, the inventor of growth accounting, notes that a common set of determinants goes far in explaining growth in most countries. "The same determinants (as in the United States) were found to be largely responsible for growth in European countries, and for differences among nine nations in postwar growth rates—except that recovery from wartime distortions was of clear importance in some countries in the early postwar years" [28, p. 149].

The unique advantage of growth accounting is that it permits a consistent, detailed, and inclusive measurement of specific determinants of growth. All growth is accounted for, in one way or another, by assigning separate growth contributions to each determinant, including a residual determinant. As empirical progress in growth accounting is made, the extent of ignorance about sources of growth will be reduced, particularly as specific determinants of growth are more precisely identified.

SPECIFIC DETERMINANTS

Analyses of the contribution to growth by the two broad groups of factor inputs and total factor productivity are of only limited usefulness. Of greater interest is the contribution made by specific determinants[5] within each of these groups. In observing the societal metamorphosis that has occured since industrialization began, Kuznets notes that "the last one and a half to two centuries represent a *new* economic epoch that reflects the emergence of a new group of factors large enough to dominate growth over a long period" [57, p. 304].

There seems to be considerable agreement among economists as to what the "new group of factors" are that dominate growth. These are the quantity and quality of labor inputs, capital inputs, and natural resources. Together these account for the total factor input group. In addition there are the components of the total factor productivity group, which include the state of technology and the way it changes; the scale of the economy; and the resource allocation efficiency of markets, including the legal and psychological attributes of economic life.

Over the twenty-year postwar interval 1948-1969, potential national income in the United States increased at a rate of slightly above 4 percent per year. About half this growth could be attributed to increases in total factor input, with the other half coming from improved total factor productivity. As estimated from Denison's data [28] this growth can be further allocated among components as follows:

Increasing factor inputs	50% of total output growth
More labor	30%
More work done	20%
More human investment	10%
More Capital stock	20%
More natural resources	0%

5. In growth accounting these contributions are measured by allocating the contribution of total factor productivity among its component determinants in proportion to the growth rates of the individual determinants. The amounts derived from labor and capital inputs are allocated among their component determinants in proportion to the growth rates of the individual determinants, each weighted by its share of income.

Raising factor productivity
Advancing state of technology	30%
Increasing scale economies	10%
Improving resource allocations	10%

These components are convenient categories under which to discuss further the sources of growth, even though they are not always conceptually distinct from one another and there are important interactions between them.

More Labor

The standard model says that population affects economic growth through its impact on changes in the quantity and quality of the labor input. Over the long run the size of the labor force is supposed to be determined primarily by changes in the size and composition of the population, which in turn are the result of demographic, not economic, factors. The quality of the labor force is theoretically determined by the extent of investment in human capital, primarily through education and health investments, but also including improved efficiency through reduced discrimination and other job barriers.

Increases in the quantity and quality of labor accounted for almost a third of U.S. growth during the 1950s and 1960s. The contribution to growth from getting more work done resulted primarily from rising employment, balanced by the negative effects of the shorter work week and a shift in the age and sex composition of the work force. The gain in human investment came mostly from increased education per worker, which is assumed to increase the skill and versatility of workers and therefore the value of their output. The large contribution attributed to this component of human investment is caused by the remarkable increase in the education of young people over the past decades. Even if this expansion of education were to stop now, the effects of past increases would have a beneficial effect on output growth for a long time to come.

As concerns about pollution and natural resource scarcities have become more widespread, this "mechanistic" view of the relation between population and economic growth has come under attack. According to Nordhaus and Tobin, "Like the role of natural resources, the role of population in the standard neoclassical model is ripe for re-examination" [68, p. 526]. What requires further discussion is not only how population and labor affect economic growth, but also how they are affected by it.

Potentially, economic growth can alter the size of the labor force through its effect on fertility, mortality, and labor participation rates. Although economists have long believed that there must be some relation between fertility and economic circumstances, it is not clear what the connection is. Specifically, there seems to be no clear answer to the question of the circumstances under which economic growth will raise fertility and those where it will be lowered. It does seem clear, however, that fertility can be significantly affected by factors other than economic growth, including the spread of birth control knowledge and devices as well as changing social attitudes about large versus small families or a large versus a small world population.

Long-run effects of economic growth on labor participation are uncertain because there are two opposing forces at work. On the one hand, economic growth provides rising incomes, which lowers the propensity to engage in remunerative activities. On the other hand, economic growth furnishes opportunities to engage in work that would not otherwise be available. For example, economic growth has been accompanied by a shortened work week, but increased moonlighting. Growth has increased the health and mobility of older workers, heightening their capability to work, but the retirement age of men has been declining. Growth has hiked the average income of families, but women increasingly seek jobs, partly to raise family income still more.

Economic growth is also supposed to provide the means for raising the share of national output devoted to human investment, thereby raising the quality of labor that contributes to further growth. Evidence for affirming a relationship between human capital and economic growth is provided by intercountry comparisons, which show that countries with a high output per capita also have a high proportion of the population being educated; and by studies of investment in human capital showing that the lifetime productivity of particular individuals is raised by such investment.

However, increases in investment may sometimes reflect a cost rather than a benefit—for example, the costs of combating the pollution that is a by-product of economic growth. Investment in human capital may have similar characteristics. Economic growth, for instance, may result in diminishing returns to education, causing a rising cost without an increase in the quality of labor. This may be of substantial importance in a post-industrial society increasingly confronted by scarcities of skilled human capital and surpluses of unskilled labor.

More Capital Stock

In the view of many observers, business investment plays a role in the growth process. Investment differs critically from consumption. Consumption is only a component of demand for current output, but investment—in addition to being such a demand component—also adds to future capacity to produce output. Over the short term it does not matter much whether additional demand comes from consumption or investment. For long-term issues of economic growth, however, the amounts society decides to invest and consume are of critical importance. There is both an optimistic and a pessimistic view regarding a high share of investment in total output. The optimistic view is that with more investment now, next year the economy will be able to produce more output. The pessimistic view is that if an economy is unable to employ its people and resources fully now, then high investment merely means that next year will bring still more unemployment. Both of these views may be correct depending on the circumstances.

The pessimistic view is of venerable origin and is based on concepts of a "mature" economy that is not sufficiently dynamic to generate sufficient demand for achieving full employment. Currently this maturity argument is reflected in the judgment that growth in overall demand will not be sufficient to warrant continued expansion in energy facilities; and, if such expanded investment does take place, it would only result in a displacement of jobs with a cumulative reduction in consumption demands [19, vol. 3, p. 148]. A related view is that the economy follows a 45- to 60-year cycle, which is peaking in the 1970s. As a result the economy now has too much rather than too little physical capital, particularly energy facilities; worse still, since society retains propensities toward high rates of investment that are not sustainable, the excess of capital will continue to grow [95, p. 79].

The rate of investment—more particularly, the rate of net investment—is a key indicator, because a high rate of investment is correlated with the rapid postwar growth in output. This has been true not only for the United States but also for European countries, the Soviet Union, and Japan [39, p. 151].

Apart from their effects on stimulating aggregate demand, high rates of investment lead to increases in the capital stock that, in turn, produce growth in potential output. Added capital stock affects output through capital by "widening," which provides new workers with the same amount of tools on the average as those already at work; through "capital deepening," which increases the amount of tools available to workers on average; and through "capital quickening," which improves the quality of tools available to workers [44, p. 214]. Capital widening increases capacity output without affecting productivity per worker. Capital deepening increases labor productivity, not by changing technology but by giving workers more tools to work with. Capital quickening improves labor productivity by providing better tools made available through invention.

In this view capital stock is the "causeway" for achieving growth in economic output. The close relationship between capital investment, technological progress, and productivity improvement is emphasized. Investment is perceived as a necessary condition for growth, not only because it is a substitute for other inputs, but also because it "embodies" the improvements in technology and productivity. On such an assumption, growth in output is particularly sensitive to growth in capital.

This view should be contrasted with the source-of-growth view, in which it is not assumed that more capital stock is a necessary condition for growth; growth can occur even if net capital formation is zero. We saw that increases in total capital stock have accounted for a fifth of the output growth. In other words, it would take a 20 percent increase in the ratio of investment to output to raise the output by 0.1 percent. In order to raise output 4 percent to 5 percent a year, it would be necessary to triple the share of investment in output. But if it is assumed that capital is the causeway through which productivity improves, then increasing the output by 1 percentage point would require a much smaller rise in the share of investment in output.

In the source-of-growth view—where capital stock accumulation is not essential to growth—"in order to stimulate growth significantly through capital accumulation we should have to increase our investment quotas enormously" [1, p. 779]. In the causeway view—in which capital accumulation is given special significance in relation to output growth—"if we could merely maintain the rate of *potential* improvement opened up by the advance of knowledge, the economies of scale, the extension of education, and whatever else contributes to the potential efficiency of resources, a fairly modest increase in rates of capital formation would provide large increases in our rate of growth" [1, p. 779].

This distinction between investment as a causeway for productivity improvement and investment as an independent source of growth helps to clarify the question of whether energy and economic growth are linked. If energy is perceived as a source of growth, then growth in national output can continue without massive investments in energy facilities; furthermore, such massive investments, taken by themselves, could increase national output only by very modest amounts. This supposition essentially reflects the beta connection view, whose protagonists believe that energy can be decoupled from economic growth.

But if the alternative view is adopted and energy is perceived as the causeway through which productivity improvements are implemented, then continued expansion in energy supplies would be needed if the rate of output growth is to be sustained. Furthermore, such investment would be socially beneficial, since without it the potential improvements in productivity would not be achieved. Advocates of the alpha connection, who believe that energy and economic growth cannot be decoupled, would agree with this proposition.

Advances in Knowledge

Advances in knowledge are generally assumed to be of special importance in spurring economic development: "All history—as well as all current experience—points to the fact that it is man, not nature, who provides the primary resource: that the key factor of all economic development comes out of the mind of man" [83, p. 79]. When economic and technological development are linked, as they have tended to be in modern times, then advances in knowledge become the source of progress in technology, which in turn is the means for growth in production.

When these connections are coupled with the view that "no highly developed society has denied that affluence is its final objective" [6, p. 60], then advances in technology must, on balance, be viewed as meritorious. There is a growing objection, however, to affluence as an objective, and to technological advance as progress. It is now feared that technology's ability to deal effectively with social and economic problems over the past 200 years has been due to unique and not repeatedly favorable circumstances [65]. Even more pointedly it is suggested that, from now on, not only will technology be unable to cope with emerging problems, but the problems are themselves the result of technological "success" [20].

Uncertainty about the long-term consequences of major technological innovations fosters a major concern over the desirability of technological advances. Foremost among these uncertainties are: What are the limits to the assimilative and food-producing capacity of the environment? For how long can there be a continued exploitation of the earth's finite resources? Does technology intensify social stress created by increased contact and interactions among persons and cultures? Is there a significantly increased probability of global disasters associated with new biological, chemical, and nuclear technologies? Does the elimination of jobs, with possible destruction of established institutions for distribution of wealth and resources, accompany continued technological change?

One response to such uncertainty is to deliberately dissassociate advances in knowledge from those in technology and to direct new knowledge toward new purposes unrelated to industrial advance. Science will ameliorate the world's problems rather than contribute to them only if there is a conscious and fundamental change in the objectives it sets and the direction it takes [83].

Such a response is far different from the traditional response, which says that the direction and pace of scientific advance are largely independent of economic activity; that advances in technology cannot be disassociated from advances in knowledge; and that growth in output over the long term cannot be separated from advances in technology. "In most of the literature on factor productivity and production functions, it is assumed that technical change is autonomous, neutral and growing at a constant rate; the purpose of these studies is mainly to determine the contribution of technical change to growth of output" [72, p. 1146].

Advancing technological knowledge is supposed to contribute to economic growth in several ways—it enables a greater quantity of output to be produced from given quantities of inputs; it facilitates the production of goods better suited to specific wants; it creates new and better ways to meet human needs; and it enables new wants to be developed that could never be met before [149].

Reasonable as these statements might seem, they are only inferences. The evidence we have that advances in knowledge add to economic growth is primarily indirect. Indeed the only way its contribution can be measured is as a residual, because no way has been devised to obtain a direct estimate [29, p. 7]. This residual has accounted for almost a third of the U.S. output growth over the past two decades. Included in this aggregate are a variety of specific items. Change in the state of technological, managerial, and organizational knowledge is the most important of these items, and accounts for 60 to 80 percent of the residual. A second component of the residual reflects the contribution made by reducing the gap between the most efficient production practices that can be achieved through current knowledge and the average of actual practices. Such reduction could take place, for example, through lowering governmental and labor union obstacles to efficient production and increasing the dissemination of knowledge about best techniques. Other ways to affect productivity involve such actions as increasing the use of multiple shifts in order to economize on the use of capital, reducing the reporting obligations of business to government in order to lower business costs, and discouraging dishonesty or raising the ethical standards in the business environment.

Scale Economies

In an economy operating under constant returns to scale, an increased input will augment the output by some amount. If the observed increase is greater than this amount, the economy is operating under increased returns to scale. Kaldor has claimed that, as resources shift from agriculture to manufacturing, efficiency improves because manufacturing industries enjoy the advantages of economies of scale. He demonstrated the existence of such economies of scale by comparing a dozen industrialized countries and showing that a substantial part of the observed expansion of manufacturing productivity could be explained by increases in manufacturing production. Increased higher returns to scale, therefore, were the main engine of fast growth.

In this view, higher returns to scale are an aggregate phenomenon and do not necessarily apply to a specific product, plant, or firm that confronts particular technological conditions of production. Furthermore, increasing returns are passive. Other factors cause output to rise, meaning that output will go up still more if increasing returns prevail. As Denison says, "A country cannot do much about its size but it can strive to maximize output within that constraint" [29, p. 12].

Two conditions are associated with scale economies. One occurs when the national market expands in size (which, of course, is itself affected by all the other determinants of growth). The second happens when the nation's population and production become more concentrated in particular regional markets. Taking these together, scale economies account for about one-tenth of U.S. output growth and one-fifth of total factor productivity [28], while among the European countries they account for between one-seventh and one-fifth of output growth [97]. For less-developed countries, however, the effects of growing returns to manufacturing are less pronounced. All in all it would seem that increasing returns are an important corollary to heightened efficiency even if they are not the "main engine" for growth.

Reducing Inefficiencies

Increases in total output can be attributed to a rising (quality-adjusted) supply of inputs and improvements in total factor productivity. Total factor productivity, over the long run, can be improved by advances in knowledge and scale. In addition, it is affected by the extent to which there are "inefficiencies" in the economic system. In general, it is assumed that market economies are reasonably efficient primarily as a result of competition. If there is such efficiency, then economic growth can be promoted only by more resource inputs and advances in knowledge or scale. But if the efficiency assumption is called into question, then an important additional avenue for output growth opens up.

Imagine that any economic system has some level of optimal efficiency at any point in time. In actuality, there are always such hazards as market failure, market imperfections, inadequate knowledge, uncertainties, poor planning, and inappropriate intervention that prevent the optimal from being reached. So the economy will fall short of the optimal by some amount, and the extent to which it falls short could be considered a measure of inefficiency.

Thus, at any given time, there is some room for improvement. Since circumstances change, so that optimal efficiency also changes, there is always room for some improvement. Therefore reducing inefficiencies can be a potential source of growth at all times. "Some observers do not believe that such a potential can be very large; others believe almost intuitively that the reduction of market imperfections, in its broadest connotation, must be of vital importance for economic growth" [39, p. 398].

If we knew what an economy's optimal efficiency was, we could then measure its actual efficiency and conclude that the remainder was the extent of inefficiency. However, we can never know what the optimal efficiency is, so we can never measure the degree of inefficiency. What we can do is estimate by how much inefficiency has been reduced over a certain time period, if we first identify the factors affecting inefficiency and then measure their changes over time. Defining what is or is not inefficient, however, depends on a particular view of the economic and social process. A listing of the factors affecting inefficiency is not only arbitrary but will involve considerable overlap among them. For purposes of discussion, these factors have been separated into legal and social, government, and resource reallocation factors.

Legal and Social Factors. The structure and enforcement of property rights significantly influences efficiency because they define the scope of benefits and costs that can be included under contractual arrangements. Not only the particular content of the law, but also its certainty and its continuity are vital in reducing inefficiencies. For without a reasonable certainty about legal decisions and their enforcement, there would be substantial additions to the costs of engaging in market transactions. In Hayek's words, "There is probably no single factor which has contributed more to the prosperity of the West than the relative certainty of the law which has prevailed here" [39, p. 397].

Social mobility also enhances the opportunities for reducing inefficiences, for such mobility encourages people to move between jobs, industries, and regions as they seek superior opportunities. Social mobility also provides incentives for saving and for innovation, and fosters a spirit of enterprise in which entrepreneurs are able to develop the most productive opportunities. Additionally, the mobility of workers and entrepreneurship interacts with the mobility of capital to make it more likely that resources will be allocated to the most socially productive sectors.

Standard economic growth analyses indicate that inequalities in income distribution will not affect the efficiency at which the economy operates, and that market interventions to reduce inequalities would probably lower efficiency. However, some historians of economic development believe that increasing economic efficiency goes hand in hand with reducing income inequalities. For example, it appears that, at least with respect to underdeveloped countries, not only is there no conflict between the goals of efficiency and equality, but egalitarian reforms are a necessary condition for sustained economic growth: "Social inequality is mutually related to economic inequality, each being both cause and effect of the other. Since undoubtedly social inequality, by decreasing mobility and free competition in the widest sense of the term, is quite generally detrimental to development, it is clear that through this relationship greater economic equality would also lead to higher productivity" [70, p. 119].

Government Factors. The classical trilogy of land, labor, and capital might be followed by government as a fourth factor determining economic growth: "The sovereign state is an important factor in modern economic growth; given the transnational, worldwide character of the supply of useful knowledge and science, the major permissive factor of modern economic growth, the state unit, in adjusting economic and social institutions to facilitate and maximize application, plays a crucial supplementary role" [57, p. 346].

We may be certain that government activities will affect performance in the economy, but whether they raise efficiency is a different question. Many economists seeking to promote growth believe that government interference with the operation of the marketplace will only lower efficiency; this belief is largely based on the view that growth is desirable and an efficacious, competitive market is possible. Other observers, fearing rapid growth, have only distrust for governments since "every effort will probably be made to continue in the same old growthmanic ways. Although the physical, ecological, social, and political situations that permitted these economic practices during the past few decades no longer exist, the fact will be ignored" [32, p. 7].

In a general sense government contributes to efficiency by resolving and preventing conflicts among private interests and by guaranteeing sufficient social justice to prevent civil disturbance. Beyond this general role of being in charge of the rules of the game, government also is involved with fiscal and monetary policies that seek to raise efficiency through the control of inflation and the reduction of unemployment.

Specific government activities purporting to raise efficiency include direct investment—or subsidizing private investment— in the development of physical and human resources that might not otherwise occur: "Public investment in such fields as health, education, highway construction, the conservation and development of natural resources, and urban planning and development have a vital role to play in spurring economic growth" [44, p. 20].

On the other hand, government regulations and changes in the human environment within which business operates may often raise the costs of doing business. Laws to prevent pollution, lower industrial accidents and disease, protect consumers, prevent fraud, and increase product safety will all increase business costs and reduce output for sale. So long as accounting conventions count such activities as costs they will have an adverse effect on measured output, and will appear to have a negative effect on efficiency. Yet if the effects of these costs on the quality of output were included, efficiency would most likely be shown to improve.

Resource Reallocation Factors. In the modern economy, resource reallocations are going on all the time. As new resources are added, they are not allocated among regions and economic sectors in the same way as the existing resources, and some existing resources are always shifting from one use or place to another.

Shifting resources are part of the process of economic growth. In particular, resource shifts to manufacturing have been a major cause of growth due to scale economies. It is also the case that growth requires resources to shift, because under growth conditions the different economic sectors do not change at the same rate. For example, suppose that some technological advance permits the development of a new, improved, or cheaper product. When this happens, society generally shifts labor and resources to their production. It has been shown empirically that technological advance tends to provide increased efficiency in producing existing products, and the final result, in general, has been lower prices and increased output of these products [52].

In addition to resource shifts that cause growth and are caused by it, resources have a limited ability to shift, and this is a major reason that there are limits to growth. The substitution possibilities among final-demand goods and services is finite, and therefore the extent to which resources can shift freely (that is, without governmental dictation) is also curtailed: "Input of thousands of manhours and capital, for example, into passenger cars and television sets, does not substitute for the equivalent or even larger volume used in producing food and clothing" [57, p. 342]. These demand limits in turn curtail the amount of resources that will flow into the high-growth, innovating sectors of the economy.

But there is another sense in which limits to resource shifts will put a ceiling on growth. Sometimes there are economically beneficial shifts that could be made but are not because of such factors as lack of knowledge, institutional or social barriers, uncertainties, and a discrepancy between private and social risks. For these reasons there are, at any point in time, resource misallocations. Reductions in these misallocations would lessen inefficiencies and increase potential output.

There are two kinds of efficiency-improving resource reallocations: first, a reallocation of those resources whose current allocation among industries, establishments, or regions is suboptimal; and second, a reallocation of particular resources or individuals that, because of discrimination or other reasons, are engaged in a kind of work that is suboptimal for them. Estimates of the economic costs of particular kinds of misallocations like discrimination have been made. In addition, Denison has estimated the contribution to growth resulting from reductions in two specific resource misallocations: the larger gains from reducing the overallocation of labor to farming, and the much smaller ones from cutting the overallocation of labor to nonfarm self-employment. These two "have been by far the most important changes" [28, p. 108] among the possible improved resource allocations. His calculations show that these reallocations have accounted for less than one-tenth of U.S. growth, but for twice this share in the European countries (excluding England).

It would be misleading to conclude from these data that resources are allocated more efficiently in the United States than in European countries; it would be misleading because resource allocations are intimately connected with all the other components of economic change. It is useful and instructive to classify separate sources of growth and to quantify, where possible, their contribution to growth. But it is essential to remember that in actuality these arbitrarily defined components are not independent. Each affects the other at the same time that it affects aggregate growth. These interactions must be kept in mind as we turn to a discussion of the role of natural resources in economic growth.

Natural Resources

According to modern growth theory, limits to the rate of economic growth are set by such factors as increases in the labor supply, technological advances, or capital accumulation. In the classical theory, however, natural resources played the role of establishing limits by setting a ceiling to the level of economic activity that is ultimately sustainable and by constraining the rate of economic growth that can be achieved within any time interval. In the classical argument, there must be some ceiling to the level of sustainable economic activity because natural resources are exhaustible; and, because there are not good substitutes for natural resources, their continued exploitation would be associated with increasing costs, which in turn would produce limits on the rate at which output could rise.

Even as it was being propounded, however, the classical argument did not appear to have strong empirical support. No visible ceiling to economic activity in fact seemed to threaten the industrializing countries; nor did the pace of economic growth in specific countries appear to be dependent on their access to natural resources. The distribution of natural resource endowments among nations apparently had no correlation with the growth of nations, and relatively little of a country's output was needed in order to obtain natural resources. Therefore, by the time modern theorists adopted a simplified two-factor labor/capital model, they were comfortable about dropping natural resources as a separate factor of production and instead considered them to be a kind of capital. Since a major characteristic of capital is that it is reproducible, this meant rejecting the idea that natural resources are endowed with some special quality that gives them a unique role in limiting output growth. The idea of uniqueness was replaced with the belief that within the ranges of their potential exploitation, natural resources are really not exhaustible, and reproducible capital is always a good substitute for them.

In principle, natural resource exhaustion can be avoided by rapid and continuous exploration and discovery or by technological innovations that respond to resource endowment changes that have the effect of augmenting the available resources. The empirical evidence suggests that both of these phenomena have characterized natural resource developments in the past. In addition, the weight of the empirical evidence is that capital has indeed been a good substitute for natural resources in the past. For example, with respect to U.S. trends, "econometric estimates . . . seem to support the alternative of high elasticity of substitution between resources and the neoclassical factors" [68, p. 523]. And essentially the same statement can be made about comparisons among developed nations [71, 143].

Therefore, so long as substitutability is possible, and prices and the marketplace continue to serve as effective allocating devices, natural resources are not likely to set a ceiling to the sustainable level of economic activity or to be a serious limit on the pace of economic growth. Furthermore, if there is a high degree of substitutability, not only will natural resources fail to limit growth, but they are not likely to show up in the quantitative measurements as an important source of growth. Denison, making the assumption that the quantity of land resources remained constant, ends up showing that the natural resource contribution to growth was zero [28].

On the other hand, if the cost of obtaining and using natural resources increases and substitutes are difficult to find, it will require larger amounts of real economic inputs to obtain the natural resource requirements. Since these inputs will not be available for adding to economic output, increasing natural resource costs will limit the rate at which output can grow. In a two-factor labor/capital model, this ceiling will show up as a reduction in overall productivity.

If rising natural resource costs set a limit to output growth, the symmetrical argument would state that falling natural resource costs would be an important contribution to output growth. To demonstrate this hypothesis, however, one would have to measure the impact of natural resource costs on overall productivity change or specifically account for natural resources as a third factor in the production function. Only recently have investigators turned to such measurements, concentrating on the energy resource.

For the most part, the crucial discussion about natural resources has not revolved around the question of whether they have been an important source of economic growth. Rather, what has dominated the discussion has been the more abstract issue of whether the impact of natural resources on economic activity in the future will be different from what it has been in the past.

There is a substantial body of opinion that contends the future will not be like the past in at least two important respects. First, it is claimed that neither new discovery nor resource-augmenting technology will be sufficient to overcome the exhaustion of natural resources. This expectation is based on the judgment that the rapid rate of resource consumption is unlikely to slow down substantially, so that future availability of a sufficient supply of food and mineral resources will be limited by rising costs and a reduced store of energy; that increasingly larger amounts of energy will be needed, particularly to maintain agricultural productivity; and that energy requirements to obtain mineral resources will not increase gradually but will jump by orders of magnitude as shifts toward barren rather than rich deposits materialize. Therefore, it is feared that the production of food, minerals, and energy itself will impose demands on the available primary energy sources that future generations will be unable to meet.

Second, it is claimed that the future will be unlike the past in the need to account for environmental costs associated with energy production and consumption. In the past the true environmental costs could be ignored due to the asymmetry between the benefits and costs of energy use. But the benefits from energy use tend to be linear, immediately apparent, and widely distributed, while costs increase more than proportionately with energy use, are often delayed in their appearance, and tend to be concentrated both geographically and demographically. Since the future will reap the whirlwind of higher, delayed, and concentrated environmental consequences of energy use, the future will incur the added costs needed to avoid environmental disaster.

So if future resource discovery and technology are not adequate to the task of overcoming resource exhaustion and environmental degradation, natural resources are best perceived as setting a limit to growth rather than as making a contribution to it. Given such a perspective, the task of analysis would not be to determine whether natural resources will curtail economic growth but to calculate by how much and under what circumstances they will so do. The task of policy then, would be to respond to these limits either by finding means for expanding the supply of natural resources or lowering the demand.

This type of analysis rests on a production-function paradigm in which the availability and costs of the natural resource are significant. There is, however, an alternative paradigm that analyzes the contribution natural resources make to economic development. In this alternative, which tends to be more concerned with the long sweep of economic development, the form of the natural resource and the way society exercises control over it are important.

Historically, new forms and methods of control over natural resources have been associated with fundamental changes in their relation to economic activity. The resulting shifts in methods of production, types of goods, and levels of economic output made available seem to extend far beyond what would be anticipated by standard production-function calculations. The central question of the alternative paradigm is apparently not even asked by the production-function paradigm—namely, What is the process by which overall economic productivity is influenced by events that significantly affect the form of and control over natural resources?

New forms of energy, in particular, have signaled major economic changes in the past—changes of such magnitude that it is difficult to imagine how they could have occurred with continued dependence on the displaced energy forms, no matter how low their cost or extensive their availability. This kind of transformation happened when coal replaced wood, when liquid fuels superseded coal, and when electric power became important to commerce and industry.

Not only the past but also the future can be viewed in terms of the impact of energy form on economic activity. Once its technical feasibility was demonstrated, the potential of nuclear energy for influencing the organization of production and the patterns of consumption captured the popular imagination. This potential was not particularly related to the (mistaken) notion that nuclear energy would be cheap or abundantly available. At the time, neither the cost nor scarcity of primary energy sources were matters of particular concern. Rather, what was articulated was the notion that new production could be designed and new goods and services could be created that would not have been possible if the world had been constrained by current energy forms. Such notions were expressed not only in the popular and speculative literature, but by the most sober of scholars. Two decades ago, for example, Schurr and Marschak conjectured that the assumed ubiquitous nature of atomic power, that is, its near equal availability in all places, would drastically change the location of people and industry with major consequences for the pace and pattern of economic activity in the nation and the world [86].

Even though this proliferation has not happened, there is still the general expectation that the future will bring with it new energy forms. Technical feasibility, changing energy cost conditions, and considerations of national security would seem to be conspiring to bring this about. The disagreements are not over whether changes will take place, but over which energy forms should—or are likely to—dominate, and how they would affect economic growth.

In one scenario, fossil fuels will continue as the primary energy source for a long time to come, even though the energy form might shift to greater dependence on synthetics, coal, and conventional nuclear reactors. Such changes in energy form would have a minimal impact on the organization of production. The most likely effect would be that rising costs would slow down economic growth or induce a significant shift toward energy-conserving methods of production and consumption.

In a second scenario, renewable energy sources such as solar or breeder reactors will become the primary energy form, inducing significant changes in the organization of production. Whether the result would be a rising growth rate in economic output, as in the past, would depend on two particular cost factors: (1) the investment costs needed to build energy producing facilities; and (2) the expenses incurred to prevent environmental degradation associated with continued high energy usage.

In a third scenario, the requirements for energy fuels will diminish as a consequence of the changed goods and services society selects to consume. Destined to replace fuels are knowledge and skilled labor, which would have a profound effect on the organization of production. The costs of fuel development and use would not be of great importance in the future, since they would not be a major factor in determining the pace and pattern of economic activity. The societal changes implied by this scenario could be so profound that conventional measures of economic growth would no longer be applicable, and quantitative comparisons between the present and future would become meaningless.

Chapter Four

Sources of Growth in Energy Consumption

CONSUMPTION TRENDS

Energy consumption in 1975 was twenty times the 1875 level.[1] However, the population is now five times the figure it was a hundred years ago and economic output is thirty times larger than before. Clearly something more than simple developments in population and output have caused growth in energy consumption. What are these other sources of energy consumption?

Since energy becomes valuable only when converted to some good, this means that the demand for energy is derived, directly or indirectly, from the nation's production of goods and services. One classification of the sources of energy consumption, therefore, can be developed by spelling out the components of this derived demand from production.

It is convenient to think of production as the product of the amount and the productivity of labor. The amount of labor (employment) is determined by combining the total population with the share of the population that is employed (employment propensity). Labor productivity can be broken into three components: (1) the average quantity of output produced by each unit of capital stock (capital productivity); (2) the average amount of capital stock associated with each unit of energy consumed (capital intensity); and (3) the average amount of energy associated with each unit of labor

1. The data described in Chapters 4 and 6 are derived from the basic data in Tables 1-9 in the Appendix at the back of the book.

(energy depth). The average amount of energy consumed per unit of output—that is, the energy intensity—multiplied by the level of production will give the total energy consumed.[2] When the energy lost in conversion, that is, in the generation and transmission of electric power, is subtracted from the total, the remainder indicates the net energy consumed by the end users. This is separated, for present purposes, between the industrial, the residential, plus commercial and the transportation users.

These components of production and energy intensity are here defined as the sources of energy consumption as depicted in Figure 4-1. It is also assumed that each source is independent of the others in terms of its effects on energy consumption. Therefore, the relative contribution each source has made to growth in energy consumption can be estimated as the ratio of its growth rate to the growth rate in total energy consumed—much in the same way that the sources of economic growth were measured in Chapter 3.[2] The significance of the sources of growth in energy consumption can then be compared with one another, and their changing importance in different time periods can be analyzed.

A Century of Growth

Energy consumption over the past century has grown at an average of 3 percent a year. Population over the same interval has increased at about half the energy consumption rate. So population growth— accompanied by rising demands for goods and services requiring energy for their production—has accounted for half the increase in energy consumption since 1880.

Also during this period, energy consumption rose 1.5 times faster than employment, and energy depth grew at an annual rate of almost 1 percent a year. So an expanded energy consumption in relation to employed workers accounted for a third of its growth over the past hundred years.

---

2. What has been spelled out is merely an identity in which energy consumption equals the product of the various components or sources that have been identified. Let O = output; P = population; L = employment; S = capital stock; E = energy consumption. O/L = labor productivity; O/S = capital productivity; L/P = employment propensity; S/E = capital intensity; E/L = energy depth; E/O = energy intensity.

$$O = P \times L/P \times O/S \times S/E \times E/L$$
$$E = P \times L/P \times O/S \times S/E \times E/L \times E/O$$

2. For example, the sources of economic growth were measured by allocating the contribution of total factor productivity among its component determinants in proportion to the growth rates of indexes for the individual determinants. Since the sources of energy-consumption growth are assumed to be independent, their growth rates will sum to the energy-consumption growth rate, and percentage shares of the total can be calculated.

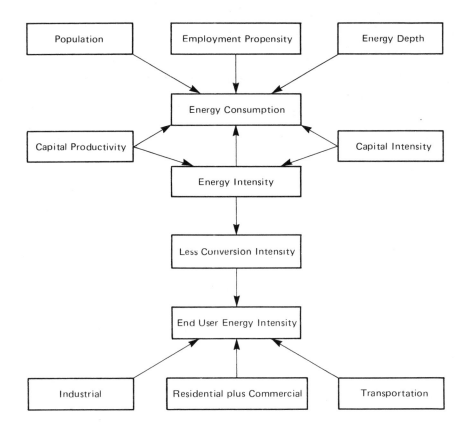

Figure 4-1. The Energy Consumption Identity

Not only has population increased, but the share of the population employed has also increased. This rising employment propensity raised energy consumption, because the added workers require an energy input to be productive. The growing propensity for employment has represented one-tenth of the energy consumption increase.

These two factors—the increased employment and the increased amount of energy associated with each employee—formally account for all of the increased energy consumption. But implicit in the energy depth ratio there are other elements—relating to the use of capital and energy—that are important sources of change in energy consumption.

The amount of capital stock has increased at a slightly faster rate than the quantity of energy consumed. Since capital stock is energy-using, its growth will tend to raise energy consumption, even though capital intensity goes up. Over the past century the change in capital intensity has accounted for 10 percent of the energy consumption increase. Since output has grown faster than capital stock, capital productivity has also risen, thereby adding to the increased production of goods and services that require an energy input. The heightened capital productivity has been the source for about 5 percent of the total energy consumption increase.

All of the preceding factors have been positive sources for energy growth over the past century. The major factor retarding still further increases in energy consumption has been the fall in energy intensity. Since 1880, energy intensity has declined by about 0.5 percent a year. Without this decline in energy intensity, energy consumption would have increased at a 15 percent faster rate than it actually did.

Over the entire period since 1880 population growth has accounted for about half the rise in energy consumption, while increases in the energy depth and employment propensity have accounted for the other half. But this can be misleading. The sources of energy consumption growth have varied from one period to another during the century. These variations are associated with changes in economic conditions and in the composition of fuels comprising the energy base. This lends support to the contention that changing energy forms are related to the pace of economic growth and the character of economic development.

It seems to take about three to four decades for a new energy form to seriously challenge or displace older forms. For example, in 1850 wood accounted for almost nine-tenths of energy consumption in the United States. By the 1880s wood accounted for less than half of total energy consumed because of the incursion of coal. Then, sometime before 1920, coal reached its highest share of almost four-fifths of total energy consumption. Also by 1920, oil and electric power clearly became energy sources to contend with as each provided about a tenth of the energy requirements; natural gas waited another decade before it reached a tenth of the energy consumed.

After 1920 the liquid fuels expanded at a much faster rate than electric power. By the late fifties oil approached half of the total energy consumed and has tended to sustain this share. Natural gas accounted for one-quarter of consumed energy by the mid-fifties and peaked at one-third in the early seventies.

Between 1920 to 1955 the increase in direct end use of liquid fuels (i.e., excluding fuel sales to utilities) was five times the growth in fuel consumption for electric power. However, between 1955 to 1977 this trend dramatically changed so that the growth in electric power fuel consumption was only one-third smaller than the growth in direct end use of liquid fuels. The result was that electric utilities provided for almost half the increase in total energy consumption.

These trends in fuel use can be used to separate the last 125 years into four distinct eras:

1850 to 1880—the *wood era*. Wood continued to provide over half the nation's energy.

1880 to 1920—the *coal era*. Coal became the dominant energy source and maintained its position.

1920 to 1955—the *liquid fuel era*. Oil and gas provided the basis for increased energy consumption.

1955 to 1977 (or beyond?)—the *electric power era*. Even though oil and gas have continued to be the primary fuel sources, electric power generation accounted for almost half the total growth in energy consumption during this interval.

The shifting importance of the sources of energy consumption can be clearly observed in Appendix Table 10. Figure 4-2 compares the relative contribution of each source to total energy consumption during each era.

During the wood era the major energy need was for space heating in the home. As a consequence, energy consumption was not closely related to levels of economic activity and increases in energy consumption could be totally attributed to population growth.

The coal era experienced the fastest rate of growth in total energy consumption—twice as fast as during the liquid fuel era and 25 percent faster than in the power era. Energy consumption growth in the coal years was faster than in the power era, almost completely because of the relatively rapid population growth in the earlier period. Thus, the rate of increase in per capita energy consumption was essentially the same in both eras.

Of the four periods, the liquid fuel era experienced the slowest growth in energy consumption. This can be largely attributed to the fact that the quantity of energy used per worker changed very little during the period, as compared with substantial increases during the coal and power eras. Another factor that distinguishes the liquid fuel era is its striking drop in energy intensity. This energy-intensity decline, by itself, cut the rate of energy consumption growth almost in half.

The difference in energy intensity between the coal and liquid fuel eras can be linked to the changing nature of fixed capital require- ments and productivity improvements. Capital stock in the coal era

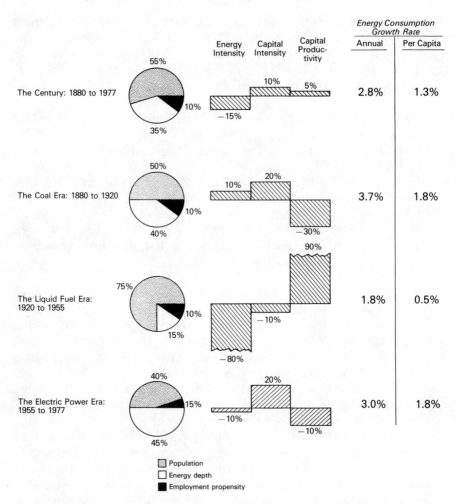

Figure 4-2.   Relative Contribution of Sources of Energy Consumption

increased at three times the rate of the liquid fuel years while its labor productivity improved at two-thirds the rate. As a result, capital productivity declined during the coal era while increasing during the liquid fuel period. What all of this suggests is that before 1920 the industrial and transportation sectors employed increasing quantities of energy-using capital in order to raise labor productivity and to prevent energy intensity from falling. The 1880 to 1920 period, in other words, was a period of *mechanization*.

During both the coal and the power eras, the capital stock grew at a much faster pace than labor productivity. However, during the liquid fuel era it was possible to achieve substantial improvements in labor productivity without having to add to the capital stock at an even faster rate. New industrial processes and a changing product mix abetted by the new forms of energy (power as well as natural gas and oil), created what appears to be a unique period in history—a substantial decline in energy intensity accompanied by rapid increases in labor and capital productivity. The 1920 to 1955 period, in other words, was a period of *industrialization*.

There are two major characteristics that distinguish the power era from the earlier periods. First, growth in the industrial sector's output and employment was at a much slower rate during the power years. Growth in industrial energy consumption, however, was at half the rate of the coal era while at about the same rate as during the liquid fuel era. Industrial energy intensity, consequently, essentially stabilized in the power era rather than increasing as in the coal period or declining as in the liquid fuels period.

The second factor that distinguishes the electric power from the other two eras is the different ways that the energy intensities of the specific end-use sectors have changed.[3] These are summarized in Figure 4-3. In the coal era energy intensity of the industrial and transportation end users increased as they mechanized their production processes; however, a decline in energy intensity of residential and commercial users substantially offset the industrial and transportation intensity increases. In the liquid fuel era each end-use sector lowered its energy intensity because each sector benefited from increased industrialization. However, further declines in energy intensity almost stopped during the electric power era, with a small decline in the energy intensity of the industrial and transportation sectors being offset by a small increase for the residential to compel a slowdown in the decline of energy intensity. At the same time, the shift from goods to less energy-intensive services has helped to prevent the intensity-increasing forces from becoming dominant. These competing forces have balanced out so that energy intensity remained essentially stable for each of the end-use sectors. The 1955 to 1977 period, following terminology developed by Kuznets, has been a *servicing era*.

---

3. The overall energy intensity can itself be decomposed into the energy intensity of each end user, customarily separated into the industrial, transportation, and residential plus commercial end users. (Electric utility sales and conversion loss are allocated among end users in this formulation.) However, changes in the energy intensity within each end-use sector do not aggregate to changes in the total energy intensity. This is because changes in product mix involve shifts in energy consumption from one sector to another. Since the level of energy intensity is different for each sector, these product mix changes would also contribute to overall energy-intensity changes. Changes in end-user energy intensity, over the past century, are shown in Appendix Table 10.

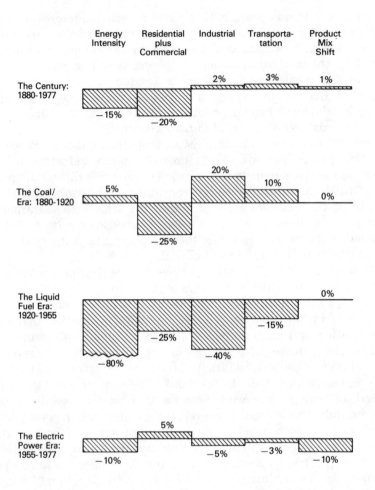

Figure 4-3. Relative Contribution of Energy-Intensity Sources of Energy Consumption

Thus, over the past century changes in energy form have been sufficiently associated with changes in economic structures and their energy intensities to provide the following distinct historical periods:

1850 to 1880—The wood/home heating era
1880 to 1920—The coal/mechanizing era
1920 to 1955—The liquid fuels/industrializing era
1955 to 1977—The power/servicing era

Not only were the relations between energy and the economy quite different as between each of these periods, but also, within each period changes in economic structure and energy use occurred from one decade to the next. The following section looks more closely at these changes.

Subperiods of Energy Consumption

Each of the major historic eras has a distinctive pattern of development in terms of the sources of energy consumption. The variety in the patterns of historical development is evidence that the future is not committed to some rigid set of relationships. We need to be alert to the dangers of extrapolating the relationships within some arbitrarily selected historic interval, as if that interval were the only relevant history. The diversity of potential responses is apparent in the following description of the differences in developments within the 5- to 10-year subperiods of each major era since 1850.

The Home-Heating Period. In 1850, 90 percent of energy consumed was in the form of wood, and the major energy need was for space heating in the home. As a consequence, energy consumption was not closely tied to levels of economic activity, and changes occurred primarily as a result of population growth.

Productivity on the farm and in the factory was, however, improving. Part of these improvements was probably related to the increasing use of coal (which had reached two-fifths of total energy consumption by 1880), as well as to the growing application of energy in the industrial sector (which accounted for one-quarter of energy consumption by 1880). These advances in productivity, coupled with a probable increased efficiency in the use of energy in the home, meant that energy intensity had to decline from 1850 to 1880. And so it did—at a very rapid rate—primarily because of rapid improvements in overall economic productivity.

The Mechanizing Period. The major change in economic structure during this period was expansion in the fixed capital of factories, railroads, shipping lines, and mining enterprises. Between 1880 and 1920 the nation's capital stock grew by a factor of six. Fueling this growing infrastructure was coal. Without coal the growth in capital stock would not have been possible. With coal the potential for mechanizing the economy could be realized. And with mechanization the growth in demands for energy, particularly in the industrial sector, was unprecedented as compared with the past and unrepeated in most periods of the future.

This growing energy consumption was fostered not only by the increased mechanization but also by substantial population increases. Even though the rate of population growth in the decades of this era exceeded the rates of most future decades, per capita energy consumption also tended to grow at a faster rate. Since the growth rates for GNP, industrial output, and labor productivity were not particularly rapid, the energy intensity, particularly in the industrial sector, rose substantially, as did the quantity of energy supplied to the average worker.

These trends, however, did not persist. By the last decade of the era, new signs were becoming visible, signs that the economic structure was again changing. The new industrial processes and changing products were not needing as much additional capital as in the past and could also get along with less energy.

The first decade of the mechanizing period saw a substantial growth in energy consumption, attributable totally to the increase in population and employment propensity. However, the quantity of energy consumed per employee declined somewhat, while energy intensity remained stable. This stability was the result of offsetting forces: an increased energy intensity in factories and railroads was balanced by declining energy intensity in the home.

In the next two decades employment growth fell off, largely because of a slower increase in the share of the population that was employed. A major spur to increased energy consumption during these decades was the rising quantity of energy consumed per worker, as both the industrial and the transportation sectors hiked their shares of economic activity and raised the intensity of their energy use. Overall energy intensity, however, still remained relatively stable, because intensity in the home continued to decline, probably as a result of improved efficiency in the use of coal.

The last decade of the mechanizing period appears to be a transitional interval in that for the first time, energy intensity declined slightly, anticipating the major declines of the later periods. This reduction in energy intensity was brought about by industrialization, which halted the substantial declines in capital productivity that had been occurring and caused a shift to less energy-intensive products. The leveling off of energy intensity, coupled with a slow employment increase during the last decade of the mechanizing era, meant that the rate of growth in energy consumption slowed down considerably, even though there was a substantial rise in the quantity of energy consumed per employee.

The Industrializing Period. The interval from 1920 to 1955 saw not only the emerging dominance of oil as the primary fuel source but also some wide swings in overall economic activity: the growth

Empirical Highlight 4-1. Changes in Sources of Energy-Consumption Growth

● Increases in population are a major source of energy-consumption growth in all of the historical intervals; and such increases are the most important source in most of the intervals. Increases in the employment share of the population (employment propensity) were an important source of energy-consumption growth only in selected periods: 1880-1890, 1930-1940, and 1940-1947. Combining population and employment propensity shows the importance of employment growth as a source of energy consumption. Employment increases were a particularly important source during the industrializing periods, but were less important during most of the periods in the mechanizing and servicizing eras.

● The increased amount of energy used by the average employee (energy depth) was an important source of energy-consumption growth during the mechanizing and servicizing periods, but not during the industrializing period.

● The increased quantity of energy used per average unit of capital stock (capital intensity) was an important source of energy consumption growth only during selected intervals: 1880-1890, 1920-1929, and 1947-1955.

● Increases in the quantity of energy consumed per unit of output (energy intensity) were an important depressing influence on energy-consumption growth only during the industrializing periods and 1960 to 1966.

● Increases in the economic output produced per average unit of capital stock (capital productivity) were an important cause of the declining energy intensity in the industrializing periods and 1960 to 1966. Declines in capital productivity acted to prevent energy intensity from falling during the other periods.

● Energy lost in the generation and transmission of electric power has been increasing substantially relative to total energy consumed. But this conversion loss relative to total output has shown only a slight upward drift.

● During the first three decades of the mechanizing era, energy intensity was stable—essentially because a decline in residential and commercial energy intensity was offset by an increase in industrial and transportation intensity. The last decade of the mechanizing period (1910-1920) was a transition decade in which industrial energy intensity remained stable while there was a shift to less energy intensive goods and services. Energy intensity declined in the industrializing periods as a result of intensity declines by each of the energy end users. In the servicizing period these declines have tapered off, and only the industrial end user has persistently held on to a declining energy intensity.

acceleration of the 1920s, the bust of the thirties, the boom of the war years, and the surprisingly rapid growth of the postwar years. But, probably of greater long-run significance than these events was the emerging importance of oil and natural gas.

The availability of liquid fuels enhanced the nation's mobility, improved its productivity, and changed its styles of living. The growing economy encouraged an increase in energy consumption. But the changing economic structure dampened the need for more energy. The energy consumption growth was usually slower than the growth in output so that energy intensity fell during most of the industrializing period. This was true for the total economy as well as the industrial sector taken alone.

The slow growth in capital stock over the entire era reflects the failure of capital stock to increase during the depression and war years. Such stability, of course, does not mean that there was no new investment; only that additions to the capital stock merely offset plant and equipment which became obsolete and were no longer used. The failure to add to capital stock during these years helped to slow down the growth in energy consumption.

However, the major reason for the slow growth in energy consumption during the liquid fuels era was that the energy requirements per worker did not increase by very much, even though labor productivity, particularly in the industrial sector, improved substantially. New technologies were being introduced that allowed for faster growth in output than in capital stock, labor, or energy use.

The result, then, was a decline in energy intensity. A decline in the industrial sector occurred because of rapid productivity improvement. A decline in the transportation sector occurred because of the use of more energy efficient vehicles. And a decline in the residential sector occurred because of a shift to less energy-intensive goods and services.

The increase in energy consumption during the twenties was supported both by a rising population and an increase in the energy depth ratio. But the growth in energy consumption was slowed down as compared with preceding decades because of a fall in energy intensity, which occurred partly because industrialization was rapidly improving for the entire economy, and partly because the energy sector itself was able to conserve. For example, the shift from coal to oil for space heating and industrial processing meant an improvement in thermal efficiency, as did the lowering of heat rates for the generation of electric power.

The substantial drop in energy consumption from 1929 to 1930 was totally caused by the reduction in employment and incomes as a result of the great Depression. However, energy consumption—particularly in the residential, commercial, and transportation sectors—does not respond rapidly to a decline in total output. Therefore, energy intensity actually rose in this one year.

Employment did not continue its decline for the entire Depression decade (1930-1940). Rather, by 1940 it had surpassed the pre-Depression levels. Therefore the slowdown in energy consumption growth that took place during the decade is not primarily attributed to a reduced rate of employment but to a decline in the average quantity of energy consumed per employee, which is associated with the 10 percent drop in energy-using capital stock that occurred between 1930 and 1940.

Improvements in labor productivity during the Depression produced declines in energy intensity. However, the pace of labor productivity improvement was cut in half, as compared with the preceding decade, which meant that the rate of decline in energy intensity slowed down. Continued improvements in thermal efficiency of specific fuels, as well as shifts to more efficient fuels, helped to sustain the decline in energy intensity for each end user.

The war and immediate postwar years (1940-1947) saw recovery to rapid growth in output and in energy consumption. Employment increases were the chief source of energy consumption growth, although a rising energy depth also made some contribution. Even though the pace of labor productivity improvement picked up, the decline in energy intensity slowed down considerably. This leveling off was probably attributable to a shifting product mix in which the fuel demands for military and freight transport were so high that the intensity of transportation use did not decline. Another cause was a shift to energy-intensive manufacturing industries, which contributed to a rise in the industrial end-use intensity. It was only in the residential and commercial sectors that energy intensity continued to decline both as a result of improved thermal efficiency and a shift toward less energy-intensive purchases.

The rate of output growth in the postwar years (1947 to 1955) was about the same as in the war years; the pace of energy consumption growth however, was almost cut in half. About half of the slowdown was caused by a reduced rate of increase in employment as the employed share of the population remained stable. The other half resulted from a speedup in the rate of decline for energy intensity. The transportation sector—no longer faced with high military demands and supported by a rapid shift to thermally efficient diesel fuels and by the spread of high-compression auto engines and fuel-efficient aircraft engines—showed a rapid decline in energy intensity. The industrial sector also enjoyed a declining energy intensity as it shifted to fewer energy-intensive goods and services and introduced energy-saving production processes. This was not so for the residential and commercial sectors, whose growing demands for energy-intensive products and, to some extent, less thermally efficient fuels prevented further declines in energy intensity. It is interesting to note that the pattern of development in the postwar decade is quite similar to the pattern of the 1920s. It is as if the economy was simply continuing the industrializing trends interrupted by the Depression and war years.

The Servicizing Period. The last two decades are probably more informative about the course of future relations between energy and the economy than earlier eras. Two characteristics of these last decades are of particular relevance to the future: the emergence of electric power as a major source for energy expansion and the steep rise in energy costs over the past few years. It is likely that in the future, electric power will become even more important and energy prices will go even higher.

However, it is well to remember that the future will not replicate the past. For example, although electric power will almost certainly continue its relatively rapid growth, it is by no means certain what the fuel sources will be. Also, even though energy prices continue to rise, the future impact will be different as the economy finds the means to make appropriate adjustments. Thus, it is fairly certain that the relations between energy and the economy will not remain as they now are; they will not even change in the same way as they have changed in the past two decades.

The major characteristic of the servicizing era is that energy intensity effectively stabilized. This occurred because output grew at about the same rate as in the industrializing era while growth in energy consumption picked up considerably. As in the industrializing era growth in output was supported by improvements in labor productivity and increases in employment. However, to determine what caused the increased growth in energy consumption we need to look more closely at the different experiences of the industrial and nonindustrial producing sectors.

The industrial sector did not account for the speed-up in total energy consumption growth. In the industrial sector energy consumption grew at about the same rate as in the previous era but the rate of industrial output growth fell off. This put a virtual stop to the decline in industrial energy intensity—perhaps because of some shifts to energy-intensive industrial processes and increased use of safety and pollution control equipment which use energy.

During the servicizing era the contribution of the industrial sector to growth in total output, employment, and labor productivity diminished. The services part of the economy became much more important, with substantial growth in its capital stock and produced output. These factors caused a significant pick-up of the energy used per worker in the service sector, which raised service energy intensity. When coupled with growing service employment, the increased energy depth in the service sector accounted for most of the increased rate of energy consumption growth for the total economy.

Thus, it would appear that several offsetting forces have been at work during the servicizing era: a shift of total activity from industry to less energy-intensive services, accompanied by increasing energy intensity within services.

But, these overall trends describing the entire servicizing era represent a balancing of differential trends that occurred during specific intervals within the era. Some new trends emerged during the second half of the 1950s. Although the growth in output was cut in half compared with the preceding decade, the rate of growth in energy consumption remained the same. As a result, declines in energy intensity as experienced in the preceding decade were halted, and a substantial increase in the quantity of energy per employee sustained the growth in energy consumption. The industrial sector was mainly responsible for preventing any further decline in energy intensity, which seems related to the decline in capital productivity that took place between 1955 and 1960. The rate of decline in transportation-sector intensity also slowed down, as suburbanization and large cars began to take their toll in fuel consumption, while increased electrification and air conditioning in the home and in commercial buildings raised the energy intensity of the residential and commercial sector.

The first half of the sixties brought an extremely rapid rise in output supported by substantial increases in employment and labor productivity. This, in turn, meant a high rate of growth in energy consumption, as both production and the ratio of energy to employment rose. However, energy consumption did not rise as fast as output. As a result, energy intensity declined, just as it had during the industrializing period, and probably for the same reason—rapid improvements in overall productivity for the economy. This decline in energy intensity was not restricted to a particular sector but was equally enjoyed by all end users.

Energy intensity began to increase in the second half of the sixties. From 1966 to the 1973 oil crisis, improvements in the heat rate ceased, rapid growth in nonenergy uses of fuel proliferated, and substantial expansion of air conditioning and electricity for space heating became more common. Each of these developments helped to increase energy intensity in the industrial, residential, and commercial sectors. Perhaps even more important was the expanded production of big cars, along with increased auto, truck, and air mileage, along with the cessation of shifts to diesel fuel, all of which helped to raise the energy intensity of the transportation sector.

In addition to these energy-use considerations, the 1966 to 1973 rate of improvement in labor productivity was slower than in earlier periods. As a result, even though the average energy requirements per worker increased substantially, growth in total output slowed down from its earlier pace, while growth in energy consumption speeded up. The resulting hike in energy intensity was channeled primarily through each of the end use sectors.

Events since 1973 are of particular relevance to the future. With rising energy costs and efforts at conservation, energy per worker has dropped considerably in spite of a slow growth in employment. This has been reinforced by substantial shifts of economic activity from industry to less energy-intensive services. As a result, overall energy consumption has barely increased over the past four years and energy intensity declined sharply both in the aggregate and for each end-use sector. Failure to recover to full employment has kept output growth relatively low during these years. Therefore, the decline in energy intensity is probably not attributable to a large increase in the denominator of the intensity ratio. Rather, it appears attributable to decline in the numerator of the ratio, resulting from rising energy prices and other factors leading to reduced energy usage.

PATTERNS OF ENERGY CONSUMPTION

The patterns of energy consumption relate to what form energy takes, who uses it, and for what purposes. The major forms of energy are the primary fuels—wood, coal, petroleum, and natural gas—as well as electricity which converts the primary fuels or other inputs (such as hydro, geothermal, and nuclear inputs) into energy. As shown in Figure 4-4, the relative importance of these forms has been changing over time. Prior to 1890 wood was the primary energy form, and then was replaced by coal. Coal retained half of the energy market until after World War II even though its share of energy consumption peaked before 1920. The petroleum share of consumption increased steadily until the mid-1950s, and has since stabilized. The natural gas share increased slowly at first, but jumped markedly in the postwar years until the early 1960s, and then leveled off. Electric power has consistently increased its share of energy con-

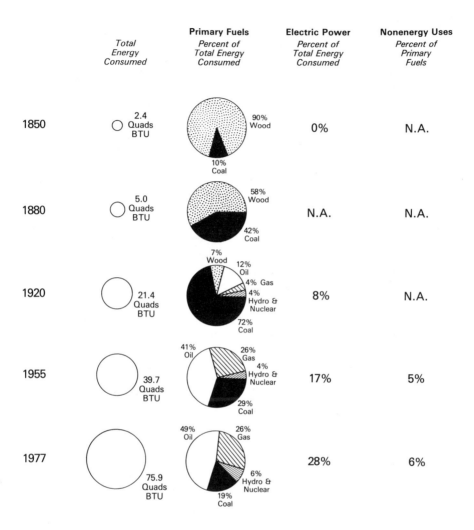

Figure 4-4. Forms of Energy Consumption

sumed and is continuing to do so. Hydroelectric power remained at a fairly constant share until the postwar period. Since then, until the most recent years, the increasing share of nuclear power has merely offset the falling hydro share.

In conventional accounting, energy consumption is measured in terms of British thermal units (BTUs), which allows for comparability among tons of coal, barrels of oil, and cubic feet of natural gas. Electricity is measured in terms of its fuel equivalent, even though some useful energy is derived from such nonfuel sources as hydro and solar power. This discrepancy creates some difficulties in international comparisons of energy consumption, particularly with countries that rely heavily on hydro power, and it will increasingly create measurement problems as the nonprimary fuel sources become more important. In addition, an increasing amount of fuels is being used for such nonenergy purposes as petrochemicals, lubricants, and fertilizer. This suggests that it will become increasingly important to distinguish between fuel consumption and energy consumption in the future.

The major users of energy are conventionally separated into the sectors that directly consume it: households for use in the home and for personal transportation; industry for producing goods and services; and the commercial sector for providing services. However, the specific components included within each of these user categories differ from one data series to the next. For example, most of the available long-term historical data series consolidate the household and commercial end users of energy. Although the small size of the commercial sector may have warranted this type of accounting 50 years ago, it is not appropriate today. Electric power consumption presents another problem. In some data sources, electric power is treated as a separate end user, and in others it is allocated to its industrial, residential, and commercial users. But even when electric power is divided among the other end users, the problem remains of how to allocate conversion losses so total primary fuel consumption can be accounted for.

Transportation presents another measurement problem because it is carried as a separate end-use sector in most of the long-term historical data series. Transportation, however, is more properly a use than a user, and each of the end-user sectors utilizes some energy for transportation purposes. The separation between personal and commercial transportation is particularly important, with the former allocated to the household end-use sector and the latter usually relegated to the commercial sector. It would be even more useful if the energy directly consumed for transportation by the industrial and commercial sectors were also identified, but this is rarely done.

Although the difference between the production of goods and services is not always clear, this distinction is used to separate the industrial from the commercial end-use sectors. The industrial sector generally—but not always—includes the energy consumed not only by manufacturing but also by mining, construction, agriculture, forestry, fishing, and utilities. The commercial sector then covers the trade, finance, insurance, real estate, services, and government energy consumers, as well as serving as a catch-all for energy consumers not included somewhere else. Some important difficulties with such coverage by the commercial sector are that government energy consumption is not separately identified, and that energy consumed in rental housing is usually included as a commercial rather than household-sector activity.

Only recently have the separate uses of energy been systematically defined by separating energy uses into three major categories: (1) transporting people and goods; (2) space conditioning through the heating, lighting, and air conditioning of structures; and (3) materials processing through the use of fuels and electricity to produce heat in order to change the molecular structure, the configuration, or the location of materials [73]. Figure 4-5 presents a three-dimensional view of energy consumption by user, form, and use.

In one way or another, each of the major end users consumes each energy form for each of these purposes. Household and industrial users each take about a third of the energy, commercial users about a fifth, and other users[4] about a tenth. Materials processing accounts for about a third of the energy uses, transportation about a quarter, space conditioning about an eighth, and other uses about a quarter. Petroleum provides two-fifths of the energy, natural gas more than a quarter, electricity (including all its primary fuel inputs) one-fifth, and coal one-tenth.

The end users vary in the ways they employ their energy as well as the forms of energy they purchase. Households depend primarily on petroleum and use energy mostly for transportation and space conditioning. Industry relies mostly on natural gas and electricity, which it uses primarily for materials processing. The commercial sector spreads its energy, most of which is petroleum, among transportation, space conditioning, and other uses, but little materials processing. Electric utilities[5] primarily consume coal in their production of power, which they put mostly into space heating and materials processing.

End-Use Sectors

Unfortunately the data are not available to show how the interrelationships among form, use, and user characteristics of energy

---

4. Other users refers primarily to coal exports and oil and gas feedstock.

5. To avoid double-counting, electric utilities are not included among all end users in Figure 4-5. However, the uses of electric power and the primary fuels that electric utilities consume are shown separately in the chart.

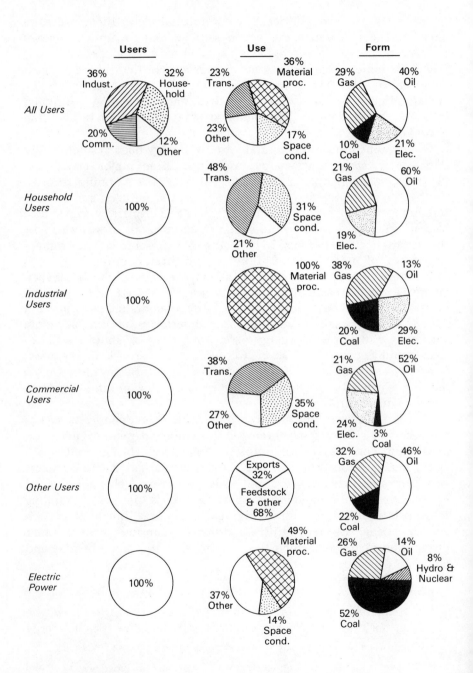

Figure 4-5.   Energy Consumption by User, Use and Form, 1970

consumption have changed over time. However, the long-term shift in energy consumption—from wood to coal to oil to gas and electric power—can be related to changes in the pattern of consumption among end users and uses. Figure 4-6 shows these relationships. The major change took place during the coal era: the household and commercial sector's share of total energy consumption was cut in half while the share of the industrial and transportation sectors doubled. Since 1920, the major changes have related to the rise of electricity. Electric utilities doubled their share of primary energy consumption during the liquid fuel era and almost doubled it again during the electric power era. So by 1975, electric utilities consumed more of the primary energy fuels than any of the other sectors. The increased share of primary energy consumed by electric utilities since 1920 has been offset by downward drifts in the shares of the household plus commercial and the industrial sectors while the transportation share remained stable.

If the energy consumed by electric utilities is allocated among the purchasers of electric power, a different picture emerges. Both the household plus commercial and the transportation sectors have essentially maintained their shares of the total energy consumed since 1920, each accounting for about one-quarter of the energy. However, the share of energy consumed through the process of converting primary fuels to electric power has substantially risen and now accounts for one-fifth of the total energy. To offset this increase the industrial sector share has declined, modestly during the liquid fuel era and more precipitously during the electric power era.

In view of the magnitude of economic changes over the past half century, it may appear surprising that essentially the same allocation of energy occurred in 1920 as in 1977, with the residential plus commercial and the transportation sectors each responsible for a quarter of energy consumption and the industrial plus electric utilities sectors accounting for a half. However, this similarity is misleading because comparisons between the major end users are too gross to identify the important changes actually taking place—those within each of the end use sectors.

The Household Sector. Households consume two-thirds of all energy—one-third directly in the home and for personal transportation and the other third indirectly through the purchase of goods and services from the industrial and commercial sectors[6] [73, p. 19]. Of the direct energy consumption, half is for transportation, a third for

6. The remaining third goes to the energy embodied in exports, capital formation, and government purchases.

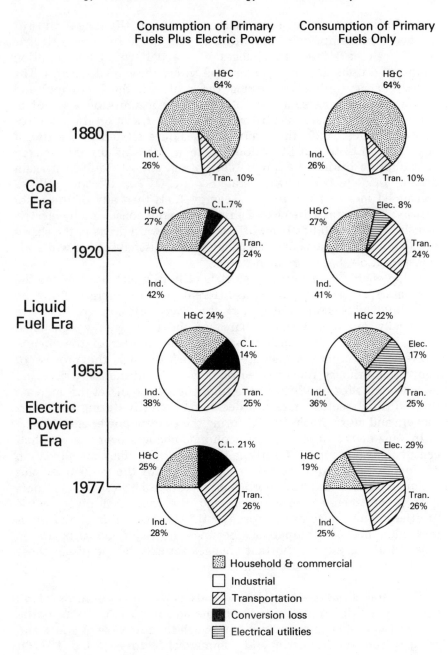

Figure 4-6.   Patterns of Energy Consumption

space conditioning, and a fifth for materials processing (such as cooking) and other uses.

Demographic and social factors have a significant effect not only on the aggregate energy consumed by households but also on its uses. For example, small families consume more energy per capita than large families, and families with children less energy per capita than families without. This occurs partly because in large families less gasoline per capita is consumed, and per capita living space requirements are smaller, lowering heating and cooling costs. Geographically dispersed units of an extended family consume more transportation fuel than those families whose members live close to each other. City dwellers use less residential energy and automobile fuel than suburban and rural families. Density in residential locations tends to lower energy consumption, while long journeys to work raise it. Multiworker families consume more energy than single-worker families. Tenants tend to use more energy than homeowners. Speed limits, building codes, climate, and social norms with respect to interior heating and lighting all influence patterns of household energy consumption.

Economic factors, particularly energy prices and income levels, will affect household energy consumption. As energy prices increase households tend to consume less, primarily by cutting back on activities that consume large amounts of energy. Also, as incomes rise the per capita amount of energy consumed goes up directly. As a consequence the poor use less energy for space conditioning, travel fewer miles, and have fewer energy-using appliances. In addition the poor get even less utility than the rich from the average unit of energy they actually consume, for they tend to possess energy-intensive appliances, inefficient energy-using automobiles, poor insulation in their homes, and few energy-saving devices such as temperature controls. It is partly because their homes and equipment are relatively energy intensive that the poor must spend proportionately more of their income on energy than the rich. But it is not only a poor-versus-rich differential that occurs. Along the entire income scale, the share of the household budget spent directly on energy also declines as affluence increases. However, there is a countering influence to this direct energy/income relationship: as affluence rises an increasing share of the family's budget is spent on the energy indirectly consumed through the purchase of goods and services that have relatively high quantities of embodied energy [45].

Energy-using capital goods—appliances, vehicles, and structures— are the channels through which changing energy prices and family incomes affect the level of energy consumption. Thus rising energy prices appear to reduce the rate of utilization, particularly for automobiles and for space-heating equipment, and thereby lower household energy consumption in the short run. But such capital goods have 5- to 20-year lifetimes, so that it is often the anticipated, rather than current, energy prices and family incomes that will induce changes in energy consumption. Expectations tend to speed up change, because if a consumer anticipates that energy prices will rise, he or she is more likely to purchase energy-conserving equipment than would be economically warranted by the current energy prices. If energy prices are expected to increase very rapidly, it may even speed up the rate at which existing capital goods are scrapped or retrofitted.

Over the long run, therefore, the amount and thermal characteristics of residential housing, personal transportation vehicles, and energy-using applicances and equipment will be primary determinants of energy consumption. But the capital goods turn over very slowly, so the primary determinant of energy consumption in the short run is the rate at which capital goods are utilized.

The Industrial Sector.   The industrial sector accounts for about a third of the total energy consumed. Over nine-tenths of this consumption occurs in manufacturing establishments. Furthermore, most of the manufacturing energy consumption takes place in a few relatively energy-intensive industries.

The reason for such concentration of energy consumption is that the physical process of altering the chemical or molecular structure of materials is inherently more energy intensive than other industrial processes. These molecular alterations tend to occur in the early stages of processing and for a relatively small number of industries—the chemical, metal, paper, and fuel industries. The physical processes required to change the state of materials (such as melting glass) is less energy intensive, while the processes required to rearrange the location of materials (such as automobile assembly) require very little energy.

Figure 4-7 shows a cross-classification of energy consumption by process and industry. The energy required by the processes that change molecular structure comprises three-fifths of the total industrial energy required, because the energy intensity of these processes is very high. The energy intensity of processes that change the state of materials is much lower, but the total energy consumed by these processes is sustained by the high level of demand for the products they produce. The processes that change the location of materials have a very low energy intensity, causing them to require less than a fifth of the total industrial energy consumed.

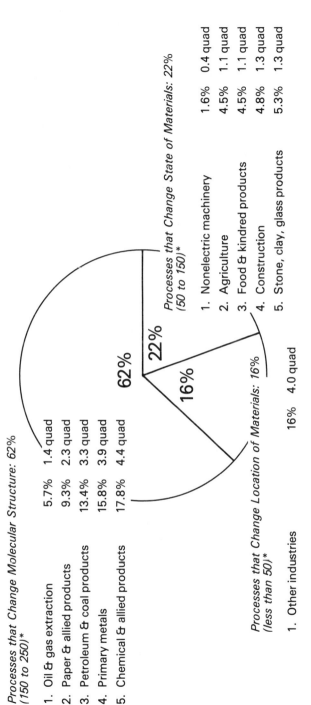

Processes that Change Molecular Structure: 62%
(150 to 250)*

1. Oil & gas extraction	5.7%	1.4 quad
2. Paper & allied products	9.3%	2.3 quad
3. Petroleum & coal products	13.4%	3.3 quad
4. Primary metals	15.8%	3.9 quad
5. Chemical & allied products	17.8%	4.4 quad

Processes that Change State of Materials: 22%
(50 to 150)*

1. Nonelectric machinery	1.6%	0.4 quad
2. Agriculture	4.5%	1.1 quad
3. Food & kindred products	4.5%	1.1 quad
4. Construction	4.8%	1.3 quad
5. Stone, clay, glass products	5.3%	1.3 quad

Processes that Change Location of Materials: 16%
(less than 50)*

1. Other industries	16%	4.0 quad

62%

16%

22%

*Thousands of BTU consumed per $ of industry output.

Figure 4-7. Industrial Energy Consumption, by Industry and Process, 1972

In the household sector the quantity and rate of utilization of appliances, vehicles, and structures are the primary determinants of energy consumption. In the industrial sector the counterparts to these determinants are the energy intensities and output levels for each industry. In the long run, as well as in the short run, industrial-sector energy consumption will change as a result of both these determinants. In the short run, changes in energy consumption are probably most influenced by alterations in the level of production. Energy consumption in specific industries can be lowered in the short run by more effective energy housekeeping practices, by some minor capital investments, and by some upgrading or retrofitting of existing equipment. Rising energy prices will encourage such changes, although the likelihood is that since the industrial sector has been greatly concerned about lowering its overall costs, it has already achieved most of the potential in these areas.

Over the long run, trends away from the intensive energy-using processes are likely to continue. In addition, new processes, materials, and equipment may all become available. What these new developments are and how rapidly they will be introduced will depend on energy prices and, to some extent, the particular forms of energy that are relatively abundant.

The Commercial Sector.   The commercial sector includes a variety of activities, some of which have little in common. The major energy users in this sector—which accounts for one-fifth of total energy consumption—are the commercial transportation industries, the structures and the equipment of the nongoods-producing industries, and the various federal, state, and local governments.[7] In 1971, one-third of the commercial sector's energy consumption went into space heating, and almost two-fifths into commercial and government transportation. The remaining quarter of the energy consumed in this sector involves a highly diverse set of materials processing and communications activities, most of which take place within commercial buildings.

Energy consumed per square foot of commercial buildings can vary by a factor of five [73, p. 59]. Such large differences are caused in part by the various types of activities in each building and the equipment they employ. But mostly the disparities in energy consumption for different structures arise from the requirements for space conditioning, which are affected by the physical and occupancy characteristics of buildings as well as their geographic location.

7. Multiple-family rental housing is here included as part of the residential sector energy consumption, and not as part of the commercial sector.

"In the nation as a whole the structural uses that consume the most energy in order of importance are: (1) heating and ventilation; (2) lighting; (3) air conditioning (cooling) and ventilating; (4) equipment and processes; and (5) domestic hot water" [30, p. 11]. This ranking may vary from one building to the next depending upon climate, type of structure, characteristics of operating the building, and type of equipment being used. For example, in cold climates, heating tends to consume the most energy, followed by lighting, and then cooling. In milder climates, cooling is likely to be more important than heating; and lighting, which is independent of climate, may exceed both. In retail stores and schools, lighting is likely to be the most important energy consumer, but in hospitals hot water needs may exceed the lighting requirements. Buildings such as hotels that are occupied on a 24-hour basis are likely to have a very different energy consumption than those often unoccupied, such as auditoriums or theaters. Generally, heating seems to be relatively more important for buildings that are occupied only part-time.

Building design and materials are an important source of differences in energy consumption. For example, buildings can be constructed to utilize waste heat, require less glass, provide self-contained air conditioning units, locate personnel so that large blocs of unoccupied areas can be shut down, use low-pressure lamps, and introduce automatic devices for providing adequate but not excessive lighting. And since the design and materials are influenced by building codes and zoning practices, they also will significantly influence energy consumption in the commercial sector.

Commercial transportation accounts for over one-third of the energy used by the commercial sector as a whole. This comes to about 7 percent of the nation's total energy consumption and approaches one-fifth of our petroleum consumption. In addition, energy used by the military for transportation purposes is about one-quarter of the commercial transportation usage [73, p. 66].

Trucks take half of the energy consumed by commercial transportation, aviation a quarter, with ships and rail each accounting for about a tenth [73, p. 65]. Energy consumption by alternative modes is significantly affected by fuel price changes. Rising prices induce changes in payload, speed, dispatching practices, use of equipment, modal shifts where possible, and technological innovations. In the long run technological changes and new regulatory practices are likely to have major impacts on the energy consumed by commercial transportation.

PRICE EFFECTS ON CONSUMPTION

The price consumers must pay for a commodity helps to determine the quantity that will be used. But for many observers the full story of how the price of energy has affected U.S. society is not told by the relationship of energy's price to its consumption. To these observers a two-dimensional demand curve does not sufficiently describe the story of how "cheap" energy has, in the past, been responsible for overall economic advance and determined the content of what society has decided is a high standard of living. Their prognosis is that the end to a low-cost reliable energy supply in the United States will bring with it major societal readjustments.

But by what standard is the price of a commodity "cheap" or are its costs "low"? When such labels are applied to energy, then its price is probably being judged in relation to one or more of the following four criteria. According to one criterion energy prices in the United States have been low as compared with those in other industrial countries. Our lower prices have encouraged patterns of energy consumption that would be judged wasteful in these other places. According to another criterion energy costs have generally been a small share of a family's budget or a firm's expenses, so there has been little incentive to seek ways to use less energy. A third criterion states the customer of energy has not been required to pay the full costs associated with its production and use (either because of regulated prices or because the market price fails to include pollution costs), and that this situation has produced a greater than optimum amount of energy consumption. According to a final criterion, energy costs and prices have increased at a slower rate than the general price level, and a cessation of such a decline in real costs signals that energy will no longer be a bargain.

Price Trends

Most closely linked to the "cheap" energy concept is the empirical observation that, until recent years, real energy prices have been declining. The long-term trends in the production costs and whole-sale prices of different energy forms indicate that the United States has had more than a half century of "cheap" energy—beginning right after World War I and ending with the oil crisis of 1973. During this interval, real energy prices (measured at wholesale for all fuel and power) declined by 0.75 percent a year. But 90 percent of this decline occurred during the industrializing era; during the servicizing period (1955 to 1973), overall real energy prices were essentially stable. Furthermore, all of the real price decline during the industrializing era took place between the ends of World War I and World War II (1921 to 1947). However, the forces that created the real price decline before 1940 were different from those that followed: prior to World War II not only real prices, but nominal (that is, actual current dollar) energy prices were falling; during the war, nominal prices increased but at a slower pace than prices in general, so that real energy prices declined.

In the postwar period, real energy prices drifted upward until the mid-1950s. Over the next decade, real energy prices declined, not because of a fall in nominal energy prices (as occurred during the first half of the industrializing era), but because of the relatively rapid increase in the general price level.

Electricity prices fell in nominal as well as real terms right up to the mid-1960s, which has given electricity a major role in lowering the real price of all energy. The real prices for electric power have fallen at three times the pace for all energy. Since electric power now accounts for almost a third of total energy consumed, the decline in electricity prices has contributed more to the overall real energy price decline than all the other energy forms combined.

The overall real cost of production (for the weighted composite of all fuels) was about the same in 1973 as in the early 1920s, but this does not mean that real costs were steady during this entire period. Rather, a sharp decline in real production costs occurred during the twenties attributable primarily to a fall in nominal costs. After 1930 real costs increased, except for the first half of the sixties. During the early sixties a relatively rapid rise in the general price level set the stage for the real energy cost decline.

If the real costs of producing primary fuels did not change by very much during the era of cheap energy, what caused the decline in real energy prices? The price of energy includes not only the primary fuel production costs but also the costs of distribution and transportation of energy. It appears that a substantial part of the long-term decline in real energy prices can be attributed to falling costs of the distribution and transportation components of the energy price.[8]

---

8. It is arithmetically appropriate to depict the price of energy as comprising the sum of the various cost components. However, such a description is not an energy price analysis. First of all there are a variety of measures for energy prices, depending on particular measurement procedures, and they do not all show the same trends. In addition a component cost breakdown of energy prices provides only a very small part of the data needed for analysis of the complex relation between energy costs and prices. For example the price and supply of imports, price regulations and industry pricing practices, short term versus long term prices, incremental versus existing production costs and effects of prices on exploration and research are just a few of the considerations that should enter into any detailed analysis of energy prices.

The share of the energy price accounted for by fuel production costs varies by energy form, region, and type of customer. It tends to be relatively low for natural gas and gasoline, small consumers, and places distant from the production sources; the reverse seems to hold for coal, fuel oil, and nonresidential electricity [36].

The long-term changes in overall energy prices are also influenced by differential trends for the various energy forms. Although the real costs of production for each primary fuel were lower at the end of the industrializing era than at the beginning, their patterns of decline were not the same. The real costs of natural gas liquids declined through the entire industrializing era, and then continued to decline through 1966. Natural gas began its real cost decline in 1930 and ended it before the 1950s; real costs of production for crude oil fell up to World War II and then rose until the mid-fifties when they again began a decade of further decline; bituminous coal declined in the decade of the twenties, increased through the postwar period, and then fell again right up to the middle of the sixties.

Energy prices in real terms began to rise in the mid-sixties, reversing their historical decline; this rise was in part related to increasing real production costs. But these increases were quite modest compared to the precipitous increases since 1973. The increased price and quantity of oil imports triggered the increased overall real energy prices, but was not the sole cause. Domestic fuel production costs also increased as production shifted to high-cost sources in order to meet rising demands.

Price Elasticities

One of the important consequences claimed for rising energy prices is that they will cut the demand for energy. To a very large extent the success of energy conservation programs depends on this result. But while there is general agreement that rising prices will reduce energy consumption from what it would otherwise be,[9] there is much less agreement about the magnitude of the reduction.

The quantitative relation between prices and demand are conveniently summarized by the "price of elasticity of demand," a ratio showing the percentage change in the consumption of an energy form divided by the percentage change in its price.[10] A review of

9. This does not mean that future increases in prices will be accompanied by falling levels of energy consumption. There are other factors, including population growth, income growth, changes in residential living patterns, and many other factors that may favor rising energy consumption. The price effects as discussed here are independent of these other factors.

10. For example, a price elasticity of —0.5 would mean that a 10 percent price increase over some time interval would result in a 5 percent drop in

recent studies that have empirically estimated the price elasticities of various energy forms shows that virtually all price elasticities have a negative sign—indicating that price increases do result in a lowered demand.

Long-run price elasticities are substantially larger than in the short run, which occurs because energy is generally not consumed directly but through the use of equipment and appliances, or is embodied in some commodity that has been produced by energy-using equipment. In the short run, ordinarily defined as the period in which the capital stock is fixed, higher energy prices would cut energy consumption primarily by lowering the utilization rate of the equipment (for example, by reducing the number of automobile miles traveled). In the long run, however, when capital stock is variable, energy consumption can also be lowered by changing the quantity and type of equipment and appliances in current use (by shifting to smaller cars, for instance). The long-run elasticity estimates indicate that, in fact, rising energy prices will slowly change the capital stock so as to lower energy consumption.

The long-run demand for electricity is relatively elastic. In other words a price increase produces a proportionately larger drop in consumption. Furthermore, electricity demand becomes increasingly elastic as prices rise [60, p. 323]. Comparable data are not available for other energy forms except for the limited information on gasoline for motor vehicles, which suggests that over the long run, demand reductions are almost proportional to price increases.

The price elasticity for all energy forms combined tends to be lower than the elasticity for any particular one because there is competition among fuels. So if the price of a particular fuel rises relatively fast, other fuels will be used instead.[11] So long as such substitutions are possible, part of the consumer's reaction to a price increase for a particular fuel will be to shift to another fuel rather than reduce energy consumption, and this means that the aggregate energy price elasticity must be lower than the elasticity for a particular energy form. The evidence indicates that few of these substitutions occur in the short run since particular types of

consumption from the level it would otherwise reach. The theoretically preferred way to calculate price elasticities is by fitting a demand function in which the consumed quantity of some energy form is a function not only of the price of that form but also the prices of other types of energy, of income, and of energy-using equipment [93, p. 75]. In this way the price effects can be kept independent of the effects of other factors.

11. These relations are formally defined by the cross-price elasticity, that is, the change in consumption of a particular energy form with respect to the change in the price of some other energy form. The empirical evidence indicates that cross-price elasticities among energy forms are positive.

equipment or appliances require particular types of energy. Over the long run, however, as the capital stock changes, these interfuel cross-price elasticities can become significant.

Because the price elasticities of particular fuels are different, the total energy price elasticity is influenced by the mix of particular fuels being consumed. Similarly, the price elasticities associated with different end users vary. The industrial sector, which tends to be cost conscious, displays a higher long-run price elasticity than the other sectors. Also, although the data are not definitive, there is a suggestion that the price elasticities of the residential and commercial sectors are about the same and that both are somewhat higher than for motor vehicle end users. Overall it appears that the effects of energy-mix shifts toward electricity and away from the industrial end use would be to raise the price elasticity of all energy.

Most of the early studies of energy systems avoided discussions of energy prices. When prices were mentioned, the assumption—implicit or explicit—was that the price elasticity was zero. In a competitive system such an assumption is valid only if energy intensity does not change. Now most observors reject the zero price elasticity assumption. There is not only general agreement that the price elasticity is nonzero, but also that its size is nontrivial. But agreement on the nontrivial aspects of the price elasticity has not yet produced agreement about its magnitude. The most that can be confidently said is that the elasticity falls between 0 and −1, with some clustering of estimates near −0.5 [48, p. 4].

From a policy perspective it is important to know more precisely the values of energy price elasticities. Over the long run even small differences in price elasticity can end up as large differences in energy consumption. For example, if the probable price elasticity is somewhere between −0.3 to −0.7, then the reduction in energy consumption from a particular price rise would be twice as high at the upper end of the elasticity range than it would be at the lower end.

Although rising energy prices will dampen the growth in energy consumption, higher incomes will work in the opposite direction. Both the short-term and the long-term income elasticities are positive, with the latter generally being larger. So over the long run, higher incomes will affect energy consumption, offsetting the effect of rising energy prices. Since aggregate real income is likely to rise faster than real energy prices over the long run, while income elasticity does not appear to be lower than price elasticity, the net effect of these countervailing forces would be to raise levels of energy consumption over the coming decade.

Yet many of the most recent studies have projected a higher energy price elasticity and lower rate of income growth than were generally being assumed in the last few years. As a consequence the growth now expected for energy consumption is considerably less than earlier forecasts—particularly compared with some of those doomsday predictions based either on insufficient energy availability or "excessive" energy consumption.

INTERNATIONAL COMPARISONS

The quantity of energy consumed per capita differs among countries. The differences between the industrialized and the developing countries are very large. But even among the industrialized countries, the disparities are substantial. The United States, for example, consumes four times the amount of energy per capita than is used in Israel, three times the amounts in Japan or in Western Europe, and about the same amount as in Canada. If the reasons for these differences could be identified we would learn much about the role of energy in the industrialized economy.

The Statistical Evidence

Many people have offered a variety of multicountry correlations as statistical support for their views of how energy and the economy are connected; or, more particularly, their views as to whether significant changes in U.S. energy consumption would affect our living standards. The problem is that the available evidence can be used to support a variety of positions. On the one hand the statistical observation that levels of GNP are closely related to energy consumption leads easily to the implication that high living standards depend on substantial energy use. On the other hand there is the statistical observation that for high-income countries further increases in energy consumption are inversely related to a rising national output, which leads to the implication that reductions in energy consumption would be desirable. Between these extremes is the view that the statistically observed intercountry variability between energy use and national output means that there are many benign policy options available for a country seeking to influence its energy consumption.

The variety of inferences drawn from the same set of data is not only a signal to be cautious in basing policy on such comparisons; it also reflects some disagreement about what the data actually show. These data support four significant findings [24]. First, multicountry correlations show a strong relation between national output per capita and energy consumption per capita. The data do not indicate that output rises proportionately to energy consumption. Rather, as we move up the scale of country affluence, per capita energy consumption increases at a somewhat slower pace: roughly, a 10 percent rise in output per capita is associated with an 8 percent rise in energy used per capita. However, some countries depart from the general relationship. Many observors believe that it is the experience of these deviant countries that is relevant to future policy and that the United States should learn from those countries that have achieved a high standard of living with low rates of per capita energy consumption.

The second finding is that changes in per capita output over time and within specific countries are roughly proportional to their changes in per capita energy utilization. For industrialized countries, the annual percentage change in output relative to the annual percentage change in energy consumption tends to be about 1.0 and to range between 0.8 and 1.3.

The third finding is that although energy intensity (that is, the energy/output ratio) in individual countries tends to change over time, there is no clear trend. During some periods the intensity increases, and in others it declines; for some countries the ratio rises, while for others it falls. In spite of the absence of a clear trend, there does seem to be some long-run convergence for the energy intensities of various countries. For example, some countries that were well below the U.S. energy intensity 25 years ago have been increasing their intensity at a relatively rapid rate while at the same time the U.S. ratio has remained comparatively stable. The result is that the disparity between the United States and Western European countries has become smaller. So in assessing whether the transfer of foreign energy consumption practices to the United States is feasible, the possibility that the transfer may actually be going in the opposite direction should be recognized.

The fourth and in many ways the most intriguing of the findings is that there is neither a positive nor negative significant correlation between energy intensity and per capita output. If there were a clear-cut positive relation it would be tempting to say that increasing energy intensity contributes to rising productivity (that is, output per capita) in industrial countries. Conversely, if there were a clear-cut negative relationship, a highly probable inference would be that increasing productivity helps to restrain the growth of energy intensity in industrialized countries.[12]

12. Another way to state the absence of a correlation between energy intensity and productivity is that the cross-country relation between energy and output is not systematically related to energy per capita. Therefore, if energy per

Taken together, these four observations identify the issue posed by international comparisons—namely, why is it that increases in per capita energy consumption (over time and across countries) are systematically related to rising per capita output, but increasing energy intensity is not? The policy analogue to this statistical question is: Can living standards in the United States continue to rise if the lower energy consumption standards prevailing in some other countries are adopted?

Only recently have empirical investigations into this question been undertaken, and they have been of two types: (1) comparisons of the energy consumption patterns among a set of industrial countries; and (2) comparisons of the United States with other specific countries that have lower levels of energy consumption with comparable living standards, most notably Sweden [82] and West Germany [40].

The United States consumes substantially more energy per capita in each end-use sector. As compared to the weighted average of the other selected industrial countries, the U.S. residential, commercial, industrial, and conversion-loss sectors consume about twice as much energy per capita, while the transportation sector uses about four times as much. The contrast in energy intensity between the United States and other countries tends to be about half of the per capita consumption difference, reflecting the fact that variation in productivity among industrial countries tends to be smaller than energy intensity differences.

The U.S. transportation sector accounts for a larger share of total energy consumption than in other countries. In some countries (such as Japan, Italy, and West Germany) this is partly offset by a

capita could somehow be held constant across countries, a different view of the relation between intensity and productivity might emerge. In order to standardize the energy per capita across countries, we asked the following question: If energy per capita for each country were the same as in the United States, would there be any systematic relation between energy intensity and economic productivity?

We first calculated the labor productivity, energy intensity and per capita energy consumption for nine industrial countries in selected years since 1950. We then transformed these indicators into index form with the United States as the base of 100. For each country we then calculated an excess productivity index, which is the difference between its productivity index and its per capita energy consumption index; and we also developed an excess intensity index, which is the difference between the intensity and the per capita energy consumption indexes. We then graphed the cross-country relationship between excess productivity and excess intensity. The results show that for each of the indicated years there is an inverse relation between energy intensity and economic productivity. This brief test suggests that—given U.S. levels of per capita energy consumption in all countries—increasing productivity tends to lower intensity. (If some other country, rather than the United States, were used as a base, the results would likely be different.) No support is provided for the contention that increasing energy intensity raises productivity.

relatively large share of energy consumption by the industrial sector; in other countries (such as the Netherlands and Sweden) the residential and commercial sectors consume a proportionately large share; and in still others (such as Canada and the United Kingdom), a relatively large conversion loss offsets the smaller transportation energy consumption as compared to the United States. The relative importance of transportation in the United States also means that it accounts for a disproportionately large share of the differences in energy consumption between the United States and other countries. For example, although transportation is less than a sixth of energy consumed in the selected industrial countries, it accounts for almost a third of the difference from the U.S. level of per capita consumption, and almost half of the difference from the U.S. level of energy intensity.

Although these data clearly indicate that the United States consumes more energy than most other industrial countries, they provide no evidence as to whether such consumption reflects "waste" or even a capability for the United States to adopt new patterns of energy consumption without serious effects on its living styles. To evaluate these questions a deeper probing for the causes of differential energy consumption is needed.

Why Countries Differ in Energy Consumption

Cross-country comparison studies indicate a limited number of factors that account for international differences in energy consumption per capita and energy intensity. For the sake of clarity these factors have been grouped into three categories: (1) geographic conditions; (2) structural characteristics; and (3) end-user intensity. The following discussion elaborates on how each affects energy consumption in particular industrial countries.

Geographic Conditions.   Compared to most other industrial countries, the United States is larger, has a warmer climate, and has more easily extractable energy resources. In the past the United States has responded to these geographic features in ways that tend to add to its relatively high per capita energy consumption.

Country Size.   The volume of United States passenger travel and freight transportation is much greater than in other industrial countries. For example, U.S. per capita passenger mileage is twice that in Germany, while per capita ton mileage is five times greater [40]. In part these differences are related to the size of the United States and the spatial configuration of its industrial and residential locations. In spite of its huge size, the spatial configurations in the United States are similar to those in other industrial countries: a number of urban areas—having densely packed central cities and nearby suburban communities, which are linked to each other through a complex system of trade. In the United States, distances between the urban areas are relatively long, not only because of the sheer size of the country but also because the large urban complexes are located on the periphery, so people and goods are transported across vast land stretches between the urban areas.

Most of the freight in industrial countries moves between, rather than within, urban areas. Since there is little indication that the per capita tonnage of intercity freight in the United States differs from other industrial countries, its higher ton mileage seems attributable mostly to the longer distances between urban centers.

Thus distance contributes to the high per capita energy consumption in the United States.[13] Although little can be done about changing the distance between urban areas, the ton mileage could be reduced if there were an increase in the share of the freight traffic between nearby rather than far-apart urban places. This choice has not been made in the United States because long-distance trade offers many advantages that overcome the costs of transportation.

Movement within urban areas accounts for about two-fifths of the total energy used for transportation in the United States. The relatively high passenger mileage per capita in this country is accounted for mostly by intraurban travel for such purposes as commuting, shopping, and recreation. For example, passenger mileage per capita within urban areas in the United States is twice as high as in Sweden; but passenger travel between urban areas is only one-third higher [82]. Urban densities tend to be less in the United States than in other industrial countries, indicating that distances between travel points, particularly for commuting, are somewhat greater. This is partly because suburbanization began earlier and has been more rapid in the United States, and partly because in European countries the population tends to concentrate in small centers near work and shopping, thus reducing daily transportation needs [80, p. 19].

The longer intraurban traveling distances account for some of the relatively high passenger mileage in the United States. However, probably more important than the fact of distance is our life style, which favors the use of automobiles for short trips. The private auto

---

13. The ton mileage involved in export and import trade is not included in these comparisons. Since such trade is greater for the European countries than the U.S., the actual ton mileage difference is less than the measured domestic ton mileage.

accounts for nine tenths of all short trips in the United States, while in Sweden it is used for only half [82]. A higher reliance on walking, bicycling, and public transit for short trips is responsible to a considerable extent for the lower passenger mileage of European countries.

Climate. The second geographic characteristic important to energy consumption is climate, which directly affects the residential and commercial uses of energy for heating and cooling. The colder climates of the European countries have raised their energy consumption per capita for heating compared with the United States. In order to counteract the resulting high energy costs, the European countries have also responded to the cold climate by adopting energy-saving tactics. For example, lower temperature settings than in this country are ordinarily considered comfortable. Even more important is the impact of climate on building design, which encourages the construction of well-insulated buildings that conserve on energy use. In the United States, perhaps because energy costs are lower, warmer inside temperatures in cold weather and colder inside temperatures in warm weather are required to meet people's standards of comfort. And at least until recent years, building construction has been unconcerned about heat loss. Building design has hiked energy consumption still further by incorporating heavy energy-using air conditioning systems.

Energy Resource Base.   An abundant energy resource endowment is the geographic factor with the greatest impact on U.S. energy consumption. Considerable energy is used up in the course of extracting, processing, and shipping coal, oil, and gas—all of which are relatively abundant in the United States as compared with other industrial countries. The energy used up in the extraction, production, and delivery of energy is called the *energy penalty*. Exclusive of energy conversion losses, the energy penalty accounts for almost a tenth of U.S. energy consumption. Since U.S. energy intensity is 25 percent above the average intensity in Europe, the energy penalty alone accounts for a third of the differential.

Countries with few energy resources import the additional energy they need. Cross-country comparisons show a strong correlation between energy intensity and energy import dependency: countries with a low energy intensity having a high import dependency. But this relation may be largely attributable to measurement conventions. Import-dependent countries enjoy a low energy intensity mostly because they do not incur a large energy penalty. Under current measurement practices, the energy penalty incurred in providing the imported energy is not counted as energy consumption in the importing countries. If it were, their energy intensity would be raised and the correlation between energy intensity and import dependency would be weakened.

The ability to import energy has widened the scope of industrial opportunities for poorly endowed countries. The absence of domestic energy resources has not seemed to discourage countries from developing energy-intensive manufacturing industries. Nor has the depletion of domestic energy resources caused countries to give up their energy-intensive industries [24, p. 27]. Countries with a small energy resource base, but otherwise suited to energy-intensive industries, have historically been able to import energy and incorporate such industries into their industrial structure.

This is not to say that the availability of domestic energy resources has no effect on industrial activities of a country. Even though a relatively small domestic energy resource base is not, by itself, sufficient to prevent the development of energy-intensive activities, a relatively abundant energy resource base encourages the adoption of energy-intensive production technologies. Furthermore, the particular energy form in the resource base also tends to influence the kinds of production processes that are adopted and the types of energy-using equipment that are employed.

The effects of the domestic energy resource base on industrial activity are closely linked to its impact on other factors, such as the price of energy, the location of industry, the design of equipment, the character of technological innovation, and the nature of the existing infrastructure and capital stock. Many of these impacts may have their rationale in history rather than in current circumstances, but their present consequences are just as real. It does seem clear that, although the precise effects of a relatively ample energy resource base in the United States are difficult to isolate, the choices that have been made as a consequence of this base have favored practices that increase energy consumption in general, and specifically raise the consumption of the abundantly available energy forms.

Structural Characteristics.   A popular technique for evaluating the differences among countries in energy consumption is to separate the difference into two components: one part attributable to a different mix of activities; the other to differential energy intensities for each activity. This distinction is useful because the structure of activities sometimes tends to reflect living styles or physical conditions in a particular country that are difficult to change; while the energy intensity of activities tends to reflect efficiency factors that might be transferable from one place to another.[14] In this section the structural characteristics in three classes of activity are considered: transport modes, fuel forms, and industry outputs.

Transport Mode. If a country favors energy-intensive modes of transport, this will tend to raise its energy consumption. In the United States the more energy-intensive modes are favored for passenger travel but not for freight. There are two reasons that the U.S. freight modal mix is less energy intensive than in European countries: (1) the longer distances have encouraged the use of such energy-saving modes as rail and water to move goods; and (2) domestic oil and gas production has meant that a large share of total transportation tonnage moves through pipelines—the least energy intensive of the transport modes.

A major factor leading to an energy-intensive modal mix for U.S. passenger travel is the extensive use of the private automobile, rather than mass transit, for intraurban travel.[15] Mass transit in the United States accounts for less than 5 percent of the intraurban passenger mileage, and cars essentially account for the remainder; at the same time, cars consume five times more energy per passenger mile of local travel than is used by mass transit. In Germany, which is also a car-oriented society, mass transit accounts for about 15 percent of intraurban travel. In Sweden, which is much less car-oriented, mass transit accounts for 25 percent of commuting and other local trips, while motor- and pedal-bikes account for another 25 percent; in addition, Swedish cars consume only twice the amount of energy per passenger mile that is consumed in mass transit.

If the U.S. modal mix were less concentrated on the auto for local travel, energy consumption would be lower. But the consequences of a private auto-oriented modal mix should not be overemphasized. For example, if the United States were to use cars for only half of its local passenger travel—the share now prevailing in Sweden—this cut would reduce the nation's total energy consumption by only 3 percent and its transportation energy consumption by about 10 percent. Local passenger transportation, which accounts for less than

14. However, caution should be exercised when interpreting country differences in energy consumption in this framework. Not only is it unable to deal directly with underlying causal factors, but also the quantitative relationship between intensity and mix is a function of the level and kind of activity aggregation that are adopted.

15. The U.S. preference for auto travel cannot be explained by higher income levels or its income distribution. "Relative to given income levels, Americans drive a lot more than Europeans" [85, p. 20].

one-tenth of total energy consumption, is simply not a large enough energy user for even significant shifts to mass transit to greatly reduce energy consumption in the United States.

Fuel Form. Since fuels differ in their thermal efficiencies, the primary fuel mix that countries adopt can potentially influence their level of energy consumption. However, the overall thermal efficiencies of industrial countries are roughly the same [24, p. 29], partly because intercountry differences in the mix of fuel consumption are not large.[16] In each of the industrial countries, at least half of the energy consumption is provided by petroleum products; for the remaining half, most of the countries adopt a mix of the primary energy forms, while at the same time relatively emphasizing a particular form.[17] Thus it is perhaps only 20 to 30 percent of primary energy consumption whose specific fuel allocation varies among the industrial countries.

In addition to the rough similarity in fuel mix, industrial countries seem to adopt practices that will compensate for their use of thermally inefficient fuels. Sweden, for example, reduces the heat loss associated with its relatively large use of hydro and nuclear power by cogenerating electricity with steam production for residences and industry purposes. Cogeneration typically needs only two-thirds as much fuel as is required by separate generation of heat and electricity. Sweden also obtains additional primary energy savings by generating a relatively large share of its industrial fuels from waste products (particularly in the paper industry, which is a large component of Sweden's industrial sector). German industry also engages extensively in cogeneration of electricity and steam in order to counterbalance its relatively large use of thermally inefficient coal. The United States seeks to compensate for its thermally inefficient transportation sector by employing a thermally efficient fuel mix that emphasizes the use of gas in its residential and industrial sectors.

Industry Mix. Manufacturing uses more energy per dollar of output than nonmanufacturing; within manufacturing, some industries are more energy-intensive than other industries; and within industries, some production processes require more energy than

16. Only the United Kingdom is out of line, having a low thermal efficiency because of its extensive use of coal for domestic heating.

17. In France, Italy, Sweden, and Japan, there is a relative emphasis on additional oil use; in Germany and the U.K. the emphasis is on coal; in the United States and the Netherlands, natural gas gets a high weight; and in Canada and Sweden, hydropower is relatively important.

others to produce equivalent outputs. Clearly the mix of activities that countries adopt at these various levels can affect their overall energy consumption and energy intensity. The question is whether this mix varies sufficiently among countries to actually have these effects.

The U.S. industrial value-added as a proportion of GNP is somewhat lower than it is for European countries in general, about the same as in Sweden, and somewhat higher than in Germany. Since U.S. GNP per capita is relatively high, the industrial value-added per capita in the United States is also higher than in other countries—by about 20 percent. If industrial output is stated in physical rather than value terms, U.S. industrial output per capita would move somewhat closer,[18] but still remain above that of other countries. From these data it can be concluded that the relatively high energy intensity and per capita energy consumption in the United States cannot be attributed to a disproportionately large industrial sector.

A similar statement can be made for the energy-intensive manufacturing industries—food, paper, chemicals, petroleum and coal products, stone, clay and glass products, and primary metals. These industries as a group have about the same share of total manufacturing in the United States as they have in other industrial countries, since proportionately high shares for some industries—such as paper in Sweden and chemicals in Germany—are being offset by lower shares for other energy-intensive industries. Furthermore, those industries that are highly energy intensive because their principal use of energy is to change the molecular structure of materials (such as chemicals, primary metals, paper, and petroleum and coal products) have a share of manufacturing in the United States that is no higher and probably smaller than in other countries. So the fact that energy-intensive manufacturing industries have a disproportionately large share does not explain the high levels of overall energy intensity in the United States.

The U.S. foreign trade mix and its production process mix do have compositional effects on the intensity and consumption of energy in the United States relative to other countries. Foreign trade transactions in nonfuel commodities have an impact on energy consumption in the industrial sector because of the energy embodied in exports and imports. In conventional accounting, the energy contained in export goods is assigned to industrial energy use, even though it does not end up being consumed domestically. And the energy embodied in imports, which should be included as a part of domestic energy consumption, is not.

---

18. Differences in the relative prices of industrial goods account for this.

In the United States and most other industrial countries, energy embodied in exports about equals the energy embodied in imports (excluding the direct export and import of fuels). However, for Sweden, Germany, and Japan, the net export of embodied energy amounts to a tenth of the total energy they consume [24, p. 20]. As a consequence, the foreign trade mix in these countries causes an increase in their apparent consumption because of an arbitrary measurement convention. Since the energy consumption and intensity of these countries is relatively low as measured, the effect of the foreign trade mix is to narrow their apparent differential from the United States. Foreign trade patterns do not, therefore, explain the relatively high overall energy intensity and consumption observed for the United States; on the contrary, they would be still higher without such trade.

The mix of production processes adopted by U.S. industry tends to raise energy consumption and intensity because, more than in other countries, U.S. industry apparently favors technologies that require large amounts of process heat and adopts processes that utilize relatively large amounts of energy to provide this heat. It is difficult to quantify the effects of industrial process mix on energy consumption. Although they tend to raise overall energy intensity, it is doubtful that the process-mix effects overbalance those industry-mix effects that tend to lower U.S. energy consumption relative to other countries. Considering the various industry-mix effects discussed here, it is likely that the overall impact of industry structure is to lower rather than raise U.S. energy intensity relative to other industrialized countries.

End-User Intensity. The energy consumed per dollar of GNP by each end user—residential, commercial, industrial, and transportation—is greater in the United States than their energy intensities in other industrial countries. The reasons for this can be traced back to very specific habits of energy consumption and requirements of energy-using equipment in each of the end-use sectors.

Residential. The major use of energy in the home is for the cooling and heating of space. The most important reason for the relatively low use of energy in European homes relates to their methods of space heating, rather than cooling. A smaller share of the U.S. energy budget is spent on residential space heating than the other selected industrial countries; but because of its higher overall energy intensity and per capita consumption, the United States uses relatively more energy per capita and per dollar of GNP. When adjustments are made for climatic differences, U.S. energy intensity for space heating is one-third higher than that of European countries [24, p. 19].

About half this difference is attributable to more residential space per capita in the United States, partly because of larger dwellings and partly because a greater share of the dwellings consists of single-family rather than apartment units. If adjustments for both climate and residential space differences are taken into account, our use of energy for space heating is considerably greater than in other countries—for example, about twice as high as in Sweden or Germany.

Several other factors apart from climate and the amount of residential space account for the relatively low space-heating intensity in European countries. European homes, particularly in the colder climates, are constructed from materials that avoid heat loss and infiltration; storm windows, double glazing, and weather stripping are more common. Apartments, which are more prevalent in Europe than the United States, inherently have lower heat losses because of a smaller per person exterior. The European preference for more energy-efficient homes is reinforced by such institutional factors as stricter building codes, mortgage practices that do not induce builders to minimize first costs rather than life-cycle costs, and the willingness of banks to make energy conservation housing loans. In addition, internal temperatures are customarily lower in European countries; in some countries, such as Sweden, thermostats are set at low temperatures, while in other countries, such as Germany, rooms are not heated when they are not being used. District heating, which is more thermally efficient than individual apartment boilers, is also a significant factor in lowering the consumption of energy in some European countries, including Sweden.

In the United States energy consumption is raised because of a widespread dependence on air conditioning rather than natural ventilation. In Europe, homes are rarely air conditioned and account for a negligible quantity of energy consumed. These differences in space cooling contribute to the lower energy intensity of European households.

There are other factors, less important than those related to space conditioning, that lower energy intensity in European homes. In Germany, for instance, water-heating systems that function on demand are in widespread use, resulting in considerable energy savings. Lighting standards appear to be much lower in European homes and commercial buildings; for example, per capita use of energy for lighting in Germany and Sweden is one-third that in the

United States. Clothes-dryers and dishwashers are not common in Europe, which lowers European energy consumption relative to the United States. Other household appliances are generally less prevalent in Europe, although this lack seems to make relatively little difference for energy consumption. What does make a difference is the kind of appliances used: European homes prefer high-voltage and more energy-efficient appliances, pilotless ranges, and nonfrostless refrigeration—all of which lower energy consumption. In addition, some social customs, such as manual dish washing, less bathing, less frequent clothes cleaning, and less outdoor lighting have smaller consequences for energy consumption.

Industrial. It has already been noted that the European industrial use of energy is less than in the United States, not because of a favorable industry mix but because the technological processes adopted are less energy-intensive. This applies not only to energy input per dollar of value-added, but even more to energy input per physical units of output; it pertains not only to the energy-intensive primary industries, but also to the light fabricating and assembly-type of manufacturing industries.

Several factors have been identified as contributing to the lower industrial intensity of European countries. In Europe there are more efficient energy-production practices, such as cogeneration of heat and electricity, use of waste materials for energy, and production of energy in the manufacturing plants. There is more attention paid to energy-saving practices that lead to better energy housekeeping, plugging energy leaks, less throwaway packaging, greater durability of capital goods, and less preference for high-energy-content plastic products.

Probably the most important source of the less energy-intensive industrial processes in Europe is the kind of equipment used in European factories. In a number of European countries, factories are newer and equipment more modern than those in the United States. This has meant that productivity is higher in Europe for a number of industrial processes, which would lower energy intensity. In addition, the modern equipment is more efficient in the use of energy, since less energy waste is incurred and the plant layout and equipment design are more oriented to energy-saving than the older capital stock.

The use of more modern equipment can have significant effects on energy consumption. For example, the United States requires 25 percent more energy per ton of aluminum than the Netherlands, where smelting equipment is of more recent vintage. U.S. energy requirements for steel production are 50 percent greater than in Germany, which uses the more modern oxygen and electric furnaces rather than open-hearth facilities. Furthermore, U.S. cement production uses 50 percent more energy than in Japan, which has more up-to-date kilns. In the Netherlands, which has adopted modern processes utilizing crude oil rather than natural gas as feedstock, petrochemicals can be produced with 15 percent less energy. In the production of flat glass the United States has adopted the modern float glass process and achieves a saving of a third in energy usage [95, pp. 106-8].

No one argues that European technologies are appropriate in the United States simply because they are less energy intensive. But it is clear that in the long run opportunities exist for substantial energy savings as U.S. industry modernizes its facilities and designs its plants in response to the more stringent conditions of energy supply.

Transportation.   U.S. automobiles require 50 percent more energy per passenger mile than European cars, primarily because U.S. cars are heavier. They also have more energy-using equipment, are less well maintained, and are less likely to use diesel fuel, all of which mean lower gas economy. And less reliance on such devices as limited street parking, higher parking costs, one-way and pedestrian-only streets, bikeways, and walkways contribute to the higher auto usage in the United States. In addition, the larger number of short trips, where fuel consumption per vehicle is very high, adds to the relatively high energy intensity of U.S. cars.

While U.S. automobiles are clearly more energy intensive than European cars, the comparative intensity for other modes of transport is more uncertain. Mass transit in Europe is not only more popular, but seems to be more efficient in the use of energy than the U.S. systems. This is partly because mass transit is more subsidized, faster, and more available than in the United States. But intercity freight traffic—whether by road, rail, air, or water—seems to require more energy per ton in European countries than in the United States. But this higher energy efficiency of U.S. freight transport is more than offset by the greater ton miles per capita required to move goods in the United States.

ENERGY CONSERVATION

At its most basic level energy conservation means using less rather than more energy, and is concerned with directly or indirectly managing energy consumption to achieve this result. Such management is desirable, it is claimed, because uncontrolled market forces or market distortions interfere with achieving particular societal objectives considered fundamental by their advocates.

Conservation Objectives

One objective is to maintain U.S. national security and international stability, which are threatened by rising oil imports. To the extent that energy conservation lowers U.S. oil imports it contributes to the independence of U.S. foreign policy, enhances foreign trade by lowering the balance of payments deficit, and increases the likelihood that more- and less-costly fuels will go to the poor regions of the world that depend on imported energy for their development.

Another objective is to provide future generations with an adequate economic base. To the extent that conservation buys time for new energy sources to develop or lowers the rate of depletion of the available energy stock, then fuel scarcities will be less likely to threaten the economic foundation of future generations.

Preventing environmental deterioration is a third objective of energy conservation. The production and use of energy place a particularly heavy burden on the environment. Energy conservation, at least in its direct effects, will lower those burdens. This will reduce the need for expenditures on environmental protection, release some energy for use in cleaning up the environment, and buy time for new techniques of environmental control to emerge.

The most widespread—and at the same time disputed—claim for energy conservation is that it will raise living standards and help to move people out of poverty. Conservation will add to real incomes, prevent sacrifices in material standards of consumption, and enhance the economic opportunities of low-income groups. This is true only if the conservation effort uses fewer economic resources than are required by energy production; slows down use of the costly marginal energy sources; prevents deterioration in the rate of overall productivity improvement; dampens the rise in energy prices; weakens the strength of the cartels; and adds to the number of job openings.

But energy conservation could cost more in real terms than energy production; could produce unemployment rather than jobs; could hamper rapid productivity improvements; could lead to a less desired package of consumer purchases; and could result in severe regional and industrial dislocations or income redistributions. If these are its results, then the conservation effort will reduce the chances to maintain a growing standard of living not only during a transitional period but also over the long term.

For a small but not insignificant group of conservationists, lowered standards of aspiration and levels of consumption represent a goal rather than a problem. For these people energy conservation is perceived as an opportunity for society to learn about the values and attractions of life styles less dependent on material consumption. The exposure to reduced energy-using patterns of production and consumption brought about by energy conservation will then lead to a rechannelling of social incentives and attitudes so that the trend toward adopting less consumption-oriented life styles will be enhanced.

Conservation Concepts

Not only is there a variety of energy conservation objectives but also there are different energy concepts that can be identified. Conservation can be conceived of as curtailment, preservation, waste reduction, technical efficiency, and economic efficiency. Figure 4-8 shows the relationship between specific conservation objectives and concepts.

Conservation as curtailment refers to the attempt to reach some rate of energy consumption that is below the historical rate or below some forecasted rate that would occur without conservation programs. Curtailment implies that some energy consumption target is set to achieve particular objectives, usually with little regard for the undesirable side-effects that might also occur. Curtailment is likely to lower imports and protect the environment, and may even change living styles. But it will not raise living standards or assure the economic future of coming generations.

Conservation as preservation refers to the attempt to extend the

Conservation Concepts	Conservation Objectives				
	Lower Imports	Raise Living Standards	Change Living Styles	Assure the Future	Protect the Environment
Curtailment	Yes	No	Maybe	No	Yes
Preservation	No	No	Maybe	Yes	Yes
Waste Reduction	Yes	Yes	No	No	Yes
Technical Efficiency	Yes	No	Maybe	No	Maybe
Economic Efficiency	Maybe	Yes	Maybe	Maybe	Maybe

Figure 4-8. Conservation Concepts and Objectives

life of the energy stock by achieving an appropriate distribution of energy use over time. In this sense the energy stock is thought of as being finite, and using energy tends to be synonymous with using it up. Since the advantages of preservation are very long term and hence subject to heavy discounting, market calculations very often need to be overridden if preservation is to be achieved. Preservation tends to assure the future, help to protect the environment, and perhaps has some effect on living styles. But it will not raise living standards. Nor is it likely to lower imports since the inclination will be to protect the domestic energy stock by using foreign sources.

Conservation as waste reduction refers to the attempt to eliminate those practices that use up energy without adding appreciably to national output or consumer satisfaction. In terms of energy usage this means introducing minor modifications in industry production processes and family consumption habits that will significantly lower the energy they use. In terms of energy production this means being more alert to the possibilities for leaving less fuel in the ground during the extraction process, reducing heat loss in the energy conversion process, and expanding the energy base through recycling processes. Waste reduction tends to lower imports, raise living standards, and protect the environment. It is unlikely to change living styles or assure the future.

Energy curtailment, preservation, and waste reduction are not precise conservation concepts. Rather, they are reflections of a widespread belief that at any given time and without negative side-effects more can be done than is being done about lowering energy consumption, preserving the energy stock, and plugging the energy leaks. The economist seeks to introduce more precision into conservation concepts by distinguishing between technical efficiency and economic efficiency.

Technical efficiency refers to the attempt to minimize the energy used up in providing some particular level of output or satisfaction. This can be done by substituting, wherever possible, some other input for energy; by designing equipment, buildings, and entire production systems to require less energy; and by consuming goods and services that are less energy intensive. But the diligent pursuit of lower energy consumption through technical efficiency must at some point become very costly in terms of goods and services that fail to get produced and potential satisfactions that families never realize. So if technical efficiency goes beyond the economically efficient point, although it will lower energy impacts and might change living styles, it will not raise living standards or assure the future. Whether or not the environment will be protected depends on whether the diminished environmental degradation because of lower energy use would be offset by increased environmental restoration available through expanded economic productivity.

Under conditions of economic efficiency, scarce resources are allocated in accordance with their value to society, which is reflected by their relative costs (and in a market system by their relative prices). As the relative costs of energy rise, it is economically efficient to discourage energy use—that is, to conserve energy. What this means is that up to some point it costs society more—in terms of final output given up—to produce and use some quantum of energy than not to do so. But beyond that point failure to supply and use the energy will mean less final output. Considerations of economic efficiency subsume the problem of conserving energy under the more general problem of using all scarce resources in combinations that get the best output results. Thus energy conservation as economic efficiency will raise living standards. It will also protect the environment and assure the future if society sets a high value to such protection and assurance. But whether imports are lowered will depend on the relative costs of imported and domestic fuels, and whether living styles are changed will depend on the size and speed of the increase in the costs of energy.

Conservation Strategies

The factors affecting a nation's energy consumption relate to the physical, institutional, and cultural aspects of the country and its population. Whether energy intensity in a country is "low" or "high" must be judged in relation to these factors in that country at that time, and not to what may be more energy-favorable circumstances in some other place or some other period. At the same time, however, energy intensity is the result of particular responses to the existing factors, so within limits the quantity of energy consumed does represent a choice made by the people of the country. Levels of energy consumption different from those actually reached are always possible if new strategies for saving energy are pursued. And many observers believe that those strategies should be adopted in the United States that have successfully achieved energy saving in other industrial countries.

Using less rather than more energy often requires changing the devices or materials being used to consume or produce energy. This strategy for energy conservation has come to be called the *technological fix*. Another way to conserve energy is to modify the processes by which energy is consumed in buildings, offices, plants and vehicles. This strategy is labeled the *managerial fix*. Energy-saving equipment and processes are often available but not being employed because they interfere with current habits and tastes. Changes in such habits and tastes that lower energy usage can be called the *attitudinal fix*. Transactions involving energy, energy-using equipment, and energy-embodied goods and services take place in the market. Changes in market prices, regulations, and standards will affect the quantity and type of energy consumed. When such changes are introduced for the purpose of lowering energy or fossil fuel consumption, the *market-fix* strategy for energy conservation is being pursued.

Specific techniques for lowering energy consumption can be identified with one or more of these strategies. Over 100 ways to lower energy consumption have been listed in Empirical Highlight 4-2. These techniques are grouped according to the strategy they are ordinarily identified with and the energy end uses that are affected.

The multitude of energy conservation techniques signifies only a potential for lowering energy consumption. Actual achievement of energy conservation falls far short of the potential. In part this is because each of the specific conservation techniques is relevant only to a limited number of energy users and uses. As a result each technique—even if maximally applied—would have only a small proportionate effect on total energy consumption. Furthermore, maximum application of a particular technique will require complementing support from other techniques. For example, the design of energy-efficient structures (a technological fix) is only a first step to achieving lower energy usage. Revising building codes and introducing some construction incentives (market fix) may also be needed. Consumers will need to be willing to accept the new design and possibly revise their living habits (attitudinal fix). And homeowners or building managers will need to monitor the energy uses in the building (managerial fix) to achieve the designed energy conservation.

Thus successful energy conservation depends on applying a package of conservation techniques. But there are a number of barriers to conservation that may inhibit the application of any one of the components of the package.

A significant barrier is the time it takes to introduce and implement conservation programs. The conservation lead time, in many cases, is longer than the time it takes to build new energy production facilities; that is, it may be measured in decades rather than years. It takes time to design new processes or equipment for conserving energy, to build new energy-efficient plants, and to make energy-efficient appliances commercially available. Even when

Empirical Highlight 4-2. One Hundred and One Ways to Conserve Energy

THE TECHNOLOGICAL FIX

In Homes and Buildings

- *Structures* can be designed, constructed, and sited to require less heating and cooling, reduce heat loss, improve heat recovery, utilize solar energy, and improve energy-storage systems for heating in winter and cooling in summer.

- *New construction materials* can be developed to reduce heat loss and improve heat recovery.

- *More efficient heating and cooling systems* can be developed, including gas and electric heat pumps, solar-assisted air conditioners, and heat-dissipating devices to reduce cooling loads.

- *Improved cascading* or total energy systems can be introduced, which utilize for space and water heating the waste energy from lighting and air conditioning.

- *Improved appliance design* can raise energy efficiency of water heaters, stoves, refrigerators, pilot lights, and lighting facilities.

In Transportation

- *Vehicles* can be designed and new materials used to improve their aerodynamic structure and reduce their weight.

- *Auto accessories* can be designed to improve their energy efficiency.

- *New engine types* can be designed and existing types improved to increase efficiency through use of smaller engines, lean fuel mixtures, nonpetroleum fuels, combined gas turbine with electricity, variable transmissions, and improved carburation, ignition, air injection, and waste-energy recovery systems.

- *Traffic control systems* can be developed to reduce congestion.

- *Highways* can be designed and constructed to improve vehicular energy efficiency.

- *Communication systems* can be improved and used as a substitute for transportation.

- High-speed and flexible *ground transportation* can be designed as an alternative to automobile use within urban areas.

Empirical Highlight 4-2 (cont.)

- *Carrying capacity* of commercial vehicles (planes, buses, trucks) can be increased.

In Industry

- *Process steam* can be generated with energy-efficient electric and vacuum furnaces.

- Development of induction heating, microwave heating, and laser welding will raise energy efficiency in *combustion.*

- Recuperators, regenerators, and low-temperature heat engine will increase *recovery of waste heat and lower heat loss.*

- Improved designs for *heat pumps and heat exchanges* will raise energy efficiency.

- *Plants can be designed* to incorporate energy-control devices and improve insulation of furnaces and pipework.

- *New industrial materials* can be developed to substitute for high energy content materials.

- *High energy content materials waste* can be reduced through substitution of such processes as powder metallurgy for machining.

- Energy efficiency in *agriculture* can be raised through development of disease-resistant and high-protein content new plants and increased efficiency of the photosynthesis process.

- New methods for *recycling materials,* particularly aluminum, steel, and paper, can be developed.

- New *manufacturing processes* utilizing less energy can be adopted, such as producing steel through reduction of iron chloride by hydrogen.

In Energy Production

New systems for making use of waste energy include:

- *Cogeneration*—Simultaneously raising process steam for use in plant while generating electric power for resale.

Empirical Highlight 4-2 (cont.)

- *District heating*—Using waste heat from electric power plant to provide heat for space conditioning and process steam in urban or industrial complex.

- *Total energy systems*—Onsite (plants or buildings) generation of electricity with small gas turbines or fuel cells, while using waste heat for space and water heating.

- *Combined cycle electric power plants*—Using steam generators in combination with gas or magnetohydro-dynamic turbines.

Improved Energy-producing Equipment Includes:

- *Stack gas desulferization devices.*

- *Safe breeder reactors.*

- *Automatic controls* in thermo-processing plants.

- Devices for recovering energy from *organic and industrial waste.*

- Techniques for obtaining energy from *nonfossil fuel sources,* including solar, wind, tide, geothermal, and hydrogen.

- Equipment for more complete *fuel extraction and refinement* and for *reducing electric power losses* in transmission and distribution.

THE MANAGERIAL FIX

In Houses and Buildings

- General *tightening up,* such as sealing, weatherstripping, operating appliances at capacity, storm windows and doors, plugging leaks, and turning off pilot lights in summer.

- Conducting *energy audits* in commercial buildings to determine areas of heat loss and excessive energy use.

- *Repair* inefficient energy-using appliances and equipment.

- *Replace* energy-inefficient appliances, motors, air conditioners, and lighting with more energy-efficient devices.

Empirical Highlight 4-2 (cont.)

- Where possible *substitute gas for electricity* in space heating, cooking, refrigeration, air conditioning, and water heating.

- *Introduce solar* or solar-assisted heating and cooling devices.

- *Use natural lighting, heating, and cooling* as much as possible.

- *Vary lighting, heating, and cooling standards* according to the task being performed rather than adopting uniform practices throughout the building.

- *Use central air conditioning* systems.

- *Reduce peak-period* use of air conditioners and appliances.

In Transportation

- Raise passenger and freight *load factors* so that vehicles are operated closer to their capacity.

- *Shift to energy-efficient modes,* particularly from auto to bus for intracity and for short-distance intercity travel.

- *Improve intermodal connections* to facilitate intracity passenger transfers from car to rail or bus and freight transfers from truck to rail or water.

- Shift to *energy-efficient fuels,* particularly from gas to diesel.

- Give *priority access* to energy-efficient modes of travel such as special bus lanes.

- Introduce *traffic-flow and congestion-control systems.*

- Provide *alternatives to single passenger auto* for short trips, including vanpool, carpool, bikeways, and buses.

- Encourage energy-conserving *driving customs,* such as lower speeds, lower acceleration, radial tires, and less use of air conditioning and power accessories.

- Introduce *aerodrag reduction devices* on long-haul trucks and between freight cars.

Empirical Highlight 4-2 (cont.)

In Industry

● Improve *equipment maintenance* procedures.

● *Retrofit* equipment to operate closer to design efficiency.

● *Replace* energy-inefficient equipment.

● Improve *insulation* on equipment, furnaces, and structures.

● Conduct *energy audits* in plant and on the farm.

● Introduce *substitutes for energy-intensive materials* such as using plastics instead of metals.

● Generate *steam* with other than hydrocarbon fuels.

● Adopt *production processes* that are not energy-intensive.

● *Substitute natural fertilizer and biological pesticides* for their chemical counterparts in agriculture.

● Introduce *cascading techniques* that control the energy flow so that energy released by processes requiring high temperature is then used by lower-temperature demand processes.

In Energy Production

● Improve *load management* practices to lower peak-load requirements.

● Increase capacity of energy and fuel *storage facilities.*

● Reduce use of *inefficient standby plants and generators.*

● Reduce fuel *extraction and energy conversion losses.*

● Energy production facilities that are efficient but might endanger the environment and safety can be *located* in isolated areas.

Empirical Highlight 4-2 (cont.)

THE ATTITUDINAL FIX

In Homes and Buildings

• Consumer acceptance of *energy-efficient design and regulation* of structures, appliances, equipment, land-use patterns, and community design.

• *Change in living habits to prefer:* lower acceptable levels for heating, cooling, and lighting; substitutes for hydrocarbon fuels and electric power; more durable equipment and fewer throwaway items; multifamily residential structures; energy-saving housekeeping practices; less energy-intensive goods and materials.

In Transportation

• Consumer acceptance of *energy efficient equipment* and customs such as: smaller cars, mass transit, living in central city, fewer cars in family, less travel-intensive vacations, energy-efficient transportation modes for passengers and freight, increase passenger load factors in public transportation and airplanes, traffic-control devices and regulations, combined auto/transit and other multimode trips, energy-saving devices on vehicles, and less energy-using auto accessories.

• Change in *driving habits* to prefer: lower speeds and acceleration, increased car pooling, fewer short auto trips, improved auto maintenance.

THE MARKET FIX

Permit *Unregulated Market* to:

• Establish fuel and energy prices.

• Allocate fuels among customers and regions

• Determine energy exploration, research, and investment.

• Find customers for energy-efficient equipment and appliances.

Empirical Highlight 4-2 (cont.)

Regulate Higher Prices or Raise Taxes on:

- Fuel and power.

- Energy-using devices.

- Energy-intensive items.

- Peak-load energy use.

Provide *Subsidies or Tax Incentives* for:

- Installing equipment and appliances that conserve oil and gas.

- Recycling materials.

- Expanding the energy resource base.

Set Minimal *Standards* for:

- Fuel performance of appliances, equipment, and automobiles.

- Product labeling.

- Advertising.

Establish *Rationing* or Allocation Procedures for:

- Fuels and power.

- Energy-using equipment and appliances.

- Transportation and travel.

Improve Government *Legislation, Regulation* and *Enforcement* of Energy-saving Practices in:

- Land use and development.

- Construction.

Empirical Highlight 4-2 (cont.)

● Building codes.

● Environment.

● Freight movements.

● Passenger travel.

● Roads and airports.

● Power and fuel transmission and distribution.

● Dissemination of energy conservation information.

Remove Obstacles to Energy Saving Created by Excessive Market Power of:

● Labor unions.

● Construction industry.

● Energy and transportation industries.

energy-efficient devices are available they are likely to be introduced only gradually, because they need to wait for the existing stock of equipment and appliances to become obsolete. Finally, it takes time for people to learn about energy-saving devices or how to conserve energy, and it takes even longer for people to adopt new habits that may be energy conserving.

Conservation techniques may also be impeded by environmental and safety considerations. For example, some techniques for conserving vehicular fuels may have negative environmental effects, reduced ventilation may affect health, substituting coal for oil in power plants may be environmentally destructive, and more complete fuel extraction may increase the occurrence of safety hazards.

Lack of knowledge and uncertainties also tend to inhibit conservation. Consumers are frequently not aware of the costs and benefits that conservation may bring to their families. They also may not be aware, or even care about, the societal benefits conservation may provide, such as cleaner air, less congestion, or increased national security. Uncertainty about the rise in future energy prices, about the advent of new energy technologies, about the likelihood of future embargoes, about the performance of new equipment, and about the stringency of new environmental standards are all likely to impede the adoption of conservation techniques.

Low energy prices are an effective barrier to energy conservation. To some extent energy prices appear to be lower than they actually are because of the many indirect costs associated with energy use, which are not apparent to the consumer. Simply informing the consumer about the magnitude of these costs may have a beneficial effect for conservation. Direct increases in the price of energy— whether brought about by increased scarcities, monopoly power, fuel taxes, pollution charges, eliminating price discounts, peak-load pricing, or charging full costs of fuel replacement—would all effectively lower energy consumption.

High costs of energy-saving devices are another deterrent to energy conservation. The buyer is more aware of the purchase price of the equipment rather than its life-cycle cost, which includes not only the initial equipment cost but also the future operating expenditures. Energy-efficient equipment may often have a higher initial, but lower life-cycle, cost. Unaware of comparative life-cycle costs, the consumer may choose a less energy-efficient appliance under the mistaken impression that it will cost less over the long run. In addition many consumers—even when aware of life-cycle costs—may choose a less energy-efficient appliance or refuse to install an energy-saving device such as insulation simply because they do not have the money needed for the expensive investment.

Industrial firms as well as households may reject energy-efficient investments with low life-cycle costs. For example, even though savings on operating costs because of reduced energy needs might recover the investment cost in 4 years, the investment will not be made if the company's standard payback period is 3 years.

There are also market forces that discourage households from purchasing conservation devices. Families are mobile and they hesitate retrofitting a house they may soon vacate. Renters cannot easily force landlords to improve insulation. Commercial and apartment landlords can easily pass on their utility costs to renters. Marketing practices for appliances tend to emphasize the advantage of low initial costs rather than life-cycle cost. Similarly, builders have incentives to keep first costs low, which makes it easier to sell homes.

The costs of investing in energy conservation are undoubtedly high. But these costs are usually less than the costs of investing in new facilities for energy production.[19] As a result, investment in conservation would not add to the total capital requirements in the nation, but may significantly lower such requirements. However, the operation of capital markets may slow down the flow of investment funds to energy conservation. For example, many homeowners, small businessmen, and industrial sectors with low rates of return who would benefit from conservation do not have ready access to lending sources; at the same time, energy producers are often able to finance capacity expansions with attractive interest rates or internal cash flows that are, in some ways, made possible by the government's regulatory and rate-setting practices.

ENERGY SAVINGS

It is clear that major energy savings are possible through technological advances, management improvements, market adjustments, and attitudinal changes. For example, it has been estimated that if already known energy-efficient techniques—the so-called soft technologies—were in place in 1973, energy consumption could have been reduced by 40 percent with the transportation, industrial, and residential plus commercial sectors each accounting for about a third of the savings [80].

Drawing on estimates such as these, Lovens has suggested that even without drastic market or attitudinal changes the soft technologies already available could double the technical efficiency of energy use by the end of the century, eliminating the need for an ever-increasing rate of energy consumption. More advanced soft technologies could increase efficiency by a factor of four or five, making it possible over the long run to have lower levels of energy consumption—particularly fossil-fuel consumption—than we currently have [58, p. 72].

But these are claims for potential energy savings. There is no assurance that such savings, or even a small fraction of them, will actually be achieved. "There is no easy path in resource conservation. In energy conservation, a program that can yield a saving equivalent to 0.5 percent of the nation's energy budget is a major one" [94, p.

---

19. The investment costs for the annual production of a quad of energy from new coal mines was about $2 billion in 1977; from new oil or gas wells in the U.S. about $4.5 billion; from synthetic oil or gas about $10 billion; from coal-fired electric utilities about $45 billion; and from nuclear plants about $90 billion. Capital costs to save a quad of energy are often less than $1.5 billion and usually less than $4 billion, but sometimes go as high as $11 billion per quad [43, p. 69].

103]. Alert to the many barriers that may inhibit conservation, the Federal Energy Administration estimates that an active conservation program, including higher energy prices, could cut in half the growth in energy demand—from an annual growth of 3.6 percent to 2.2 percent [101]. On this basis conservation would lower the 1985 level of energy consumption by about 15 percent.

The impact of particular conservation techniques on the nation's life styles, work conditions, and living standards will vary. Some impacts may be highly desirable, while others are less so, if at all. Energy prices are important in this regard. The relative price of energy can often serve as a signal indicating whether increased energy consumption or intense application of a conservation technique is more desirable. Also, imposing higher energy prices will almost certainly lower energy consumption and expand adoption of conservation techniques. This is particularly apparent from cross-country comparisons.

Energy prices in the United States are generally lower than in other industrial countries. This lower price accounts for a sixth to a half of the lower energy intensity in the United States as compared with other countries [24, p. 24]. In addition, the relative price differentials among the specific fuels helps to explain some of the differences in fuel mix among the countries, such as the relatively extensive use of natural gas in the United States, hydropower in Sweden, and coal in the United Kingdom.

The increasing use of oil—and in particular of imported oil—tends to reduce energy price differentials among countries. This is because the costs of imported oil and petroleum products are roughly the same among the industrial countries. Consumer prices, however, are not the same, because countries impose different gasoline and fuel taxes. In some of the industrial countries the price of gasoline is more than doubled because of taxes, while the price of heating and fuel oil is increased by a fifth.

Thus the relatively low energy intensity and per capita energy consumption in the United States is, to an important extent, related to the relatively low rate at which energy—at least until now—has been taxed. This particularly applies to transportation, the end-use sector where the United States differs most from other countries in terms of both energy consumption and energy tax rates. The differential tax impacts apply to a lesser extent to the residential, commercial, and industrial sectors. Even for these sectors, as shown by the demand-elasticity studies, the energy consumption response to an energy price change is not trivial. Thus it can be expected that rising energy costs will significantly lower energy consumption, and imposing additional taxes on top of the rising costs would lower consumption still more.

There are a few conservation techniques of particular importance to slowing down the growth in energy consumption. Improving the gas economy of the U.S. auto fleet is probably the most important of these. However, since this depends primarily on reducing the weight of cars, it can be achieved only slowly as new car purchases replace the existing fleet. Presumably, mandated gasoline consumption standards and auto weight taxation will speed this process.

Reducing the number of short trips made by cars would have a more modest impact. This could be achieved in the short run if rising gasoline prices discourage some of the short trips presently made or increase the auto occupancy rate on these trips. Also, many mass transit systems now operate at less than capacity, and their use could be quickly expanded to balance the reduced auto usage. Over the long run, however, improvements in transit systems and attitudinal changes toward their use would be needed for nontrivial reductions in energy consumption.

Space conditioning, hot water heating, and lighting in homes and commercial buildings offer potential for reducing energy consumption. In the long run this would involve improved building and equipment design that will probably be achieved as reduced expenses through energy saving are sought and as energy conserving building codes are enforced. Even in the short run, however, retrofit can plug leaks, energy-efficient appliances can be installed, and lower settings for heating, cooling, and lighting can be adopted. Again, rising energy prices would speed up this process as would various financial inducements and more favorable mortgage practices that would make energy conservation investments more attractive.

In the last few years U.S. industry, under the pressure of rising costs, has introduced many energy-conserving practices. It is doubtful that substantial further tightening will be achieved in the short run. In the long run, however, it can be expected that increased consideration will be given to adoption of less energy-intensive industrial processes and equipment, which will constrain growth in industrial energy consumption. In addition, industrial cogeneration of steam and power, product recycling, energy recovery from industrial waste, and increased thermal efficiency in energy production all have a long-run potential for energy saving in the United States.

If economic and social progress are to be pursued, it is not only appropriate but essential for the United States to apply some of the energy-saving lessons that have already been learned; just as it is appropriate and essential to consider additional strategies for conserving energy and expanding the sources of energy supply. But it is not enough to be alert only to the contributions energy conservation makes to the achievement of economic and social progress. We should also be alert to how energy conservation influences society's view of what constitutes economic and social progress.

✳ *Chapter Five*

Channels for Economic Growth

Economic growth has been the target of government policy and the victim of market forces; offered as panacea to social ills and decried as source of these ills; perceived as a resource problem or a labor problem or a technology problem or a monetary problem; expressed as a short-term concern or a long-term concern; seen as an efficiency issue or an equity issue. Clearly, "growth has meant different things to different people and at different times" [68, p. 511]. What are these different things that growth has meant, and still means, to different people?

Growth has meant *economic recovery*. When an economy is not fully employing its available resources, output can be expanded considerably by putting these resources to work. Economic recovery involves filling the gap between the actual and potential output of an economy.

Economic expansion takes over once there is full employment and relates to increasing the economy's capacity for production. In an expanding economy the capacity potential to produce moves from one level to a higher one. If economic expansion continues, there is a sustained increase in potential output.

If this continued expansion of output is accompanied by transformations in the economic structure, such as fundamental changes in production, trade patterns, working conditions, and methods of resource allocation, *economic development* is taking place. If this economic development is compatible with the ultimate aims of the society in the sense that it contributes to society's welfare as well as to the nation's product, then *economic progress* is taking place.

These are the four channels for economic growth. They are not mutually exclusive; nor are they dependent on one another. All, or none, or any combination of the four may be occurring, or be perceived as occurring, at any time. Furthermore, the analytical and empirical distinctions among them are not very precise.[1]

Yet the differences among these four channels are also crucial. The causes of growth and the relationship between energy and growth will vary depending on which channel is being traveled. Growth as economic recovery is a demand phenomenon, because overcoming the insufficiency of aggregate demand provides the opportunity for increasing national output. Growth as economic expansion is a supply phenomenon, because increasing capacity paves the way for a sustained expansion of national output. Growth as economic development is a structural phenomenon, because fundamental economic, technological, and social changes make it possible to change the nation's output. And growth as economic progress is a value phenomenon, because changes in the national output and methods of providing this output are judged according to their effects on the welfare of present and future generations.

ECONOMIC RECOVERY

Since World War II economic policy has been guided by two major concerns. Full employment policy has been directed toward economic recovery, which would reduce the gap between actual and potential output. Generally this policy has produced a focus on the short run rather than on the long run, and has influenced aggregate demand rather than the capacity to supply.

The second concern, typically identified as growth policy, directs its attention not primarily to raising the actual output but to speeding up the growth of potential output through increasing productivity, improving the quality and employability of labor, and accelerating the pace of technological progress. Thus the emphasis of growth policy is on the long run rather than the short run, and on upping the capacity to supply rather than on raising aggregate demand.

Between the two—full employment or growth policy—greater attention has been given to the former over the last thirty years, partly because short-run concerns tend to dominate political considerations. Also, however, both economists and decision-makers seem

1. Because of this there is no concensus on the terminology employed to label each channel. Most particularly, what is being labeled economic recovery is sometimes referred to as economic expansion, while what is here called economic expansion is often called economic growth.

more confident in their ability to influence economic recovery than to control economic expansion.

The argument for seeking to promote economic recovery goes something like this: at any point in time the difference between actual and potential output reflects the degree to which available resources are unemployed and underutilized. Increasing the aggregate demand for goods and services will also raise the rate at which available resources, the work force, and capacity are used, and as a result the level of output will go up. The customary policies adopted to achieve this increase are cutting taxes, raising federal expenditures, and pursuing an expansionist monetary policy.

Since the increase of output under these circumstances results from the employment of idle resources, it is sometimes argued that the ensuing growth is free of any cost. But even if this were so, the process cannot continue forever. For once capacity operation and full employment have been reached, further stimulation of aggregate demand will only foster inflation, unless capacity also increases.

During short periods of time, putting idle resources to work and increasing the rate of utilization of capacity is of great importance to the economy, and particularly to those resources that are underemployed. But over long periods of time, running into decades, reducing the underutilization of capacity is much less significant for economic growth than is the expansion of capacity.

In recent years the ability of fiscal and monetary policy to put idle resources to work without creating inflation has been brought into question. Only a decade ago, 3 percent rates of unemployment in the work force were the standard target of full employment. Today rates set at 5 or 6 percent are considered unachievable.

These policy failures can be interpreted as indications that the gap between actual and potential output results not only from insufficient aggregate demand but also from inadequacies on the supply side. During the 1960s the source of these inadequacies were usually found in that part of the labor force lacking the skills needed to fill job opportunities. For this reason, public programs to a large extent were directed toward overcoming the presumed skill deficiencies of the unemployed. More recently, an additional source of the inadequacies is seen in the shortages of natural resources. This raises the specter of production bottlenecks that would contribute to the deficiency between actual and potential output. Such shortages were often more feared than actual occurrences in the past. But with the 1973 oil embargo, the impact that energy shortages could have on reducing output and raising prices in the economy was realized. Higher oil prices had the distinction of contributing to recession by depressing aggregate demand in the economy and of adding to inflation by raising business costs and wages [37, p. 103].

ECONOMIC EXPANSION

Modern neoclassical growth theory focuses on the annual rate of change in potential output, that is, on the change in productive capacity. The theory examines whether potential output must eventually settle into some steady rate of growth, which would be the best possible economic situation that society could sustain. Achieving a steady state is not dependent on any particular assumptions about the conditions of energy supply. However, energy conditions will influence the magnitude of the growth rate in the particular steady state into which the economy finally settles.

According to the theory, expansion of potential output is dependent on population growth, technological progress, and growth in the stock of human and physical capital. If population and technology grow smoothly at rates determined exogenously—that is, by noneconomic forces—then it is these rates that will determine the pace of the underlying steady state or "natural" rate of economic growth. Because these factors that determine the natural rate of growth are not themselves dependent on economic forces, then neither economic policy nor energy policy would be able to affect this long-run natural rate.

But the long-run applicable to the natural rate is measured in generations. Until that sustainable natural rate is reached, society can make a choice that will influence the rate of growth in potential output: namely, the choice as to what share of the national output will be spent on investment rather than consumption.

Investment provides future consumption at the expense of present consumption. If society invests higher and higher shares of output, it raises the rate of growth to ever higher levels. Of course, the amount of output invested cannot continue to grow indefinitely, for eventually there would be no output for households to consume. Actually, the limit to investment would be set long before this, and will be governed by the thrift of the population, which in turn determines the growth in the human and physical capital stock. The willingness of the population to save will be influenced by a variety of economic factors. Under certain strict assumptions these will balance out in such a way that over the long run the growth rate in capital stock must equal the growth rate in population, which in turn equals the natural growth rate in output. What are these assumptions?

The neoclassical theory of growth usually begins with the assumptions that the population (more precisely the labor force) is growing at a constant rate (n); that the share of saving in output, termed the saving rate, is a constant (s); and that the ratio of fixed capital stock to output, called the capital coefficient, is also a constant (v). Furthermore, it is tentatively assumed that these constants do not affect each other and that they depend on demographic, social, and technological factors that cannot be influenced by economic forces.

Given these assumptions, a steady rate of growth in output is possible if two conditions exist: (1) if the growth rate in output is equal to the growth rate in population (that is, the labor supply); and (2) if the growth rate in output is also equal to the saving rate divided by the capital coefficient. This relationship leads to the well-known equation $s = vn$; which means that steady-state growth occurs when the saving rate equals the product of the capital coefficient and the rate of growth in the labor force. By implication, then, the growth rates in output, population, and fixed capital stock are all equal in the steady state.

There are many ways to illustrate these assumptions. For example, if s is greater than vn, then either the labor supply will be inadequate or excess capacity will continually increase. If, on the other hand, s is less than vn, then either unemployment will spiral or needed capacity will disappear. So forces are set into motion that will lead to the condition that $s = vn$.

However, if population growth, the saving rate, and the capital coefficient all need to be constant and independent of each other, then it would be only by the sheerest accident that the steady state would be reached. It is thus more appropriate to assume that these factors are constants when the steady state is reached; but, in the process of getting to the steady state, it is better to allow for the possibility that they might be variable and interdependent. Therefore, different paths for reaching the steady state might be followed, depending on which of the factors is allowed to vary.

If $s = vn$, then there is enough investment for the labor force to be fully employed. If s is less than vn, investment will not be sufficient to employ fully the growing labor force. If society is unwilling to accept the resulting increases in the unemployment rate, it will try to expand by overcoming deficiencies in demand. But if society is willing to accept these increases, then it acknowledges, in effect, the reality of a lower level for potential output. In this case the path to a steady state is achieved through "adjusting" the socially acceptable rate of unemployment.

Suppose that rising unemployment, perhaps accompanied by falling wages, depresses the rate of population growth. If s is less than

vn, the gap between s and vn will be narrowed. If there is more investment than is needed to employ the growing labor force (that is, s is greater than vn) the opposite process will occur and a hike in population growth will result. In order to eliminate the gap between s and vn and reach the steady state, it may be necessary to go to the extreme of dropping wages to the subsistence level. The process is more likely to stop short of this point, depending on how population growth responds to changes in wages and in the saving rate. In any case, society moves toward a steady state by "adjusting" the population growth rate.

Suppose that total income in the economy is separated into the income of workers (wage income) and that of asset owners (nonwage income or profits). Then the economy's saving rate can be defined as a weighted average of the saving rates of workers and asset owners. The latter are generally assumed to have a higher saving rate, so the lower the share of wages in total income, the higher the economy's saving rate. If the income distribution between wage-earners and propertyowners is such that s is less than vn, the share of wage earnings in total income might fall in order to increase the saving rate and thereby close the gap between s and vn. In this instance, the path to a steady state is attained through "adjusting" the income distribution in society.

The assumption that there is a fixed ratio between capital stock and output is particularly unrealistic. It is somewhat more practical to imagine a production process linking output to capital and labor in the form of a continuous function, thereby making the ratio of capital to output a variable. Now what would happen if s is greater than vn and the production function describes a situation where there is no technological progress and output grows proportionately to the growth in inputs (that is, there are constant returns to scale)? Because saving is more than sufficient to cause the capital stock to grow at the same rate as the labor force, there will be an increase in the capital-to-labor ratio (known as capital deepening). This increase will raise the capital coefficient and reduce the gap between s and vn. The capital deepening cannot continue indefinitely because there is a limit to the saving available for investment. In this case, the economy travels toward a steady state by "adjusting" the amount of capital stock made available to each worker.

Increasing returns to scale means that output will grow faster than the needed inputs as the level of economic activity rises. So if population is growing at a constant rate and the production process provides increasing returns to scale, output will spiral faster than population. The result will be a steady state in which per capita income grows faster than population, and the more population grows, the higher will be the growth rate in per capita income.

Suppose that not only labor and capital could produce output, but also a fixed supply of natural resources such as land. Because natural resources are limited to a fixed supply, there will be a tendency toward diminishing returns. If there is no technological progress, diminishing returns will make it impossible for a steady state of growth to exist. If technology does advance, the steady state of growth is possible, but diminishing returns will lower the growth rate more than it might otherwise go. How much lower will depend on the importance of the natural resource to production and on how fast the population is growing.

Without technological progress or increasing returns to scale, a steady state will be reached in which output per worker is constant. However, in industrial economies, productivity shows a tendency to rise over the long run, mainly because of technological progress, which raises output over time but is independent (at least conceptually) of concurrent capital accumulation.

If technological progress continues, it can contravene the effects of diminishing returns and produce a steady state in which output per worker and income per capita grow at a steady rate rather than remaining constant. This means that over the long run labor productivity and material standards of living would be determined by how rapidly technology improves.

However, for this type of steady state to emerge, technological progress must be of a particular type, called labor-augmenting. Under labor augmenting it is as if labor is worth more from one year to the next—that is, in any year each man-hour of labor is equivalent to some multiple of the preceding year's man-hour efficiency. If the quantity of labor, as measured in efficiency units, grows at a constant rate, then under labor-augmenting technological progress, both capital and output will rise faster than man-hours of employment. Without this type of technological progress, a steady state cannot be reached. For example, if technology advances through capital- rather than labor-augmenting, and there is a constant saving rate, the capital-to-output ratio will rise consistently, causing a fall in the rate of profit. If it is socially desirable to maintain some constant rate of profit, then in this situation it would be necessary to save and invest a decreasing share of total output.

The kind of technological progress will therefore determine whether a steady state will be achieved, whether per capita consumption will grow or remain stable, and what the distribution of income will be under the steady state.

It is possible and customary to discuss the theory of steady-state growth without reference to the availability or costs of energy. Thus the natural rate of growth in output and consumption—that is, the long-run equilibrium rate—is determined by the growth in the labor supply adjusted for technological change; while a transitional component—achieved in the process of getting to the natural rate—is determined by the thrift, or savings, of the population. The neoclassical theory holds these statements to be accurate no matter what conditions surround the supply of energy.

However, if it is desirable to make empirical statements about future levels and rates of growth in output and consumption, it would be necessary to introduce more detail. Included in such detail would be the supply and demand for energy, because their relationship to variables in the theory directly influence growth. For example, it has been suggested that one way to reach the steady state is to adjust the "acceptable" rate of unemployment. The availability of energy might influence the extent and type of unemployment in the economy, and might also shape the growth in population and its location through its effects on consumption standards. The income distribution, as has been seen, influences growth in output; but it could also affect the changes in demands for energy. Capital depth, which alters output growth, may in turn be affected by energy costs. Diminishing returns, as a consequence of a finite availability of energy, could mean stagnation or decline in economic activity. Technological progress, on the other hand, might assure rising levels of consumption; but the type of technological progress—whether it is labor- or capital-augmenting—could be affected by the availability of energy.

These illustrations do not exhaust the possible ways in which energy may be a channel for economic growth. They do suggest, however, that energy may be an important factor influencing the characteristics of the steady state. Energy is particularly relevant for two variants of the steady state—the stationary and the doomsday states.

The Stationary State

The theory of steady-state growth indicates the conditions required to reach a rate of continuous growth, including a rate greater than zero. The stationary state, or no-growth situation, is a special variation of the steady state that, according to neoclassical theory, would be reached in the absence of technological progress and population growth.

The idea of a stationary state is not new in economic theory. In the classical view economies could not be in a continuous state of expansion or decline, for eventually some limit would set in, such as diminishing returns, which would slow down the rate of expansion or decline, and a stationary state would be reached.

The theory of the stationary state as seen by the early classical economists included essentially the same elements as does the modern theory. Earlier economists believed that economic growth resulted from capital accumulation, which depended on the distribution of income between profits and wages. Real wages, in turn, were affected by the availability of land, the source of food production. But land was subject to diminishing returns, either because of an absolute limit to the available quantity or because of diminishing quality. The diminishing returns to land would force profits to zero. Then capital accumulation would cease and output would keep at a subsistence rate so that population growth would stop.

In the modern view of the stationary state, it is not so much diminishing returns to land as it is the extent of energy consumption and environmental degradation that make it desirable to achieve a no-growth society. The present-day proponents of no growth point out that the constant rate of growth in population and capital stock reached under the steady state may occur at a relatively high rate or a relatively low rate. A low rate of growth—that is, a zero rate— is preferred because it will mean less production and consumption, and therefore less energy depletion and environmental pollution [23, p. 14]. Opposition to further economic growth is not, by itself, irrational. Rather, it is characterized by a value system that includes great concern about the risks imposed by economic growth on the environment, on safety, on social interactions, and on psychological well-being. Because of these concerns, advocates of the stationary state argue not only that achieving a stationary state is desirable, but that achieving a state of no growth cannot be left to chance. And the sooner we get there the better, since each generation has a moral commitment not to endanger the long-term preservation of humanity.

It is claimed that the failure of neoclassical theory to deal effectively with depletion and pollution is more than a theoretical or circumstantial oversight. Rather, it reflects "an obsession with growth and with growth models in economics in which the ultimate consequences of growth are lost in the discussion of the process itself" [78, p. 89].

Yet discussion of the process of growth is not irrelevant to its ultimate consequences, for such analysis does describe what is ultimately feasible and how it can be achieved. Thus it can be demonstrated that under the right conditions, other inputs can be substituted for exhaustible and polluting resources, or that added consumption may be worth the costs of some exhaustion and pollution. Thus what may sometimes appear as an "obsession with growth," reflecting a lack of concern about long-run consequences of depletion and pollution, may really be a considered judgment that the right conditions exist for morally acceptable societal adjustments. But those who are less sanguine about the future extrapolate global trends of energy consumption, particularly the trends of energy consumption in the United States, and come to the conclusion that all the wrong conditions exist for any acceptable adjustment other than the stationary state.

First, they observe that the deleterious impacts of energy consumption trends are no longer localized but have become global in nature, which makes them difficult to stop or reverse. Second, benefits obtained from these trends are highly localized, accruing mostly to current generations and developed nations, which means they are inequitable. Third, the pace of these trends is picking up rather than slowing down, indicating the necessity of some policy intervention. Fourth, there are no substitutes for currently depleting energy sources available at reasonable cost, which means the technical fix will not work. Fifth, the capacity of political systems, social engineering, and technology to control their own side-effects has diminished, so that rather than providing solutions they become the problems of the future.

What, then, is the theory of the stationary state? Essentially it is the same as that of the steady state under specific assumptions, with two added normative stipulations: (1) that population "should" be held constant; and (2) that technological progress "should" be directed toward maintaining "the given total stock with a lessened throughput [that is, less production and consumption]" [23, p. 127]. A constant population is judged to be the best means for holding down growth in output, while appropriate technological change is the best way to lower the rate of throughput, thereby reducing the long-term environmental and depletion consequences.

But lowering the rate of throughput may lead to consequences other than less depletion and pollution. It may produce a slow-down in the expanding consumption of many goods that people now value. It could also lower the probability of reducing poverty. And it might damage the prestige and security of countries that are forced to adopt this route. Yet it may be that to future generations, with adjusted value systems, such concerns would be of little importance.

Advocates as well as opponents of the stationary state recognize that serious social problems could develop. The advent of the stationary state does not mean the millenium, even to its proponents. Although physical problems might be reduced, enormous problems of equity requiring political and social reform will increasingly confront a society under the stationary state.

Doomsday States

The doomsday state is the modern version of the classical declining society. It is an expression of the view that "mankind has blown its chance for a smooth transition to an equilibrium society, each decade will be worse than the preceding one for the average American to say nothing of the average human being" [32, p. 92]. The doom in the doomsday state applies to future generations—not only to their welfare but to their very survival.

Why should this fate be of concern here and now? Even if there were time to reverse the doomsday trends, why should society make the choice to give up some present welfare for the sake of future generations, even for their survival? What is so special about perpetuation of the human species? "There is no rational answer to that terrible question" [43, p. 170].

There is some evidence that societies that ignore posterity weaken their capacity to deal with present problems. However, a concern for future generations is not based primarily on reason or self-interest, but primarily on moral grounds. It is morally reprehensible to ignore the possibility that humanity may currently be engaging in acts that could be suicidal for the species. It is equitable for society to accept responsibility for passing on to future generations at least what it has inherited from the past. It is democratic that unborn generations be given consideration in current consumption. And it is ethical that current consumers not be given the right to keep using up the options of future generations.

So let it be conceded that there is a bond with the future and that there are reasons beyond reason not to break this bond. Yet society is still confronted with the problem of how much it owes the future. In everyday living, society discounts the future; that is, present consumption is worth more than future consumption, as evidenced by a positive rate of interest in both market and planned economies.[2] "The question of society's regard for the future goes to the core of the issue of economic growth, for it raises an age old issue, one which has always intrigued and preoccupied economists. How

2. Even if this rate of interest were only 5 percent, it would cut the value attached to future consumption by half every fourteen years. On this basis, people would only be willing to give up one and a half cents of today's consumption to provide one dollar of consumption one hundred years from now.

should society divide its resources between current needs and pleasures and those of next year, next decade, next generation?" [44, p. 87].

The mere asking of such a question implies that present generations have a choice about what standards of living future generations will enjoy. Steady-state theory indicates that in the really long run this choice depends on how fast society permits population to grow. In a somewhat shorter time frame, however, by consuming less now and investing more, a larger growth in output is achieved on the way to a steady state, and generations in the future will be better off.

The market mechanism, in which investment and savings respond to the market rate of interest, creates a certain amount of growth. Why should society desire growth at a different pace? One reason is that the social rate of discount (the rate applicable to society) differs from the market rate (the rate adopted by the private sector) because individuals have inadequate information about the future and because they are less willing than society as a whole to take some kinds of risks. Another reason relates to the effects of technology on growth. Suppose that impartiality between generations (that is, not giving the current generation favored treatment over future generations) is defined as occurring when consumption per capita is the same tomorrow as today. In order to achieve impartiality when there is no technological progress, there could be no discount or rate of return on saving. However, if technology does progress, future generations would have a built-in increase in per capita consumption. An impartial rate of return in this case would provide an amount of saving which, along with the technological progress, would keep the per capita consumption constant. Finally, there is the problem of exhaustible resources. If economic production is dependent on exhaustible resources, can impartiality, in the sense of a constant per capita consumption among generations, ever be reached?

Koopmans brings all these issues together by inquiring into what would happen if an economy required a capital stock, but not exhaustible resources, in order to produce; and, alternatively, if the requirement were for resources but not capital [60]. He finds that in the capital model a positive rate of discount favors present over future generations, and after a sufficient lapse of time, it benefits all subsequent generations about equally. Technological progress, however, benefits future generations. If technological progress is associated with capital investment, this benefit would be diminished by a positive rate of discount. In the resource model there is no capital to produce further resources, as they are consumed from the available stock. Therefore, a positive rate of discount will shorten the period of survival, and those who live closer to the present will live better. Thus the choice of a social rate of discount depends on whether the advance of technology will provide future benefits that will overcome resource exhaustion and the greed of the current generation for present consumption.

The choice that the people of the United States have made in the past is not patently greedy. New generations have been equipped with growing stocks of more efficient equipment. Technological knowledge has expanded and education has become more widespread. And, although exhaustible resources have been used in great quantities, this does not mean they have been used voraciously. Rather, a good part of them have merely been converted from below-ground capital into above-ground capital [2, p. 188].

These observations, however, relate to the past, whereas "the pure theory of exhaustible resources is trying to tell us that, if exhaustible resources really matter, then the balance between present and future is more delicate than we are accustomed to think" [89, p. 10]. Even slight miscalculations about technological progress or available energy resource reserves on the pace of resource consumption could have disastrous consequences for the future. In the doomsday view these miscalculations have already been made, and the balance between present and future has already been violated.

There are two categories of events that may result in doomsday. In one, doomsday will be brought about by some immovable physical barrier; in the other, it will be the consequence of processes working within the social system itself. The external physical barrier can be population growth, the rate of industrialization, pollution, inadequate food production, or resource depletion. The social barriers can be related to growth and crowding, which cause frictions to develop between individuals, political conflicts to intensify, intergroup rivalries to increase, family ties and traditional values to break down, psychological stress to become common, and armed conflict to become likely [95, p. 73].

According to the computer-based calculations of the initial *Limits to Growth* study [61], the ultimate collapse will probably occur because of nonrenewable resource depletion. But if it is assumed that natural resource reserves are doubled or made infinitely renewable because of technology, then the end will come because of a sudden increase in the level of pollution. If pollution controls are introduced, then food shortages will destroy us. If our capacity to provide food is increased, then population growth will do us in.

Scarcities of food, natural resource limits, and population growth have long been associated with doomsday. Nuclear devastation and environmental degradation have recently been added to the list. Nuclear attacks may be avoided, population may be controlled, food may be supplied, and infinite natural resources may be found. But, in the end, according to the confirmed doomsayer, "there is an absolute limit to the ability of the earth to support or tolerate the process of industrial activity" [43, p. 47], and environmental degradation will be the ultimate destroyer.

It is recognized, of course, that technology has the potential for moderating some physical and social trends. Doomsday models, however, tend to play down this potential for several reasons. First, there is no assurance that needed technology will continue to evolve. Second, even if the technology did emerge it would ultimately have detrimental environmental side-effects. Third, even if technology's side-effects could be controlled, society would still have to contend with the social forces set into motion by economic growth.

The present doomsday models are less concerned with the particular barrier that represents the ultimate limit than with the speed at which the barrier is being approached. The process of economic growth tends to speed up the pace at which natural resources are consumed, population grows, pollution sets in, and social stress is engendered. The concern of the doomsday models is that the time still available to stop these trends is at best very short and at worst has already passed. These concerns are reinforced by the long lead times involved in implementing pollution control, lowering population growth, achieving the dissemination of new technologies, or reducing the stresses of urban living. Therefore, after growth-abatement policies are adopted, there will still be a time interval in which the growth trends will continue at increasing rates. Thus uncontrolled economic growth appears not only to guarantee that the fatal barrier will ultimately be reached, but that it will do so in a destructive manner. Both these factors underline the urgency of slowing down growth trends, if it is not too late already.

What is at issue between the doomsday characterization of growth on the one hand and the steady or stationary state interpretations on the other is whether traditional balancing mechanisms, such as a functioning price system, still have an important role to play in averting the doomsday predictions by slowing down and then diverting the forces bringing us closer to the ultimate barriers.

ECONOMIC DEVELOPMENT

Neoclassical economic expansion theory, with its vision of steady equilibrium growth, is a dull story compared to the historian's view of economic development. Neoclassical theory "conceals, either in aggregation or in the abstract generality of multisector models, all the drama of the events—the rise and fall of products, technologies, and industries, and the accompanying transformations of the spatial and occupational distribution of the population" [68, p. 510].

The drama of events that the theory and concept of economic expansion conceals is that economic change can be part of a larger process of fundamental changes in the way people live. Adam Smith's vision of this larger picture led him to discuss more than capital accumulation, economies or diseconomies of scale, and rising productivity. He also anticipated emerging industrialization, changing standards for political and economic liberty, and expanded social mobility of the production factors, none of which are easily included in neoclassical theory. Analyses of economic development force questions about the total society and where it is headed, which are ignored by economic expansion theory. Under economic development the structural transformation of a society becomes the issue.

According to Aron, such structural transformation has had considerable impact on societies in the past.

Instead of hand implements, man now has at his disposal more and more complex machines; the amount of energy available per worker makes it possible to increase the worker's output, to revolutionize agriculture and mining so as to satisfy human needs, and to evolve technical devices which solve the age-old problems of housing, clothing, transport, and communication in a variety of ways undreamed of even by utopians. The exploitation of natural resources has to be recognized as a major characteristic of modern society, without precedent at least as regards quantity. At the same time, this technical mastery expresses a new attitude: the will to dominate the natural environment instead of being dominated by it and, in addition, a concern for measurement, rational organization, and forecasting the future [6, p. 14].

It is worth noting the rhetoric in this quotation from a scholar interested in economic development rather than expansion. "The exploitation of natural resources" is "a major characteristic of modern society." Energy "makes it possible . . . to revolutionize agriculture and mining." There is a "will to dominate the natural environment instead of being dominated by it." Transformations such as these are fundamental to understanding the relationship between energy and the economy and how this relationship will affect the directions in which society is moving.

There are two aspects of economic development.[3] One is concerned with *resource shifts* and emphasizes the transfer of economic resources from one producing sector to another over time. The second involves *production organization* and stresses the changes that occur over time in the organization of the work process. The first is concerned with such events as the growth of the service economy, the second with such issues as the decline of capitalism.

Resource Shifts

Kuznets has provided an empirical account of how resource shifts[4] have affected the growth of nations. His account considers events only up to the decade of the seventies, and perhaps as a consequence has little to say about the role of energy scarcity and pollution in this process.

According to Kuznets [57, p. 303-14], growth in output and output per capita in developed countries has been much more rapid since the beginning of the nineteenth century than it was in preceding centuries. Although growth has been continuous, it has followed long (20-year) swings in the growth rates. Population and labor-force growth have been relatively independent of economic change. The rapid growth in per capita output is credited more to productivity improvement than to the expansion in labor or capital. There has not been a trend toward retardation in overall growth, because new industries with rapid growth rates are continuously being introduced.

The low current per capita incomes in undeveloped countries can be attributed to the low base at which these countries began the nineteenth century, as well as to the slow growth since. The relatively large labor force and low productivity in agriculture that these countries now have was not characteristic of the developed countries at their early stage of development. Since World War II there has been a shift away from primary-sector to industrial-sector output, which has not been matched by a labor-force shift.

There has been a marked shift in the share of total output from the agriculture sector to the industrial sector, particularly manufac-

3. There are many theories and descriptions of economic development. Only those have been selected for discussion that can highlight, in some particular way, current views about how energy is related to economic growth.

4. The word resources is commonly applied to both natural resources and economic resources. The former includes energy, minerals, land, and so on; the latter is more comprehensive, referring to all inputs required for production, including labor and capital as well as natural resources. In the text, when natural resources is meant, that is the term used. However, if economic resources is meant, then either economic resources or resources is the term adopted.

turing, with a more modest shift to services.[5] These shifts have been more rapid than in earlier centuries. However, for some countries the shift out of agriculture continued to occur even when per capita incomes did not rise. The rapid increases in agricultural productivity have only been occurring since 1920.

Not only output but also the work force shifted from agriculture to industry and services. The modest output shift to services has, however, been accompanied by a rapid labor force-shift, which led Kuznets to conclude that while the structure of product was "industrialized," the structure of the labor force was partly "industrialized" and partly "servicized." The increases in per capita product account for some but not all of the shifts in output and work force. Thus there are other factors at work in addition to rising incomes that account for the changing structure of production.

The shift of manpower from agriculture to industry and possibly to services was first noticed by Clark [18]. He suggested that such a shift was not accidental but reflected the fact that labor moved to manufacturing where its wages would be higher, and that manufacturing could afford to pay these wages because of productivity improvements. As a consequence, economic development could be perceived as consisting of growing per capita incomes accompanied by a shift in labor and improvement in productivity.

Quantitative testing of these assumptions in a sample of countries found that rising per capita incomes were indeed associated with resource shifts to manufacturing—but only up to a point [17]. After per capita incomes become high enough, incomes no longer rise as resources shift. In other words, the process of resource transfers among sectors may not be unilinear but might proceed in stages, each stage typified by different characteristics of production and levels of income.

But what stage will emerge if there are energy scarcities or if mass consumption leads to environmental degradation? Three directions seem possible. One is that the physical realities will compel diminishing returns, and growth will be reversed, as in the doomsday models. A second is that some stimulus, the usual candidate being technological progress, will overcome the physical constraints, and growth can continue. The third direction is that there will be a reduction in those activities that impose the most severe burden on

---

5. The agriculture sector includes fisheries, forestry, and hunting, as well as farming. The industrial sector includes mining, construction, utilities, transportation, and communication, as well as manufacturing. The service sector includes trade, finance, insurance, and real estate, as well as private and government services.

limited natural and environmental resources—usually manufacturing and the consumption of manufactured products.

Curtailment of manufacturing could result in resources shifting to services accompanied by a decline in the rate of output growth. In other words, economic growth depends on "appropriate" intersector resource shifts. If the appropriate shifts are to stop, then economic growth would have to slow down.

On the basis of his examination of post-World War II developments in Western countries, Nicholas Kaldor came to exactly this conclusion, although his analysis did not draw on energy-related considerations. In his view aggregate economic growth was caused by a rise in manufacturing output, which in turn was caused by the shift of labor from agriculture into manufacturing. Since there is a limit to the labor transfer out of agriculture, the rate at which the economy can grow is also finite. When a country's surplus agricultural labor disappears, its rate of economic growth will slow down.

The view that economic growth depends on reallocation of economic resources constitutes a challenge to what had been one of the customary hypotheses in the neoclassical theory of growth. According to this hypothesis, if output increases faster than the labor force, it is due to technological progress, which occurs independently of economic forces—that is, efficiency improvement is the cause of output growth.

Kaldor took the opposite view, namely, that output growth is the cause of efficiency improvement. He observed that in most countries the growth in manufacturing output was faster than that of industrial employment, which he interpreted to mean that productivity in manufacturing depended on output growth. So manufacturing productivity improved as the quantity of manufacturing activity increased. And as labor shifted into manufacturing, the scale of manufacturing activity increased and productivity rose due to economies of scale, which in turn contributed to aggregate economic growth. In these circumstances the growth process is one of internally generating an increased efficiency in the allocation of a nation's resources, rather than externally imposing some technological progress.

This heightened efficiency has spatial as well as intersector dimensions. Most apparent is that a shift of resources out of agriculture tends to be accompanied by urbanization and movement of population and industry among regions of the country. These migration trends and capital movements then continue even after the intersectoral shifts slow down.

Such events as development of a new industry or depletion of an energy reserve occur in specific places, so that some areas decline while others expand. Often, instead of equilibrating forces being set disequilibrating forces are established to reinforce the expansion of the growing region and further depress the declining area. The result is that as economic development proceeds, it may be accompanied by increased inequalities among regions of a country, between urban and rural areas, and also between the developed and undeveloped nations [69].

Spatial movements of resources can contribute to economic development, whether or not they reinforce inequalities, by improving the economy's overall efficiency. Usually an area develops a capability to export (to other regions in the country as well as to other countries) some commodity or service. This development draws capital and people into the area not only to produce the export but also to provide materials and equipment needed by the exporting industry and to furnish the goods and services consumed by the families attracted to the area [147].

Thus high rates of growth in productivity and per capita incomes seem to be associated with large intersector and interregional resource shifts. Kuznets suggests that this happens because the advance of knowledge spurs technological innovation whose subsequent diffusion causes both rapid increases in productivity and shifts in the production structure. These dual effects of diffusion are inevitable because innovation is selective, hitting different branches of production at different times. Thus to the extent that innovation results in productivity improvements in the innovating sectors, it not only raises output in those sectors but also in the total economy. To the extent that diffusion is selective, it produces a shift in production structure, reinforcing output and productivity growth in the sectors to which resources shift, that is, into the innovating sectors.

Under these circumstances the process of growth is cumulative. The advance of knowledge brings about innovations that are diffused, causing a direct increase in output and also a shift in the production structure, which produces a further hike in output, which in turn creates more resources for knowledge advancement and innovation diffusion.

Although the growth process is continuous over time, there is a limit to growth during any particular period, brought about because the noninnovating sectors of the economy absorb resources. So a ceiling is set on the resources available to the fast-growing, innovating sectors. The limit to growth is set by the proportion of its total resources that society is willing to devote to its rapidly growing sectors, or—what comes to the same thing—the proportion it needs to devote to its slow-growing sectors. Whereas in the theory of the steady state a ceiling is set to the transitional component of growth by society's need for consumption, in this view the limit is imposed by the need for the products of slow-growing sectors.

Suppose the dynamic sectors are relatively intensive energy consumers. Rising energy costs would then lower the rate of output growth, while falling costs would raise it. Precisely something of this sort had been anticipated by Schurr and Marshak as early as 1950 in their study of atomic power. "Not only would a reduction in the cost of energy cause an expansion of energy intensive processes already in use but it would also bring into use new processes that had not been previously economical, and cause them to be substituted for present processes" [86, p. 221].

Although the dynamic sectors have been high-energy consumers in the past, it seems doubtful that this will hold true in the future. If this view of the growth process is accurate we can infer that the ready availability of energy in the past has directly contributed to the growth of the economy, and the fall in relative energy prices has also spurred growth. However, in the future, output growth will be less dependent on the availability of energy and low energy costs.

Production Organization

The concept of the industrial society was forged in the nineteenth century to distinguish it from other societies of the past; it was not a theological or a military or a hierarchical society. It was an industrial society because it was run by the producers and not by "the priests, warriors and feudal lords—the parasites and consumers of wealth" [9, p. 49].

It is the producers who are responsible for the organization of production. As we shift our focus from the quantity of production to its organization, and from resource relationships to social relations, we become involved with humanizing production, and this distinguishes the grand sociological descriptions of economic development from the more strictly economic ones. In their humanist emphasis, sociologists have raised some fundamental questions. Who are the producers in society? Are the producers also the rulers? What is the relation between the ruler/producer and other social classes? And how does this relationship affect the underlying trends in the social order?

Some of the characters that have been assigned leading roles as producers are the engineer, the owner, the entrepreneur, the manager, and the worker. For Marx the functions performed by these five characters were more appropriately assigned to the two main producers: the owner and the worker. Under capitalism, it was the owner who had the power but the worker who was the true producer. This split set up the economic contradictions that were supposed to lead to the collapse of capitalism and the rise of socialism.

For Weber, however, the significant social process was not the antagonism between owner and worker but rather the drive toward rationality and efficiency. This drive led to the preeminence of administration (whether under capitalism or socialism), the rise of the manager, and the bureaucratization of government, business, and social institutions. The critical actors were to be found not in the working class but in the bureaucracy. And this bureaucracy, as later writers would point out and as current data demonstrate, would increasingly absorb the work force, as workers left the factories to become white-collar employees and managers in offices.

The engineer is also an important actor. Veblen believed that industrialization would create a technocrat society whose emphasis on rationality would require the development of experts in the applied sciences. Further, society's need for the technocrat would endow him with authority and would cause him to become the driving force in a rational industrial society.

Schumpeter, however, perceived some dangers in rationality. To him the power in capitalist society went to the innovator/entre-preneur—a person who unsettled rather than settled things. In Schumpeter's dynamic society, innovation was the essential force to growth, and innovation had little to do with careful calculations comparing well defined choices. The decline of capitalism was to be the result of excessive rationality, as entrepreneurs became useless, innovation grew routine, owners gave way to managers, and the bureaucratic enterprise became the dominant social form.

These capsule characterizations of four major bodies of thought seek not only to hint at the importance of the organization of production to economic development, but also to indicate that the moving forces are described in terms of such ideological phenomena as capitalism, bureaucratization, technocracy, and innovation, rather than in terms of the characteristics or supply of energy.

Discussions of the role of energy in the organization of production can, however, be framed in terms of these four ideological phenomena. It is sometimes suggested for example, that energy scarcity has the potential to resolve the Marxian struggle between capital and labor, because increasing the amount of capital available to workers will be of little use in an energy-scarce society [20]. Thus the organization of production, including the types of goods produced, will have to shift in favor of labor-intensive activities.

The postindustrial society has its roots more in Veblen than in

Marx. In this society, energy will have little effect on the organization of production, as opposed to the industrial society where energy played a key role in production, and economic growth was a basic objective [9]. In the postindustrial society information is the key production input, the professional and technical scientists are the most important producers, and the codification of knowledge is the primary objective.

The Weberian tradition provides the basis for a still different resolution of energy crisis. The bureaucratization of production leads to the emergence of the service economy, which requires less energy because white-collar rather than factory workers dominate production and because households turn to the consumption of services rather than goods.

Finally, Schumacher [83] has revived the Schumpeterian innovator. Energy scarcities have introduced incentives that will encourage innovators to develop a less capital-intensive organization of production. The result will be the decline of industrialization as we know it, the demise of bureaucratization, and the triumph of small-scale industrial organization.

ECONOMIC PROGRESS

It is widely believed that economic progress should be defined in terms of well-being, involving much more than increases in goods and services. Such an interpretation of economic progress would probably lower our need for energy, since goals other than expanding gross national product would become important. For example, attending to the psychological as well as physical needs of individuals; improving educational and cultural rather than production systems; making the job environment rather than the job output rewarding; lowering discrimination rather than raising productivity; creating livable communities rather than efficient factories. "All such alternative rational goals would be significantly less energy demanding than our present goal of industrial productivity" [71, p. 4].

The relation of economic progress to increases in goods and services will be evaluated here by first describing how economic growth is generally measured. Then the question of whether the production of goods and services and household consumption are adequate measures of economic progress will be considered. Finally, some empirical findings will be given on the connection between the increase of goods and services and economic progress.

Measuring U.S. Output

The United States has become accustomed to the press releases issued quarterly by the U.S. Department of Commerce that announce the current level of national output. The news media, politicians, corporations, and labor unions all anxiously wait to hear and to judge whether the nation's economy has created more output or less than in the preceding quarter, and by how much; whether these changes were expected or came as a surprise; and whether economic policy needs revision or is on track.

It is surprising that so much attention and so much concern are focused on what is merely an arbitrary statistical artifact, "a figment which . . . would not as such exist at all, were there no statisticians to create it" [39, p. 439]. But simply because output is measured in an arbitrary manner does not mean it is measured incorrectly; and because measured output is an artifact does not mean it is useless.

What the economic statisticians are seeking by creating this "figment" is not a single all-purpose indicator of some mythical output. Rather, they are looking for a way to measure, interrelate, and summarize transactions of business, of households, and of governments—both domestic and foreign. Thus, what is being created by the statistician is not a single number, but a set of accounts. And implied by these accounts are numerous measures of economic performance.

One of the more important measures of performance is the gross national product (GNP). The GNP seeks to summarize all the measured transactions that have taken place during the year: the total amount of goods and services that are produced for final sale to households for their consumption, to businesses for their investment, and to government for its public services and facilities. The GNP is a flow of goods and services to the "final" consumers arbitrarily defined to include households, governments, and business investment. The GNP is not a measure of accumulated assets, or of the stock of wealth, or of "throughput" goods and services needed to produce the final sales, or of family consumption. It is what it says it is—a measure of the goods and services, valued at their market prices, that are provided to the final consumers. Because of various accounting conventions this figure is also equal to the sum of the values produced by labor, governments, and business as they engage in their economic transactions.

The GNP as a measure of economic performance emphasizes transactions that take place in the market, and values these transactions as the market values them. In part this convention is adopted because the market automatically produces the quantity and value information that go into creating the accounts, while nonmarket information is more difficult to develop. But there is also some conception, or model, of how the economy "really" works which determines what should be included in the accounts. Because GNP includes all the final sales to households, business, and government, it is well suited to considerations of overall economic policy, particularly as it relates to employment and inflation. It is not, however, equally well suited to considerations of economic growth, even when these considerations are restricted primarily to market transactions. The reason is that the GNP implicitly includes the value of the wear and tear on the nation's plants and equipment that occurs during the year, and it is "gross" because it includes such depreciation. Ordinarily we would not want to include the value of capital consumption in a measure purporting to describe economic growth. For this reason, the nation's economic accounts specifically identify a measure called the net national product (NNP), which is defined as the GNP less depreciation. It is the NNP, measured after adjustments for price changes over time, that is most properly used as an indicator of economic growth and as a measure of the degree of success in achieving a high level of output.

But the GNP and the NNP tend to grow at comparable rates in the United States, so for many policy purposes it would not matter which indicator is used. The most important aspect of the difference between GNP and NNP is that if capital consumption increases over time, then the use of GNP will overestimate the contribution of capital to growth.

For many purposes we are concerned not only with production but also with the earnings of those involved with production. These earnings are summarized in the measure of national income produced (NIP), which is equivalent to the NNP less indirect business taxes. The factor cost of a product—that is, the earnings labor and asset owners derive from its production—differs from the market price of the product because of the value of indirect business taxes. Therefore, NIP can be seen as the NNP valued at factor cost rather than market price. The NNP valued at factor cost is the most appropriate aggregate measure to analyze productivity change and to make intercountry comparisons. In the past, however, the difference between NNP at market price and factor cost has been trivial and the choice between the two unimportant.

For a number of analyses, primarily those that claim to be concerned with welfare considerations, it is appropriate to focus on the household sector only—that is, business and government transactions would be treated as if they were "throughput" rather than final transactions. This measure of household growth can be found by adding government transfer payments and subtracting corporate savings and corporate taxes from NIP to arrive at a measure of personal income, which indicates the money received by households (and some other agents) for the services they provide. Then, when personal taxes are subtracted from personal income, a measure of disposable income is derived, which represents the money made available during the year for household spending. Finally, if household savings are deducted from the personal income, the result is personal expenditures. Personal expenditures then can be used as a possible measure for tracking family welfare.

Economic statisticians have been accused of not recognizing the difference between the measures they produce and "true" measures of growth and welfare. This is generally an unfair accusation, as can be seen by the complexity of even these few measures. Even more, economists are making efforts to improve the national accounts and to provide distinctions among varying measures, which would permit more useful analyses of growth and welfare.

The concern with correcting deficiencies in current measurements reflects an effort to include within the formal accounting system the important quantifiable dimensions of welfare. But even though many dimensions of welfare can be measured, they cannot easily be incorporated in an interrelated system of accounts based on a single homogeneous unit of measurement such as dollars. The distribution of income, the number of persons in poverty, the level of education, and the rate of crime cannot fit within the accounting framework as we know it. For this reason, many people propose that there be developed a supplementary system of social indicators to quantify dimensions of welfare that cannot be incorporated in the conventional economic accounting.

On balance it would appear that economic accounts, particularly if supplemented by social indicators, can tell us much about changes in human welfare. Even though they do not directly measure human welfare, and do not purport to do so, the economic accounts do reflect changes in welfare closely enough so that the biases and inaccuracies inherent in the measurements are only qualifications and not negations of the results.

As Kuznets points out, the problems associated with defining and measuring national output are not new but have been "discussed at length by generations of scholars in the field" [68, p. 583]. He separates these problems into three groups: (1) how we distinguish between economic and social (or noneconomic) activities; (2) how we decide what is a cost and what is a return, or what is a "throughput" and what is a final product; and (3) how we combine diverse costs and multitude of economic products into acceptable totals through valuation.

Economic versus Noneconomic activity. When activities are thought of mainly in terms of market functions, then a number of nonmarket activities that are still part of the economy are not included. Nordhaus and Tobin have valued these nonmarket activities at almost half the size of the GNP in recent years [68]. The major component of these is the unpaid housework of family members.

There has tended to be a shift over time from housework to market work, as women increasingly participate in the labor force. Therefore, since part of the observed increases in national output is attributable to this change, there is an upward bias in the measured rate of output growth. For similar reasons the output of developed countries has an upward bias as compared to the less-developed ones, where market activities are not as pervasive.

Leisure time of households is not valued in the GNP. The worth of such time is estimated to be about equal in size to the measured GNP [68]. Further, as the workweek is reduced, leisure time value increases, suggesting that the rate of output growth has been underestimated by customary measuring techniques.

Separating economic from noneconomic activity is necessary for improved measurements of economic growth to take place. Such distinctions also create difficulties, however. What is considered an economic activity and what is not will probably change over time in response to alterations in the pattern and pace of economic growth. It is sometimes recommended that nonmarket activities be accounted for by developing a system to measure household activity according to the allocation and evaluation of householders' time. The major objection to such a system is that the measurements of the value attached to the nonmarket time of households would necessarily be arbitrary.

Costs versus Return.   One of the most serious accusations against the customary output measurements is that they include as output those factors that are really costs to society. This has been described as "Alice-in-Wonderland accounting," because many of the costs associated with economic growth are not deducted from output, and some of the expenditures associated with controlling the deleterious side effects of production are actually added to output to make GNP grow even faster. "Since the net benefit of growth can never be negative with this Alice-in-Wonderland accounting system, the rule becomes 'grow forever' or at least until it kills you—and then count your funeral expenses as further growth. This is terminal hyper-growthmania" [23, p. 150].

Thus, according to Daly and many others, economic accountants are adding where they should be subtracting. To the extent that this accusation is meant to point a finger at the confusion of the economic statistician or the materialistic bias of the economist, the accusation is unwarranted. Economic accountants have been debating these issues from the very inception of the statistical measurement of output. Yet if this accusation is meant to show that some cost items are actually measured as part of output, then it is well founded.

The reason for including costs as a part of output, however, has more to do with the social process than with the economic accounts. As the real economy becomes more complex, there is a tendency to increase the intermediate or the cost activities required to produce the final goods and services. No matter how hard the economic statisticians try, they are unlikely to keep their accounts up to date and including the latest intermediate costs generated in an increasingly complex society.

One response to this situation is to develop and hope for a less complex society [83]. The response of the less ambitious economic statistician is to painstakingly and belatedly try to measure the so-called regrettable necessities and then deduct them from output. What are these "regrettable necessities"?

One class of such items includes the overhead costs of a complex urban, industrial economy; for example, time and money spent on travel to work, on drugs to combat illness, on education, on national defense, or on job training. The argument that these are intermediate costs, rather than outputs, is essentially based on the idea that they are needed to preserve the "fabric of society at large," and therefore they are similar to the costs required to maintain physical capital. Others argue that no line can be drawn between the situation where such costs are incurred for their own final utility and the situation where they are inputs for some final product. Therefore, no measurements requiring this distinction are possible. For example, how can we know what portion of educational expenditures is to prepare for finding a job (a cost), and what portion is for learning to be a good citizen (an output)?

Another group of costs is associated with urban living and large-scale production. These are generally expenditures counted as final consumption, even though they are required simply to maintain rather than enhance utility. Outlays for sanitation, policing, pollution control, or even research and development might fall into this group. In this view air and water are assets, and economic production and consumption are causing a deterioration in their value. So any expenditures made for environmental restoration or abatement to offset deterioration should be subtracted from output. This seems to be a sounder argument than the U.S. Commerce Department position that since we are better off with antipollution devices than without, government and household spending on such equipment should be added to output.

In addition to the actual market outlays for pollution control or abatement, there are social costs, including changes in the environment, that are simply not contained in output measurements. So long as these externalities were not considered substantial, they were discussed as another relatively minor market failure; such failures can be taken care of by proper market pricing, which takes full account of environmental costs and benefits. It appears, however, that environmental diseconomies tend to increase rapidly with growth in population densities and GNP. Thus, even if efficient solutions could be reached with proper pricing of the externalities, it does not necessarily mean that the nation is better off with economic growth and pollution than without them. And, of course, many of those concerned over issues of environmental degradation insist that we will be worse off rather than better off as a result of economic growth.

Economic Valuations. When Schumpeter referred to output as a "figment," he had in mind the concept that millions of different items are somehow added together. The only way that such addition can take place is if each of the items is assigned some weight. By convention and by necessity, the weights ordinarily used are market prices. The reason for this is that market prices are presumed to reflect socially set priorities and economically efficient transactions. Yet market prices are not a perfect solution to finding the right weights. Among the possible pitfalls are these: there are many instances of monopoly and government intervention that prevent market prices from reflecting ideal weights; market prices rarely reflect the social aspects of a maldistribution of income; some items, particularly government activities, do not have a market price and are priced at factor cost; and many activities that should properly affect output are not priced at all on the market, leaving a void that only arbitrary imputations can seek to fill.

Another aspect of economic valuation relates to changes over time in its standard. For purposes of growth analysis the interest is in "real" production or consumption rather than in their monetary value in each year. Thus the monetary value of output must be adjusted so that changes in output from one year to the next exclude changes attributable only to shifts in prices. Price indexes are customarily used to express each year's value of output as if it were in constant prices. "The adjustment for price tells us how much less of an unchanging basket of standard goods one could buy in 1964 than in 1947 if he had a fixed dollar income" [44, p. 147].

There are two things wrong with this procedure. First, price indexes are notoriously deficient in their ability to pick up quality changes, which tends to lead to an underestimate of growth in products. "The introduction of new and improved final products provides the user with a greater range of choice or enables him to meet his needs better with the same use of resources, but it does not, in general, contribute to growth as measured; it results in "noneconomic" or "unmeasured" quality change" [27, p. 280].

The deficiencies of unmeasured quality change could, perhaps, be overcome by more refined measurements. But a second difficulty inherent in any weighting process is far more serious: the price relations of some particular year have to be selected to provide a constant price series. If we choose the price relations of an early year, we will overestimate the growth rate, since prices on costlier items will most likely be reduced relative to other items as time goes by. Similarly, if we select price relations from a later year as the base, the growth rate will be underestimated.

Production as a Measure of Progress
The nation's output is equal to its production of goods and services. An increase in national output after adjusting for price changes signifies economic growth. Whether it also signifies economic progress depends largely on which effects of the output increase are considered important. "Some, like economists, care about the effects on man; some, like ecologists, about the natural world as a whole; and some, like oil company executives bemoaning the energy crisis, about the effects of growth on potential for further growth. Some discussions focus on health, others on aesthetic, others on recreation opportunities, and still others on social, psychological or political ramifications" [78, p. 119].

For those who perceive output increases as economic progress, growth provides not only more per se but also more of what people want. This school of thought perceives economic growth as a basis for social and political stability because it raises the material standard of living for most families, which makes them more tolerant of their working conditions, their governments, and the social and environmental stresses to which they are subjected.

Output increases also provide specific economic gains. In addition to improving the overall standard of living, higher living standards reach more families, more people are employed, inflation is reduced, the poor are raised from poverty, education and health are advanced, and resources are made available to reduce environmental degradation, maintain world peace, and feed the people of the world.

These are the claims for growth. But even if they accurately portray its benefits—and some would dispute that—the question arises whether growth can continue to provide such benefits. It seems to require more and more effort simply to maintain the quality of life. For example, as natural resources are depleted, an increasing part of the nation's output needs to be allocated to recovering them. Similarly, as the environment becomes degraded, the costs of environmental protection and restoration increase more than proportionately. And as our cities deteriorate, it requires still faster increases in economic resources to make them viable places to live and work. Where, then, is economic progress if it requires more and more of the growth in output simply to stay in the same place?

Even if technology could overcome these physical constraints, there are those who believe that increases in output cannot measure progress, because such growth itself is destructive of cherished values. "We must sacrifice some individual security, some of our claims to protection, priority, and precedence. We must be prepared to change occupation, to move from one place to another, to accept loss of status or prestige, if not of income. . . . On the larger scene, economic growth has necessitated or has been associated with such imponderables as the growth of large cities, the shift of employment into the large, faceless corporation, the decline of self-employment, and the expansion of the bureaucratic state. Growth has brought with it the assembly line and the computer. It has meant the decline of the extended family, loss of sense of community, the reduction of regional and ethnic diversity" [44, p. 152].

One response to the destructiveness of growth is to adopt policies that will reduce or eliminate it. But if we prefer such policies, we must believe not only that growth is *on balance* negatively related to progress, but also that it is impossible to reduce the costs of growth while retaining its benefits. There is little empirical evidence that such a pessimistic view is warranted.

The alternative response would be not to give up growth but to find ways for its benefits to be greater than its costs. This approach has been customary in the past and is the challenge to the future.

Consumption as a Measure of Progress

A basic assumption of economic analysis is that well-being depends to a significant degree on consumption; that welfare increases as consumption grows. Household consumption comprises about three-fifths of national output. It is considered a more appropriate measure of well-being than production because it excludes some expenditures that are inputs to, rather than final components of, economic welfare. Prominent among these expenditures are those relating to investment, depreciation, regrettable necessities, and some categories of public spending.

Flowing from the adoption of consumption as an index of well-being are some strategic views regarding economic progress and how to measure it. Consumption becomes the goal of economic activity. Households, individually or collectively, become the ultimate consumer whose standards are the criteria for evaluating economic activity. Public expenditures are judged by the collective consumption they provide. Investments are valued because of the future consumption they make possible.

Since consumption defines what is valuable, it also provides the guidelines for measuring economic output and for deciding which activities are costs or inputs, or intermediate products rather than final outputs in the economic system. If some other attribute than consumption were assigned primacy as an index of well-being—such as political power, emotional stability, or religious conviction—then consumption would most likely be viewed as a cost or an intermediate input required to obtain the output.

Some critics of economic growth challenge the view that consumption is a final product unequivocally contributing to well-being. Specifically they reject the assumption that a person who consumes more is better off than one who consumes less. "A Buddhist economist would consider this approach excessively irrational: since consumption is merely a means to human well-being, the aim should be to obtain the maximum of well-being with the minimum of consumption" [83, p. 57].

If consumption is an intermediate rather than a final product, and if it is perceived in terms of the costs rather than the benefits it imposes on society, then an efficient economic system would seek to keep it as low, rather than as high, as possible. At the very least, "wasteful" consumption that does not contribute to well-being would be eliminated. Going beyond the elimination of waste, such a society would seek optimal patterns of consumption rather than exert the effort required to achieve maximum consumption. And, in view of the stresses and strains imposed by modern living, it is possible that such optimal patterns are associated with nonindustrial methods of production and low energy-consuming economies.

Not only critics but also proponents of consumption as a measure of well-being recognize that it is only one among a number of possible components to welfare. Proponents argue that since it is a major component, and the appropriate economic component, then it is likely that trends in consumption accurately reflect economic progress and well-being. Critics argue that consumption is not the only economic component, that it may contribute less to well-being than other components, and that emphasizing consumption may obscure the relation between nonmaterial dimensions of well-being and economic progress.

For example, working conditions are an important part of economic well-being, and their trends may run counter to those of consumption. The shift from craftsman to machine-hand, from artisanship to work discipline, from a lack of distinction between work and living to an emphasis on this distinction, may all lower well-being even as goods and gadgets have poliferated. Material progress may be gained at the expense of other aspects of economic progress, and economic progress may result in the reduction of noneconomic dimensions of welfare.

More likely, material progress, on balance, is complementary rather than competitive with these other goals. But we really don't know. Comparisons of industrial with other societies may be misleading because the nonmaterial aspects of life are difficult to quantify, and those comparisons that are available have been made by industrial societies emphasizing industrial rather than nonindustrial values.

Even if consumption is accepted as a measure of economic progress and well-being, there are aspects of its measurement and assumptions about its relation to well-being that must be taken into account. For example, is it aggregate or per capita consumption that measures well-being? This is not an easy question, since it raises not only the long-debated issues of obligations to future generations and the validity of interpersonal comparisons, but also the more current issues of right to life and women's role in society.

It can also be questioned whether it is the quantity of consumption or the ratio of actual to desired consumption that measures well-being. If the latter, then the level of well-being will not have grown as much as the level of consumption, because the expansion of consumption creates additional wants. Therefore, the proportion of wants that are satisfied will not increase as rapidly as the quantity of consumption, and in some cases the proportion may even decline.

A further question can be raised as to whether the relation of consumption to well-being is influenced by who is doing the consuming. If overall well-being is increased more through additional consumption by the poor than by the rich, then increases in the aggregate well-being will be greater, the smaller the share of increased consumption going to the rich.

The welfare implications of consumption are also influenced by how people regard their position relative to others. If well-being is increased simply because consumption differentials are reduced, then comparisons of the quantities of consumption in different countries or in different periods must be supplemented by considerations of the real income distribution that prevails.

For a variety of measurement reasons the trends in price-adjusted consumption have a downward bias as a welfare measure, which results from failing to include in the price adjustments the benefits of widening consumer choice, improvements in quality of consumer goods, and the introduction of new products. Further, there are some upward biases because the measurements do not take account of the shifting of some activities from the home, where they are not paid for, to the marketplace, where they are compensated and therefore counted in measured output.

A number of elements in well-being are simply left out of the consumption measure. This includes the apparently increasing quantity of leisure time that is available and the improvements in the work environment that are being made. Also excluded are a range of injurious effects on society at large or particular segments of the population incurred through the production and use of some consumer goods.

Finally, in using consumption as a measure of well-being, account must be taken of the fact that tastes are different from one time to the next and from one country to another. As a result, if the taste for consumption—in the aggregate or for particular classes of goods—differs from place to place and time to time, comparisons of the quantity of consumption must be adjusted before statements about differences in well-being are accepted.

Some Empirical Tests of Progress

It is clear that there are fundamental challenges to the viewpoint that economic welfare corresponds to changes in social welfare. There are three ways to test the validity of this view. One is to adjust the measured estimates of consumption so that they more closely approximate welfare, and then to compare the two statistical series. The second is to obtain measures of welfare through selected social indicators and compare them with measures of economic growth. The third way is to measure subjective feelings of well-being and see how they are related to economic growth.

Adjusting Measured Consumption. Nordhaus and Tobin [68] have developed a measure of economic welfare (MEW) that corrects some deficiencies of consumption as such a measure. The MEW excludes those parts of consumption that the authors believe do not add to welfare, such as expenditures for national defense, costs of overcoming the unpleasant conditions of urban living, environmental disamenities, expenses associated with getting to work, and depreciation of consumer durables. The MEW adds to consumption the values of leisure, household work, and the services obtained from the use of various public and private capital goods. In addition the MEW includes a "growth requirement" adjustment that allows capital stock to increase at the same pace as the population, so that consumption by future generations is not lowered. Examined in this way, MEW is measured at four times the level of consumption. This is primarily because of the imputations for leisure time and nonmarket activities. Consumption, GNP, and MEW have all been increasing. GNP, however, has been rising at a faster rate than consumption, and consumption more rapidly than MEW. The conclusion that emerges is that not only has economic progress been achieved over the last 30 years, but that measures of consumption also somewhat overstate the progress. In the words of the authors, "The progress indicated by conventional national accounts is not just a myth that evaporates when a welfare-oriented measure is substituted" [68, p. 521].

Comparison to Social Indicators.   King [54] collected data for seventeen social indicators in twenty developed countries for the years 1951 and 1969. The indicators included health, education, communication, and demographic variables. He combined these indicators for each country to arrive at a summary measure of well-being for each year. He then compared the change in this overall measure from 1951 to 1969 with the change in the per capita gross domestic product for each country.

He found that countries with a high level of gross domestic product per capita also have a high summary measure of welfare; and, although there is a weak positive association over the two decades between change in output and in welfare, the intercountry correlation is not statistically significant. On the basis of these data, King concludes that in developed countries, economic growth certainly does not move in an opposite direction to economic progress as defined by his summary measure.

His assumption, however, is that high measures for the social indicators reflect high levels of well-being. Challenging King's conclusion is the argument that in modern, energy-intensive societies the opposite is probably true, since high levels of expenditures for particular social purposes indicate only that deficiencies in well-being are present—not that they are overcome.

Comparison to Subjective Feelings.   Easterlin [68] assembled the results of thirty surveys that queried individuals on their subjective happiness. The surveys were taken between 1946 through 1970, and they covered a total of nineteen developed and underdeveloped countries.

When U.S. citizens were asked what considerations most affected their personal happiness, economic considerations were mentioned by three-fifths of the respondents, while health and family issues were each named about half the time. Other areas, such as job situations and personal values, received much less attention. Similar responses were obtained in other countries. Easterlin concludes that economic considerations dominate the perceptions of happiness by individuals in the United States and in other countries.

Easterlin then asked whether greater happiness is associated with higher income. He first compared a group's income or class status with its happiness within a country. In each of the surveys, those in the highest income or class status group were happier, on the average, than those in the lowest status group. So there is a clear positive association between income and happiness for a nation's population.

Easterlin also put together a time series for the United States for the period 1946 to 1970. He found no consistent rise in the happiness index. Since income rose during this interval, it would seem to be the case that over time happiness in the United States does not necessarily increase with income growth. In addition, Easterlin concluded from his intercountry comparisons that people in rich countries are not significantly happier than those in poor ones.

Why should a cross-section of income class and happiness within a country show a positive relationship while intercountry comparisons or changes over time indicate that income and happiness are not related? Easterlin suggests this is because happiness depends on one's relative income position compared with others, as well as on the absolute income level attained.

Overall the empirical evidence suggests that increases in a country's real output or consumption means that economic progress has also occurred—at least according to what most people would consider as being economic progress. But it is likely that economic progress has been less rapid than measured output growth since the regrettable necessities—that is, the costs associated with maintaining the fabric of society—disproportionately expanded. Furthermore, the historical relation between output growth and economic progress may not continue into the future. Physical, environmental, and social challenges to this relationship are increasingly apparent. Views differ a to whether these challenges will be met, and if so, how. What does seem clear is that energy's role in the economy will not only define part of the challenge but will also comprise part of the response.

Chapter Six

Energy's Role in the
Channels of Growth

In the early 1950s the Paley Commission, in the first modern investigation of the nation's resources, noted that "the drama of the industrial revolution and a century of remarkable progress in the United States' living standards can be written in terms of constantly improved technology and ever-increasing use of energy, mineral fuels, and water power in our factories, farms, and homes" [79, Vol. 1, p. 103].

That there has been "remarkable progress" in material standards of living is virtually without dispute. That there has been an "ever-increasing use" of energy can also be documented. But there is considerable uncertainty about how and to what degree these two phenomena are related.

In tracing events from 1850 to 1950, the Paley Commission could observe that energy consumption rose by about 2.5 percent per year, compared with a national output increase of more than 3.5 percent and a population and per capita output hike of almost 2 percent. While the pace of growth for these variables was not identical, all trends were up.

It seemed clear that there was an energy connection—a mutual interaction between energy and the rest of the economy. The "ever-increasing use of energy" was, in part, attributable to the growth in population and economic output; the "remarkable progress" in economic output was partly due to the favorable conditions under which energy was being supplied.

When energy is provided under favorable conditions—that is, when its supply is reliable without causing persistent real price increases—

then it is not considered to be a particular impediment to growth in economic activity. Since there are many other obstacles to economic growth, the Paley Commission saw little to be gained from a precise determination of how energy affects economic activity. But favorable conditions can change, and for this reason there was an expressed concern that adverse conditions of energy supply in the future might constrain further growth in economic output.

Under these circumstances, attention inevitably turned to the second part of the energy connection, namely a focus on how economic growth affects energy consumption. In terms of policy concerns, the dominating question of this century has been whether energy resources would be adequate to meet the demands imposed by a growing economy, rather than how the pace of economic growth might be affected by the energy supply. In terms of economic analysis, this means that the energy sector has been viewed in the context of its response to overall economic events, but not as the creator of these events. In terms of energy models this means that until the 1970s "the energy sector was typically treated as a satellite vis-à-vis the rest of the economy. Demand for energy, supply of energy and energy technology were assumed to be influenced by the economy. But no influence was allowed to carry over from the energy sector to the rest of the economy" [53, p. 4].

What has recently caused a modification of this analytic and policy focus has been the shift to more unfavorable conditions of energy supply and the expectation that these unfavorable conditions will not only continue but probably deteriorate even further. Specifically, the rising costs of energy have forced consideration of their impact on general economic activity as well as their effects on energy consumption.

The long-term record described in Chapter 4 provides clear evidence that overall economic developments have had a major impact on the pace and composition of energy consumption. This impact will continue, although its specific pattern will differ from the past due to the new unfavorable conditions of energy supply.

The extent to which the energy sector has had a significant feedback on the rest of the economy is more difficult to assess. For example, Appendix Tables 1 and 2 show that not only have long-term trends in key energy indicators been different from the trends in key economic indicators, but these differences have altered during different time periods. In interpreting such trends it is helpful to distinguish the effects of the energy sector on economic recovery (that is, the movement toward full employment of resources); the effects on economic expansion (that is, increasing the overall capacity for production); and the effects on economic development (that is, changes in the underlying structure of the economy).

The recent record indicates that sudden shifts to more unfavorable conditions of energy supply can have a major impact on economic recovery, both in the United States and worldwide. What is more uncertain is whether energy supply has had or will have a strong effect on economic expansion and economic development.

The supply of available energy will clearly limit the economy's potential for growth so long as technology and the level of other inputs to production are fixed. In this sense there can be no question about the fact that unfavorable conditions of energy supply have an influence on economic growth. Indeed, it is because the supply of other inputs and technology do not markedly change in the short run that unfavorable energy supply conditions so severely curb economic recovery. What is at issue is whether the conditions of energy supply in themselves will have a sufficiently large impact over the long run on either technology or other inputs so that economic expansion and development will, in turn, be significantly affected.

The large-scale quantitative models that currently chart future developments generally conclude that energy's long-run impact on the economy is relatively small. The following comments are typical:

> Given the substantial reduction in energy use, the question arises as to the effects of the reduction on the performance of the economy. The effects are noticeable but far from catastrophic, and can be accommodated within the existing economic structure. [8, p. 148.]

> The basic properties of the model are illustrated by the result that, in the 1980 simulations for example, energy input can be reduced by 8 percent at the cost of only a 1 percent increase in average prices and a 0.4 percent decrease in real income. In other words, the flexibility of the economy in adapting to changing resource availabilities and the power of the price system in securing this adaptation, mean that substantial reductions in energy use can be achieved without major economic cost. [50, p. 512.]

> One important conclusion of this study is that growth potential is more sensitive to changes in the propensity to consume than to increasing costs in the energy sector. [14, p. 579.]

These "optimistic" views are in striking contrast to the forecasts that:

> Inexorably accompanying energy-use reductions are costly effects on the economy, specifically unemployment, productivity, income distribution, and on GNP and its attendant growth. [5, p. B-1.]

Sharp reductions in real income growth per capita or in labor productivity or sharp increases in unemployment would all reduce electricity need. *Conversely, constrained energy supply will certainly force such reduction.* [91, p. 20.]

What accounts for these competing views is different perceptions about the extent to which there are available substitutes for energy. If there are few substitutes, then reductions in energy use will produce significant reductions in national output. If substitution possibilities are ample, then major reductions in energy usage can be accommodated without corresponding drops in national output.

Whether, over the long run, substitution is high or low depends to a significant extent on the relation between energy and technology. The econometric energy models tend to assume that the conditions under which energy is supplied will not seriously impede future technological developments. As a result, what may be the major factor in economic growth and development is assumed to be immune from the conditions of energy supply.[1]

What is at issue here is whether the changing conditions of energy supply have made historic productivity improvements an inadequate guide to the future. If so, then technological development cannot be treated as some function of time, for it can no longer be assumed that the historic pace of technological development is feasible. Rather, the effect of energy supply on technological development must be made explicit.

Close observers of the relationship between energy and the economy believe that, in the past, certain improvements in productivity would not have been feasible without suitable conditions of energy supply. For example, the replacement of wood by coal "changed the economic history of Britain, then of the rest of Europe and finally of the world. It led to the industrial revolution, to new methods of manufacture, to the expansion of existing industries and to the exploitation of untapped natural resources. . . . Coal was not only a source of energy but also a spur to technological development" [74, p. 140]. Similarly, for more recent times, "The impact of electrification in industrial processes is the clearest case in point. A significant but not well-recognized aspect of electrification was in its effect on the overall productive efficiency of the economy, particularly in the manufacturing sector" [85, p. 6].

---

1. In most of the econometric models, population, labor force and unemployment are exogenous. That part of productivity improvement linked to expansion of the capital stock is sometimes determined within the model structure. However, that part of productivity improvement affected by technological advance is exogenous in most models and usually based on extrapolations of postwar trends.

There seem to be two processes through which changed conditions of energy supply affect overall productivity in the economy. In the "energy crisis process"—typified by the shift from wood to coal—the important available fuel sources become insufficient either because of their depletion or because of a large increase in their demand. This creates incentives to eliminate the undesirable properties of alternative fuels so they can become an effective replacement. New technologies are developed for this purpose. For example, the reverberatory furnace was developed to eliminate the undesirable property of materials coming in contact with coal; and the steam engine was first successfully used to improve the drainage systems in British coal mines. These new technologies then bring about overall improvements in productivity by being adopted for use in other industries. "It was to no small extent [that] the needs of coal mining and coal transport . . . led to the steam engine and the railroad" [74, p. 150].

In the "energy opportunity process"—typified by the expansion of electric power—a new energy form, with properties not previously available in energy sources, appears on the scene. These properties of energy then provide the opportunity to develop new technologies, or ways of producing and living, that would not otherwise have been possible. For example,

> Electricity, which made possible the use of electric motors to which the power was delivered by wire, paved the way for a major reorganization of the sequence and lay-out of production more in keeping with the logic of the productive process than with the more rigid locational requirements imposed by a system of shafts and belting (e.g., locating heavy energy uses close to the prime mover). This was a factor of enormous importance in the growth of manufacturing productivity and thereby in the productivity of the total economy." [85, p. 6.]

If favorable conditions of energy supply has furthered rising productivity in the past, then it is equally possible that future productivity improvement may be retarded if energy conditions change. The question then becomes whether technological ingenuity will adapt enough to keep productivity improving under a new set of energy conditions. Unfortunately this question does not easily lend itself to either empirical confirmation or refutation.

The energy impact on technology is only one of the factors influencing the relationship of energy consumption to GNP. Other factors are also important. Some are found in the structure of the economy and their effect on energy consumption; others belong in the structure of the energy sector and their influence on national output.

Chapter 4 described how the structure of the economy affects energy consumption. The remainder of this chapter probes more deeply into how the structure of the energy sector affects the economy. The following characteristics of the energy sector are particularly important in their influence on the economy: changes in energy cost, energy supply, energy form, and efficiency in energy production and use. These elements are seen as influencing economic recovery, economic expansion, and economic development through their effects on such components of the economic structure as the supply of labor and capital; the degree of substitutability among energy, labor, and capital; economies of scale in industry; the composition of goods and services; new technology; the pace of productivity improvements; and industrial location.

The relationship among these various characteristics needs to be analyzed to judge whether energy consumption can be decoupled from economic growth, and to interpret trends in the ratio of energy consumption to national output. This ratio is called *energy intensity.* Energy intensity is a partial measure of productivity in that it relates total economic output to a single input. Following customary terminology, the label "productivity" applies to the relations between output and the other inputs: *labor productivity* being the ratio of labor to output, and *capital productivity* the ratio of capital to output. When all inputs are combined—each with appropriate weights—and related to total output, a measure of *total factor productivity* is found.

In addition to relating inputs to outputs, we are interested in showing the relationships among the inputs. Depth is the term that has been assigned to the relation of employment to other inputs. Thus *capital depth* is the label for the capital-stock/employment ratio, while *energy depth* is the label for the energy-consumption/employment ratio. Finally, *capital intensity* is the label used to describe the ratio of energy consumption to capital stock.

There are a number of variants for each of these key relationships, depending on the data sources used and the scope of the economy covered. The glossary, presented as Empirical Highlight 6-1, provides definitions for the more salient variants used in the following discussion.

ENERGY INTENSITY

Energy-intensity—the ratio of BTUs of energy consumed to the GNP produced—is a summary indicator of the role of energy in the

Empirical Highlight 6-1. A Glossary of Key Variables

ECONOMIC VARIABLES

GNP refers to the overall U.S. national output produced. Since it is measured in terms of the 1972 price level for each year, changes over time in the "real" or physical quantity of output are shown. The 1972 price level has been selected simply because this is a commonly used base in much of the recent literature on energy trends (see Appendix Table 1, Col. 1).

Producing Sectors of the economy are grouped into those sectors that produce goods and those that produce nongoods. Goods production includes manufacturing; agriculture, forestry, and fisheries; and mining plus construction. Nongoods production includes the transportation sector and services plus other nongoods. Services refer to the provision of business, professional, repair, and personal services. Other nongoods refer to other types of services provided, including wholesale and retail trade; finance, insurance, and real estate; communications and public utilities; and government activities. This classification of production sectors has been used for describing various employment, production, and energy-consumption trends.

National Income Produced (NIP) measures the earnings of the factors of production in the U.S. economy. (Capital consumption and indirect business taxes are the main items deducted from the GNP in order to obtain NIP.) NIP has been stated in 1958 price trends by arbitrarily using the GNP price deflator. NIP is shown for each of the producing sectors as well as for the aggregate (see Appendix Table 7) and for manufacturing only (Table 8).

Personal Consumption Expenditures refer to the purchases made by all persons and households in the United States. It includes durables, nondurables, and services (see Appendix Table 7).

Employment refers to the full-time equivalent employment in the nation. By adjusting the part-time employees to a full-time basis, a more consistent picture is obtained of trends in U.S. employment (see Appendix Table 1, Col. 3).

Persons Employed refers to the number of full- plus part-time employees in the United States. Persons employed by each of the producing sectors are shown (Appendix Table 7), as well as persons employed in manufacturing (Table 8, Col. 5).

Employment Propensity measures the ratio of full-time equivalent employment to population. It is, therefore, a type of labor participation measure (Appendix Table 1, Col. 10).

Empirical Highlight 6-1 (cont.)

Capital Stock measures the constant dollar value of fixed nonresidential business capital. This includes the equipment and structures of the business sector. The value of the stock is measured in 1972 prices; that is, all assets are valued at their 1972 prices. Therefore this series shows trends in the physical volume of the nation's capital stock (Appendix Table 1, Col. 4), and separately for manufacturing (Table 8) as measured in 1958 prices.

ENERGY VARIABLES

Gross Energy Consumption refers to the total quantity of energy consumed in the United States. It is usually stated in terms of quads of BTU consumed; a quad measures a quadrillion—10^{15} BTU (see Appendix Table 2, Col. 1). The gross energy consumed is separated into its separate sources—wood, coal, oil, gas, and hydro, plus nuclear power (Table 2, Cols. 4-8). Gross energy consumption includes not only the energy obtained from fossil and other fuel sources, but also the nonenergy uses of fossil fuels.

Net Energy Consumption refers to the gross energy consumption less the energy lost in the process of converting fuels to electric power. For some purposes net energy provides a better indicator of trends in the nation's energy consumption than does gross energy consumption (see Appendix Table 2, Col. 2). Since it excludes conversion losses, net energy consumption equals the sum of energy consumed by the residential, commercial, industrial, and transportation sectors.

Energy Consumption by Sector disaggregates U.S. gross energy consumption into the consumption by each of the "final users." Following the standard classification, end users are separated into the household plus commercial sector, the industrial sector, the transportation sector, the electric utility sector, and a miscellaneous sector (see Appendix Table 4, Col. 5). Since electric utilities are an intermediary—that is, they sell to the other final users—data are also shown that have allocated electric power sales and the conversion loss to each of the final-user sectors. The text will make clear whether final-user consumption with or without the electric power allocated is being used. Each sector's consumption of each fuel source is shown in Table 4; gross energy consumed in manufacturing is shown in Table 8, Col. 2.

PRODUCTIVITY VARIABLES

Labor Productivity for the economy as a whole is measured by the ratio of GNP to full-time equivalent employment (Appendix Table 1, Col. 8). Labor productivity for the specific producing sectors is measured by the ratio of income produced per person employed in each of the sectors (Table 7).

Empirical Highlight 6-1 (cont.)

Capital Productivity is a measure analogous to labor productivity in that it is described by the ratio of GNP to the value of capital stock (Table 1, Col. 11).

Total Factor Productivity refers to overall efficiency in the economy. Both labor and capital productivity are "partial" measures of productivity, in that they refer to a single input as if that input were solely responsible for production and productive efficiency. In order to describe trends in the overall productive efficiency of the economy, it would be necessary to relate the nation's output to an appropriately weighted composition of labor, capital, and natural resources— including energy. Data for total factor productivity have not been shown in this book, although the relation of energy to total factor productivity is discussed in a number of places.

DEPTH VARIABLES

Capital Depth refers to the relationship between the nation's capital stock and its employment. Ordinarily it is expected that, within limits, as workers are provided with more tools (that is, as capital deepening occurs), productivity will be improved. Capital depth is measured by the ratio of capital stock to full-time equivalent employment (see Appendix Table 1, Col. 9).

Energy Depth is a measure analogous to the capital depth in that it measures the relationship between the nation's energy consumption and its employment. One of the key questions to be discussed is whether improvements in productivity are dependent on maintenance of or increases in the energy-depth ratio. It is often important to distinguish among the various kinds of energy depth. The *gross energy depth* is measured by the ratio of gross energy consumption to full-time equivalent employment (see Appendix Table 3, Col. 4). The *industrial energy depth* is measured by the ratio of energy consumed by the industrial sector to full-time equivalent employment (Table 8, Col. 13). The *industrial energy depth for manufacturing* is measured by the ratio of energy consumed by the industrial sector to persons employed in manufacturing (Table 8, Col. 15). The *manufacturing energy depth* is measured by the ratio of energy consumed in manufacturing to persons employed in manufacturing (Table 8, Col. 16). The *nonmanufacturing energy depth* is measured by the ratio of energy consumed outside of manufacturing to persons employed outside of manufacturing.

INTENSITY VARIABLES

Capital Intensity shows the relation between energy consumption and capital stock. *Gross capital intensity* is measured by the ratio of capital stock to gross energy consumption (see Appendix Table 3, Col. 6). However, since considerable

Empirical Highlight 6-1 (cont.)

energy is consumed directly and not through the use of equipment, we also have included some variant capital intensity measures. *Industrial capital intensity* is defined as the ratio of total capital stock to the energy consumed by the industrial sector (Table 8, Col. 19). *Manufacturing capital intensity* is defined as the ratio of total capital stock to the energy consumed in manufacturing (Table 8, Col. 20).

Energy Intensity is a measure of the relationship between the nation's energy consumption and its production of goods and services. It is useful to distinguish the several variants of this measure. *Gross energy intensity* is defined as the ratio of gross energy consumption to GNP (see Appendix Table 3, Col. 2). *Net energy intensity* is defined as the ratio of net energy consumption to GNP (Table 3, Col. 7). *Industrial energy intensity* is defined as the ratio of energy consumption in the industrial sector to the total national income produced (Table 8, Col. 10). *Manufacturing energy intensity* is defined as the ratio of energy consumption in manufacturing to the national income produced by manufacturing (Table 8, Col. 12). *Nonmanufacturing energy intensity* is defined as the ratio of energy consumed outside of manufacturing to national income produced by the nonmanufacturing sectors. *End user energy intensity* is defined as the ratio of energy consumed by each end-use sector—residential plus commercial, transportation and industrial—to a measure of overall activity by that sector. Changes in gross energy intensity are brought about by changes in these end-user intensities and changes in the mix of products consumed (Table 10).

economy. It is not a measure of energy efficiency, which involves consideration of the thermodynamic characteristics of energy use; it does not measure energy productivity, which involves consideration of other inputs to production as well as energy; nor does it measure energy demand, which involves consideration of the prices at which energy is sold. However, energy intensity is influenced by each of these, just as it, in turn, has an effect on these other indicators.

Energy intensity has both the advantages and disadvantages of any summary indicator. It suppresses all the details and complexities which are of significance in understanding the relationship between energy and the economy. But, it also provides an intuitively meaningful measure which, when appropriately monitored, can be a signal of emerging distress or opportunity in the ways that the nation is handling its energy affairs.

Energy intensity does not stay constant as economic circumstances change. One way to interpret a change in energy intensity is to see it as resulting from differential trends in GNP and energy consumption. From this perspective the forces affecting production of output and use of energy can be identified or modeled and their impact quantified to forecast GNP and energy consumption. The ratio of these two forecasts—the energy intensity—is then used as a summary descriptor of the expected consequences of changing economic circumstances.

Energy intensity can also be interpreted as playing a more active role in economic affairs. In this view if the future change in energy intensity could be identified, then the alternative levels of energy consumption associated with different growth paths of GNP could be predicted. Similarly, varying prospects for energy intensity would change projections of energy consumption even without altering the growth in GNP. By using energy intensity in this fashion, it becomes possible to identify not only the change in energy consumption likely to occur but also how much is attributed to expansion or decline in the level of national economic activity and how much to changes in the relationship between energy and the economy.

Until recently this simple procedure was the basis for most forecasts of national energy needs. However, such forecast methodologies have fallen into disrepute because they were ordinarily based on naive extrapolations of energy intensity rather than on explicit accounts of forces affecting the intensity. Most of these extrapolations tended to disregard the potential effect changing energy prices might have on energy use and to ignore the feedback impact of changing energy usage on technology and productivity advance.

Presently available econometric and simulation models have improved on the naive procedures through bypassing energy intensity and explicitly accounting for the impacts of price changes and substitution possibilities between energy and other factors. However, they have not yet been able to effectively incorporate the energy feedback on productivity. The sophisticated models are superior to their naive predecessors in many ways: they are theoretically sound, they produce more reliable quantitative results, and they permit analyses of the impacts of alternative energy or economic policies.

However, unlike energy-intensity trends, the models are difficult to comprehend. Too often, what gets lost in the detail of the models is a grasp of the relations between energy and the economy. To provide a basis for such understanding several hypothetical scenarios shall be described which outline the interplay among forces having differential effects on GNP growth and energy consumption.

The future holds prospects for both increases and declines in energy intensity. These prospects shall be considered in terms of four major concepts.

- *Substitution* refers to the potential for substituting one input for another in the production process. This can include a substitution of energy for labor or capital and a replacement of energy by labor or capital.
- *Product mix* refers to the energy content of consumer purchases. This can include a shift in favor of energy-intensive goods and services or away from the energy-intensive purchases.
- *Technology* refers to changes in the production process which would raise the economy's total productivity. Energy-intensive technologies refer to changes that shift the production inputs in favor of energy usage while nonenergy-intensive technologies do the reverse.
- *Constraints* refer to the factors making it more difficult to utilize energy, including increases in the relative price of energy and decreases in the accessibility to energy.

A relative absence of constraints characterized the historical experience of the United States until recent years, while a fear of significant constraints underlies concern about the economic future. It is desirable to consider the forces affecting energy intensity in terms of alternative scenarios reflecting the absence of constraints (the historical experience) and the emergence of constraints (the probable future).

The Historical Scenarios (see Figure 6-1)
The Naive Model: Growth in national output will tend to directly increase energy consumption because of the energy embodied in goods and services production as well as the increased energy directly used by final consumers as their incomes rise. In the naive model it is not only assumed that there are no energy constraints but also that the causes of economic growth are not specified and potential indirect consequences of output growth are not considered. Since economic growth causes are not explicitly stated there is no way of knowing whether they would directly affect energy consumption in a manner different from their effect on output. Since growth consequences are not considered, there is no way of knowing whether they could have a further indirect impact on energy consumption which runs counter to the increased energy demands imposed directly by output growth. In the absence of constraints, causes, and consequences, it is appropriate to expect output and energy consumption to grow roughly proportionately. In this case the energy intensity remains constant.

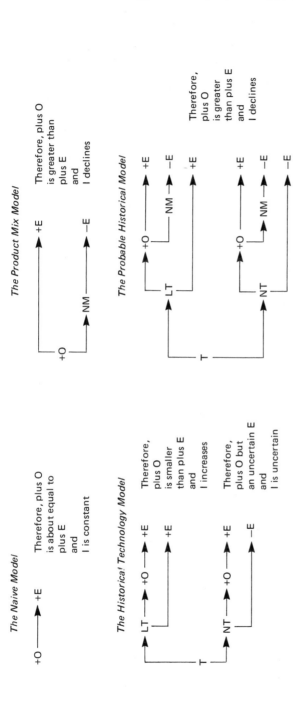

Figure 6-1. Energy Intensity: The Historical Scenarios

O = output growth; E = energy consumption growth; LT = energy intensive technology; NT = nonenergy intensive technology; T = technology; I = energy intensity; NM = nonenergy intensive product mix; T = technology

The Product Mix Model: One of the side effects of economic growth is to change the composition of consumer purchases. There is some indication that the trend has been in favor of a nonenergy intensive product mix. The result is that the growth in energy consumption as depicted in the naive model is dampened because of the product-mix effect. The consequence would be a decline in energy intensity.

The Historical Technology Model: A substantial part of economic growth is attributable to advances in knowledge, skills, and technology which raise economic productivity. If the new technologies are energy intensive they will not only increase output but also increase the energy used to produce each unit of output. Since, as we have seen in the naive model, output growth directly generates an energy consumption increase, the positive effects on energy are reinforced. Therefore, energy consumption is likely to grow faster than output and intensity increases.

But suppose the technology is nonenergy intensive. The new technology will still induce output to grow, which will lead to an increase in energy consumption. But the nonenergy-intensive aspects of technology will cause energy per unit of output to decline and either partly offset or reverse the increase induced by output growth. Therefore, although the increase in output is certain, the increase in energy consumption is not. As a result energy intensity could either increase or decline. Any increase that occurs would be less than the increase in the energy-intensive technology model.

The Probable Historical Model: Most interpretations of the past seek to account for a growth in output, a shift toward a nonintensive-energy product mix, and new technologies that are both energy intensive and nonenergy intensive. Both the energy-intensive and nonintensive technologies cause output to grow, which leads to an energy consumption increase, offset by a trend away from an energy intensive product mix. However, the nonenergy-intensive technology has the further effect of lowering the energy needs in production. As a result, the growth in output would be at a faster pace than in energy consumption so that intensity declines.

The Constrained Scenarios (see Figure 6-2)

There are two different effects resulting from energy constraints. The simulation effect would raise or lower energy intensity from the level it might otherwise reach in the absence of constraints; the forecast effect is the constraint's contribution to decreasing or

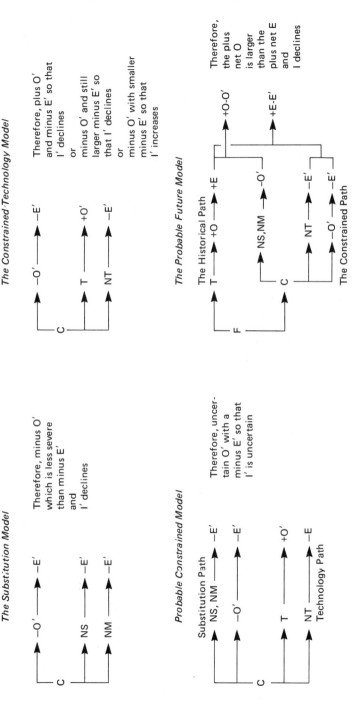

Figure 6-2. Energy Intensity: The Constrained Scenarios

increasing energy intensity over time. For example, although the simulation effect could be to lower energy intensity from the level it might otherwise reach, an increase in energy intensity over time could still occur. The first three of the following scenarios consider only the simulation effect, the fourth considers both the simulation and forecast effects.

The Substitution Model: Energy constraints imply a simulated loss in real output, which would cause a decline in energy consumption. In addition, the constraint would induce a substitution of other inputs for energy as well as speed up the shift away from an energy-intensive product mix. The result would be a decline in simulated output with a still larger decrease in energy consumption so that there is a simulated intensity decline.

The Constrained Technology Model: As in the substitution model, the energy constraint induces a simulated real output decline followed by an energy decline. However, new technology responds to the constraint, causing productivity, output, and energy use to increase. If the new technology is nonenergy intensive, there would be an offsetting energy use decline because of the reduction in the energy needed per unit of output. Several possibilities emerge from this set of events. Simulated output could increase while energy consumption declines, providing a reduced simulated intensity. Or simulated output could decline while energy declines even more, again resulting in an intensity decline. It is also possible for output to decline while energy falls at a lesser rate. The result in that case would be a simulated intensity increase.

The Probable Constraint Model: The most probable simulated consequences would occur from a combination of the substitution and technology effects. The constraint would cause output to decline, while the product mix and the faster input mix shift away from energy. All of these would lead to an energy consumption decline. However, new technology would cause output to increase while nonenergy-intensive technology induces an energy decline. The probable result of these offsetting forces would be to reduce simulated energy consumption, but whether output would be raised or lowered is uncertain. The direction of simulated intensity, therefore, cannot be predicted.

The Probable Future Model: Taken together, the probable constrained model and the probable historical model suggest the directions for the future. The future holds prospects for both energy constraints and the development of new technology. The new technology would be expected to lead to a forecast growth in output and in energy consumption, as it has in the past. The energy constraints—working through output reductions as well as less energy-intensive product mix shifts, substitutions, and new technologies—would have the effect of lowering simulated output and energy consumption. This simulated reduction, however, is not likely to reverse the forecast increases in output and energy, but merely dampen them. As a result, we would expect a net increase in output which is greater than the net increase in energy consumption. Intensity would decline.

It is important to note that not only can energy intensity increase or decline in the future but that it can do so with a rising or falling level of economic output and energy consumption. A declining energy intensity may be associated with supporting economic growth (the probable historical model), or slowing it down (the probable future model), or preventing it (the substitution model). An increasing energy intensity may be linked with adding to economic growth (the historical technology model) or preventing it (the constrained technology model).

ENERGY IMPACT ON
ECONOMIC RECOVERY

Primarily because of oil import price increases in the early seventies, the most visible impact of rising energy costs has been on economic recovery. The large hike in oil-import prices within a limited time period produced a loss in real income for consumers of energy in the United States. This loss (reinforced, perhaps, by expected fuel-supply disruptions) meant that demand for other goods and services was reduced, creating multiplier effects that lowered GNP still more. Income, meanwhile, leaked out to oil-producing countries without returning to the United States through the usual channels of trade and finance. The higher energy costs and resulting negative balance of payments were inflationary. Conceivably, tight monetary and fiscal policies introduced to combat the inflation, as well as international financial disorder, contributed to still further reductions of economic activity, which reached a recessionary order of magnitude.

A comparable sequence of events could be initiated domestically, if production costs were to rise and result in added energy-related revenues shifting to consumers or industries with high propensities to save. However, although some redistribution of income would result, the depressing effects on economic activity would probably not be so severe, since the leakages to savings would most likely not be as large as the import leakages.

Dramatic as they appear, such results of economic recovery are probably not the most important, for the demand effects of a one-shot energy cost increase eventually dissipate. And although the loss of real output is gone forever, this does not mean that the growth rate of output is permanently lowered. Thus the realized output loss becomes proportionately insignificant as time goes on, and the level of overall economic activity rises because of other growth forces. Of course, continuous injections of energy price increases would cause continued demand-related output losses. However, adjustments to such price policy would probably occur, and these would reduce the shock effects and lower the multiplier consequences that have been the major source of demand-induced loss in economic recovery.

The worldwide impact of increased energy costs is also expected to significantly affect the recovery of U.S. output growth. In this view the increased dependence of the United States on oil imports has substantially contributed to the ability of the oil producers to raise prices and to maintain the increases. The effects of these increases are to lower productivity in both developed and less-developed countries, resulting in reductions of multicountry trade that cuts down productivity still further.

The non-oil-producing, less-developed countries are particularly affected because they incur a massive debt in order to pay for their higher energy bills. Debt diminishes their ability to make investments that will improve productivity and expand capacity, which in turn slows down their industrialization process and further reduces international trade and productivity. In addition the developed countries may be compelled to expand their financial aid to the less-developed countries and may even be motivated to increase their defense expenditures as a hedge against oil diplomacy. This spending would then make less funds available for internal business investment in developed countries.

The massive debts and accumulated funds likely to result from the above process make the international financial situation uncertain, which could further require restrictive fiscal and monetary policies in the developed countries as they seek to protect themselves from worldwide economic events.

The web of potential economic and political interactions on an international scale is too complex to permit even a hint as to what the final impact on U.S. output will be. It is worth noting, however, that the major international concerns are specifically related to oil rather than to energy costs in general. A reduced oil dependency in the United States, therefore, may have particularly beneficial international responses.

ENERGY IMPACT ON ECONOMIC EXPANSION

The depressing effect that rising energy costs have on economic expansion may be more serious than their impact on economic recovery, because the former would be more durable. Whether caused by increases in oil import prices or the real costs of domestic energy producers, the consequences may be such that "the economic growth *rate* that is achievable by the industrial world has been *permanently* lowered" [12, p. 44 (emphasis added)]. But critics of this view argue that it does not allow for the economy's ability to adjust to new situations over the long run. Gradual reductions of energy consumption over the long run, when the economy has time to adjust, have very different consequences from sudden and sharp reductions compelled by some unexpected event.

Also over the long run, the impact of unfavorable conditions of energy supply on economic growth is moderated because a large share of energy consumption is a result rather than a cause of growth. For example, consumer expenditures on energy and energy-using equipment are largely "proceeds" from growth, since they contribute little directly to the productive process. Therefore, the energy used as a "springboard" for growth is consumed mostly by the business sector [85, p. 11]. And even for that portion of energy consumption that acts as a springboard for growth, the consequences of unfavorable energy-supply conditions may be diminished by technical advances and input substitutions.

A production-function framework can be adopted to measure the effects of energy supply and price on economic output. When energy is included along with labor and capital as inputs in a production function, it accounts for less than an estimated 1 percent of the growth in national output over the 1948-1971 interval [3, p. 133]. Using this kind of estimate to simulate the future, a tripling of energy prices would lower GNP and labor productivity by less than 1 percent in the year 2000 [3, p. 151]. Such estimates measure, however, the energy consumption impact on economic growth as if it were independent of other growth sources. The feedback of energy consumption on the quantity and productivity of labor and capital is critical as to whether there will be a permanent effect on the rate of economic growth resulting from unfavorable conditions of energy supply.

The story of the role of energy in economic expansion goes something like this. Output growth depends on energy, labor, capital, and technology inputs. The supply of labor and technology, however, is independent of the other inputs. Therefore, although they affect output growth they are not affected by changes in the energy sector. Energy changes not only affect output directly but also indirectly through their impact on the demand for labor as well as on the demand and supply of capital.

If energy affected only output then a reduction in the availability or use of energy would proportionately lower the output. However, in actuality labor can, to some degree, be substituted for energy. Therefore, added demand for labor would replace some of the energy reduction so that a portion of the lost output is restored. The end result from this would still be reduced output but less than proportionate to the energy reduction.

At the same time, the reduced energy availability will affect the demand for capital. Although the evidence is not yet all in, most observers believe that capital and energy are complements rather than substitutes for each other.[2] That is, reduced energy availability will be accompanied by a reduced demand for the capital input which needs energy to function. The impact of reducing the capital input would be to lower output. Thus, the result of including the capital input effect is to remove some of the output restored by the labor substitution effect.

Putting these various forces together, the effect of reduced energy usage, resulting perhaps from an energy price increase, would be to lower output by proportionately less than the reduction in energy but proportionately more than the substitute labor employed. Energy use would decline more than output and energy intensity would fall; there is little disagreement about this end result. The disagreement occurs over the quantitative assumptions about substitution and complementarity—that is, how much of a decline is likely to occur.

In order to examine these issues a little more closely, it will be useful to inquire into the validity of the assumptions that the energy sector does not affect the labor supply, while it does affect labor demand and the capital supply and demand.

---

2. The concepts of complementarity and substitutability can be the subject of highly arcane discourse. They are used here in the intuitively meaningful sense proposed by Hogan [33, PC-2]. Capital complementarity means that higher energy prices or reduced energy use will decrease the demand for capital. Labor substitutability means that higher energy prices or reduced energy use will increase the demand for labor.

Energy Effects on Labor Supply

Rising energy costs can conceivably affect the labor supply through their impact on population growth and on the labor participation rate. For example, rising energy costs may lower living standards and thereby slow population expansion. It is not likely that this would be significant in the United States. Perhaps more important in this country are the concerns about environmental destruction through energy conversion, which probably have already contributed to smaller families. Even if these concerns are somewhat mitigated in the future, the already diminished population guarantees to constrain growth of the labor force for many years to come.

The share of the population in the work force has increased over the past century. For example, currently one-third of the population is employed (as measured by full-time equivalent employment), compared with one-fourth of the population a hundred years ago. Most of this increase occurred before World War II. Since the war this ratio has fluctuated between 30 and 35 percent, partly in response to cyclical business conditions but also with an upward drift during the last decade.

We would anticipate that increases in life expectancy and in the amount of schooling considered necessary would reduce the ratio of employment to population. But these factors have been largely counterbalanced by increased participation of women in the labor force, which to some extent was probably facilitated by lower costs of energy and increased energy usage in the home.

As the conditions of energy supply become unfavorable, some effects on labor participation can be expected. For example, energy-induced changes in the product mix of consumption are likely to make some skills obsolete, which could result in early retirements, higher unemployment, and increased worker training—all of which would mean a reduction in the effective work force, although not necessarily a permanent one. On balance, however, it appears unlikely that rising energy costs in the future would cause a reversal or material slowdown of labor participation trends, which most demographic projections show as rising slightly in the future.

Energy Effects on Labor Demand

The empirical studies indicate that labor is a substitute for energy (as well as for capital), although the extent of substitutability probably varies among different producing sectors in the economy. A sense of what has been happening in the past can be obtained by tracking the energy depth, that is, the quantitative relation between energy consumption and labor.

Substitutability would suggest that during a period of decline in real energy prices (characteristic of the past century) energy depth would rise. This has been essentially the case over the past one hundred years. However, changes in energy depth may also have something to do with changes in labor productivity. For example, if increasing energy depth contributes to rising labor productivity, then decreased use of energy will lower output.

Changes in labor productivity and energy depth were compared for different intervals in the past century. No clear-cut relation between the two could be established. But, perhaps this is no surprise since a possible reason for the long-term increase in energy depth since 1920 is the increase in indirect consumption of energy by households. The direct use of energy by households is not particularly related to employment. It is the indirect energy consumption by households, that is, the energy embodied in goods and services, that is related to employment because it is associated with the producing sectors of the economy. Therefore, to the extent that the increase in energy depth is caused by an increase in household energy end use, we would expect total energy consumption to increase faster than total employment.

It, therefore, may be appropriate to examine not only what has happened to energy depth in the total economy but also to industrial energy depth—the ratio of industrial sector energy consumption to industrial employment. The substitution of energy for labor during the years of real energy price decline has been particularly important in the industrial sector where increasing quantities of capital could effectively use increasing quantities of energy. Since the 1920s the industrial work force has increased at a much slower pace than the total number of persons employed. Also there has been a slower increase in industrial energy consumption than in total energy consumption. The result of these changes has been that industrial energy depth has persistently increased and at a faster rate than the gross energy depth. The relation between changes in industrial energy depth and industrial productivity has been reasonably close in the past, suggesting that a future slowdown in the industrial energy depth might cause a future slowdown in productivity improvement.

From an economic standpoint it has made sense for the industrial sector to "buy" improved labor productivity at the expense of increased energy depth. In most manufacturing industries the labor bill is probably twenty times the size of the energy bill; and until recently the cost of man-hour of labor has been increasing while the cost of a BTU has been falling. Because of this the importance of energy in the economy has been underestimated. "Concentration on productivity as a function of man-hours, has completely overshadowed the contribution of energy simply because direct energy use has been such a very small part of the cost of doing business" [25, p. D-2].

Whether we conclude that because of substitution, unfavorable conditions of energy supply will significantly expand the demand for labor depends on which energy-consuming sectors we believe will be most affected. If the cut in energy consumption occurs through the reduction in direct energy use by households, there may not be a significant increase in labor demand. If the cut affects industrial energy consumption, a rise in labor demand will serve as a partial offset. Indeed, the rise may be cumulative as energy costs spiral, since consumers may be encouraged to spend their money on labor intensive, rather than energy intensive, products and industry may develop more labor-intensive technologies.

However, raising demands for labor by expanding labor intensive production processes may not bode well for long-run growth in output. It is true that given the need to reduce energy use, a substitution of labor for energy would permit output to grow faster than if the substitution did not take place. However, this output growth would still probably be slower than actual growth in the past. Diminished levels of productivity and output could reduce opportunities for business expansion which, over the long run, would lower labor demand. Under these assumptions, the worst combination of events would result from unfavorable conditions of energy supply— not only lower productivity but less employment as well.

Energy Effects on Supply of Capital
Rising energy costs and increased investment needs by the energy sector may permanently slow down growth of the nation's plant and equipment in other sectors. This possibility is of great concern because continued productivity improvement is assumed to be tied to plant and equipment growth.

Business investment is now about a tenth of GNP, a share that it has fluctuated around since 1950. Even if this share does not fall in the future, the loss in real output, resulting from rising energy costs, would mean that growth in the stock of plant and equipment would decline and the pace of modernization would slow down. Furthermore, many believe that a 10 percent investment share of GNP is too low to support a rapid advance in productivity for reasons mainly unrelated to the costs of energy. However, it is feared that the rising costs of energy could dampen the nation's overall investment enough both to prevent a long-awaited modernization program and to convert a threatening situation into a crisis.

In addition to the overall decline in available investment funds, growing energy demands for investment are likely to result in an important diversion of capital funds. More and more funds will need to be spent on exploration, research and development, and capacity increase in the energy sector itself, which could mean less investment in other business sectors, lowering their opportunities for productivity improvement and output growth. Such diversion could also stimulate inflation, constrain residential investment, and reduce government expenditures.

The energy industry, particularly its petroleum and electric utility components, is highly capital-intensive. Currently (and prior to 1960) the energy sector accounted for a third of business investment and probably an even higher portion of the nation's investment that is financed with borrowed funds. Energy's current third of business investment has grown from the postwar low of a quarter share in 1965.

According to the Federal Energy Administration, energy investment over the coming decade will be about $600 billion, which, on an annual basis, is almost double the current levels, although about the same share of business investment [101, p. xxxiv]. Electric utility investment alone might account for half this total, with oil and gas supplying most of the remainder. Capital costs are now about half the price of electric power, and contribute twice as much as fuel costs contribute to the price of power. These shares are likely to increase, and, because of the way utility rates are set, increasing investment will inevitably produce rising electric power prices.

Thus the need for investment funds may impose serious constraints on the energy sector itself, and beyond that may threaten to disrupt the rest of the economy. Other industries will not readily consent to a large part of the nation's productive resources shifting to the expansion of energy facilities.

Energy Effects on Demand for Capital

Available investment funds and their diversion to energy facilities account for only one limit to the expansion of capital stock. Another constraint relates to the benefits anticipated from investment, which accrue due to the increase in overall economic activity typically associated with growth in energy consumption and capital stock. One argument is that energy consumption and capital stock complement one another—as the stock of energy-using business plant and equipment grows, not only does quantity of energy consumption rise, but also labor productivity ultimately expands, resulting in increases of overall output. Therefore, if the conditions of energy supply become more unfavorable, the growth in capital stock will slow down, followed by a slowdown of growth in output. Another argument is that capital stock and energy are substitutes. Therefore, unfavorable conditions in energy supply will induce growth in the capital stock, leading to improvements in labor productivity, which will prevent a slowdown in expansion of economic output.

If energy and capital were perfect complements (that is, changed at the same rate), then the capital intensity—the ratio of capital to energy—would be constant. But the data show that neither industrial nor total capital intensity remain constant over time; rather, they fluctuate widely, declining as often as they increase. The diversity occurs partly because of changes in product mix and in the efficiency with which capital stock uses energy.

The diversity of the historic trends, as described in Empirical Highlight 6-2, indicates that there are different relationships among

Empirical Highlight 6-2. Trends in Relationships among Capital, Labor, and Energy

- Trends before the Great Depression were very different from those after World War II. Since the war, labor productivity has increased at almost twice the pre-Depression pace. Yet both gross energy and gross capital depth rose at about the same pace during the two periods.

- The fact that capital productivity did not decline after World War II (although it did during the Depression) is apparently related to the accelerated pace of labor productivity after the war. The decline in energy intensity after the war was very rapid compared to pre-Depression near-stability.

- Trends during the Depression and war years were totally different from those before and after. Increases in labor productivity were comparatively slow, while increases in capital productivity were very rapid.

- As a result of declines in the stock of plant and equipment, both capital depth and capital intensity declined from the pre-Depression to postwar period. Consequently, energy depth began and ended the period at the same level, while energy intensity showed a substantial decline.

- Dissimilarity in trends can also be observed during subperiods within the major intervals. For example, postwar improvements in labor productivity have substantially slowed down since the mid sixties, accompanied by a decline in capital productivity and substantial slowdowns in the growth of capital depth and gross capital intensity. These slowdowns occurred in spite of a pickup in the rate of increase of the capital stock and energy consumption. As a result, from the mid-sixties to the time of the oil embargo, gross energy depth increased very rapidly and energy intensity reversed its historic decline.

capital stock, labor, and energy consumption in various time periods, and that the relationships within manufacturing are not the same as in the economy as a whole. Some studies indicate that in the economy as a whole both capital and energy have been substitutes for labor [15], and that energy and capital are substitutes for each other [50]. Within manufacturing the opposite seems to have occurred, with energy and capital enjoying a substantial complementarity to one another [10; 50]. This may, however, be changing. In recent years the manufacturing sector has been able to substitute capital for energy, because "in many manufacturing processes it is possible to recover waste heat, or to reuse wastes to produce energy. . . . Such operations often require capital investment, which is, in fact a substitution of capital for energy" [63, pp. 2, 9].[2]

Perhaps the best conclusion to draw from the data is that capital and energy have been mostly complementary inputs, particularly in the manufacturing sector. However, the degree of complementarity has varied from one period to the next, and it is even likely that capital and energy have been substitutes in some periods.

The ease or difficulty the economy has in substituting capital or labor for the energy input—that is, the elasticity of substitution—is a matter of more than academic importance.[3] If capital or labor is easily substitutable for energy (that is, the elasticity of substitution is numerically high), unfavorable conditions of energy supply may produce adjustments that do not seriously lower national output or increase unemployment. If the elasticity of substitution is numeri-

---

2. Hogan [33, PC-2] calls such substitutions "engineering substitution." This reflects a situation where if the level of output can be maintained while holding all other factor inputs constant, then capital and energy must be substitutes. Hogan says that engineering substitution is a different concept than aggregate substitutability and that its existence is not incompatible with aggregate complementarity.

3. If feedback to the economy or other inputs are ignored, the elasticity of substitution is numerically equal to the price elasticity of demand (that is, the percentage change in energy demand relative to the percentage change in energy prices, as discussed in Chapter 4). Technically the elasticity of substitution is measured as the "relationship between the ratio of two inputs and the ratio of their marginal productivities" [48, p. 14]. A zero elasticity of substitution means that total output cannot increase unless the inputs increase in fixed proportions. This means that energy intensity (the energy-to-GNP ratio) remains constant when the elasticity of substitution is zero. An infinite elasticity of substitution means that inputs are totally substitutable for one another, so that output can be increased indefinitely without any particular input, such as energy, having to increase at all. The elasticity of substitution theoretically may take any value between these extremes. A benchmark value often used for illustrative purposes is unitary elasticity. When the elasticity of substitution between energy and other inputs is 1, this would imply that (under optimal conditions) as the price of energy goes up, the dollar value share of energy in the GNP remains constant.

cally low, then adverse conditions of energy supply will not be adequately compensated by the use of labor and capital, resulting in reduced output and increased unemployment.

Many complex interactions among capital, labor, and energy lie behind a measure of the elasticity of substitution. These interactions are not made explicit by the elasticity of substitution, which might be best interpreted as a convenient summary of the results of these interactions.

Analyses of the elasticity of substitution for energy indicate that, given our present economic structure, there is a fairly broad range within which the elasticity could fall, and that small differences in the magnitude of the elasticity could lead to very large differences in the impact of energy-consumption changes on the economy. For example, the Energy Modeling Forum has compared the studies that have directly estimated the elasticities of substitution for primary fuels. They conclude that "the elasticity of substitution is between 0.2 and 0.6, although there is evidence for higher and lower values" [33, p. 13]. This range is narrowed somewhat—from 0.3 to 0.5— when the elasticities are calculated indirectly from detailed econometric energy models.

The Energy Modeling Forum made further simulations to evaluate the consequences of elasticity differences. Stated in even rough orders of magnitude, their conclusions are eye-opening. If, between now and the year 2010, conservation measures were introduced that lowered energy consumption by 50 percent but kept other inputs constant, then the GNP would be reduced by 30 percent if the elasticity were as low as 0.1; by 4 percent if the elasticity were 0.3; and by 1 percent if the elasticity were as high as 0.7 [33, p. 11]. It appears that if the "true" elasticity is above 0.5, the impact of an energy reduction on GNP will be relatively small and the differential impact on GNP for all elasticity values above 0.5 would be relatively narrow. But the "true" value seems to be below 0.5, where the impact on GNP may be large and the differential impact for small changes in elasticity can be substantial.

It would seem that, as based on current and historic data, the elasticity of substitution falls in a grey area that includes the possibility of an elasticity of substitution so low that adverse conditions of energy supply will significantly lower national output; but it also includes the possibility that the elasticity of substitution is so high that the economy can be expected to adjust to adverse energy supply conditions with only a smallsimpact on the national output.

There is no particular reason, furthermore, to expect that the degree of substitutability that existed in some arbitrarily set historical interval needs to be reproduced in the future. Substitutability depends on technology as well as on relative prices. In the past there was no great incentive to develop production processes that would permit substituting other inputs for energy. It may well be that as the conditions of energy supply become unfavorable, new processes will be developed that will enhance the possibilities of making substitutions for energy.

ENERGY IMPACT ON
ECONOMIC DEVELOPMENT

The discussion of channels for economic growth indicated that economic development involves structural changes in the economy requiring fundamental economic resource shifts that raise productivity. These resource shifts involve those among producing sectors and among types of innovators. If unfavorable conditions of energy supply affect economic development, they do so by slowing down such resource shifts.

The story about energy's role in economic development is as follows. Economic development is not simply expansion in economic capacity but involves fundamental transformations in the economic structure, such as changes in the methods of production, patterns of trade, working conditions, and methods of allocating economic resources. Accompanying and facilitating economic development are resource shifts among producing sectors and regions. These shifts stimulate structural transformations and productivity advances through their influence on economies of scale, product mix, and innovation. Since the conditions under which energy is supplied will influence resource mobility, the energy sector potentially has a significant impact on economic development.

But even more important, economic development involves changes in the organization of production. Economic development becomes part of a larger process of changes in the way people live and work. Historically, a factor in these changes has been the means humans have used to seek control over the environment. Among these has been the use of energy. As energy use has shifted from one type to another, its consequences for economic development have been profound.

Resource Shifts Among Producing Sectors

The analysis of economic expansion described the economy's structure primarily in terms of the factors of production. In turning

to economic development the economy's structure is better described in terms of the relationships among its producing sectors. The
dynamics of economic development involve adjustments in these
relationships since the various producing sectors are changing in
different ways. Resource mobility—including not only the actual
shift of existing resources but also the implicit shift occurring
because new resources are allocated differently than the existing
ones—is the essence of development. Each sector's change in output
is seen as resulting from changes in that sector's ability to attract
economic resources.

Resource shifts can add to a sector's output by responding to or
creating productivity improvements in that sector. In their responsive
mode, economic resources move toward the high-productivity sectors, which provide the highest earnings. This resource shift then
supports rapid output growth in the receiving sectors. The shifts are
continually changing, since productivity is largely determined by
external forces and changes at differential rates for each sector. In
their creative mode, resources move away from sectors where they
are redundant and toward sectors where they are needed. The
increased application of resources in the receiving sectors then leads
to economies of scale, which improve productivity and are the source
of overall growth in national output per capita. In the former case
resource shifts are responsive to improved productivity because they
transfer from low- to high-productivity sectors; in the latter case the
resource shifts themselves create productivity improvements through
economies of scale.

In the responsive mode, just as in the economic expansion models,
technology is assumed to be independent of economic forces so that
a sector's productivity is also exogenously determined. The resource
shift does not add to a sector's productivity, only to aggregate
productivity because of a shift in input weights favoring the high
productivity sectors. In the creative mode the story is very different.
The resource shifts are the cause of a sector's productivity improvements because economies of scale can be exploited as the sector
obtains an increased quantity of resources. It is the productivity
improvement and not a weight shift that causes output to grow. The
growth process is one of internally generating an increased efficiency
rather than adopting an externally imposed technological progress.

The question now raised is whether either the responsive or the
creative resource shifts which add to output are likely to be slowed
down because of reduced use of energy. If this does happen then
future growth in output would slow down to accompany the lower
rate of energy utilization. Energy intensity would be more likely to

remain stable than to fall significantly under these conditions of reduced economic circumstances. On the other hand, if unfavorable conditions of energy supply do not inhibit resource mobility, then productivity will not be affected and output will grow. The energy intensity would fall under these conditions of improved economic circumstances. This question will be investigated by first examining whether the facts of long-term sectoral economic development in the United States better fit the responsive or the creative mode of resource mobility. For this purpose we will concentrate on mobility of the labor resource (see Empirical Highlight 6-3).

Labor resources have been remarkably mobile in the United States, and most remarkable has been the farm worker. From providing half of the nation's employment in 1880, agriculture is now responsible for less than 5 percent. Until the Depression the number of agricultural employees increased, although it dropped in relative terms; since the Depression, the level of agricultural employment has declined continuously.

Where did the employees go when they could not go into farming? Only some went into manufacturing, where employment increased both relatively and in actual numbers until the early fifties. After that the proportion of manufacturing in national employment stabilized, although the absolute number of manufacturing employees continued to rise until the most recent years. Currently the manufacturing share of total employment is not much different from

Empirical Highlight 6-3.   Labor Mobility

- During each of the historic eras, nongoods employment has increased at a faster rate than either agriculture or manufacturing; however, in each of the intervals, nongoods labor productivity improvement has been at the slowest pace.

- Similarly, while agriculture employment has grown at the slowest rate in each of the indicated eras, agriculture productivity improvement has always been faster than either manufacturing or nongoods.

- Manufacturing employment growth has generally been slower than for nongoods and faster than in agriculture; manufacturing productivity improvement, however, has been faster than nongoods for each interval and more rapid than agriculture until the most recent period.

what it was in the early decades of the twentieth century—about a quarter of total employment as compared with a peak share of a third in the early fifties.

Most of the employees who did not end up in agriculture found their way into the nongoods-producing sectors. In 1880, nongoods production accounted for one-quarter of employment. It has increased consistently and currently accounts for three-fifths. Thus in the United States, long-term labor shifts have not followed a path from agriculture into manufacturing that is then replaced by a shift from manufacturing to services. Rather, right from the beginning of the industrialization process the labor shift has been among all three sectors; right from the beginning the economy has been "servicized" as well as "industrialized."

The data also indicate that labor shifts are, by themselves, no guarantee that output in the sectors receiving the labor will grow rapidly. For example, even though the nongoods sector's share of employment has increased from two-fifths to three-fifths of the total since 1930, its share of income produced has remained the same. The relatively slow growth in labor productivity of the nongoods sector accounts for this stabilization.

If the creative mode accurately describes resource mobility, and labor shifts by themselves resulted in productivity improvements, one would expect that the sectors whose employment has grown most rapidly would also grow the most rapidly in output and labor productivity. This does not seem to have happened. For example, since 1920, nongoods employment has increased at twice the rate of manufacturing, while nongoods labor productivity has improved at less than half the manufacturing rate. The periods in which a rapid employment increase and a rapid productivity improvement occur together appear to be relatively rare.

In the United States, nongoods have historically been the high productivity sectors (as measured by income produced per employee), and it is to these sectors that resources have flowed. Furthermore, as resources have flowed into nongoods, their productivity has improved at a slower pace than either manufacturing or agriculture. As a result, labor productivity in the nongoods sector, which was twice the level of the rest of the economy in 1880 and 50 percent higher in 1920, is now at about the same level as the average for the economy as a whole.

It would thus seem that long-term trends do not support the hypothesis that labor shifts, by themselves, are a particularly important factor in creating productivity improvements in the sector receiving the labor. Apparently what is more likely is that labor transfers from low- to high-productivity sectors. As this shift occurs a greater weight is automatically given to the high-productivity sectors in the economy. Thus aggregate productivity in the economy is improved as a consequence of the labor shift, even though productivity within each sector may not be improved. In short, the shift in product mix seems to have had a more important effect than economies of scale on aggregate productivity in the economy.

If the change in product mix favors energy-intensive activities, then there would be a strong possibility that labor shifts could be slowed down by difficulties in shifting energy usage from one sector to another. But this is not the case. The product mix is shifting toward nongoods, which generally have a lower energy intensity.

Nongoods tend to require less energy than goods, not only in terms of the energy directly utilized in their production, but also in terms of the energy used indirectly for the supplies, materials, construction, and other inputs needed for production. The direct plus indirect energy embodied in a dollar's worth of a particular product or service sold to final consumers has been called "specific energy intensity." Specific energy intensity for the economy as a whole is defined as the direct plus indirect energy content per dollar's worth of all goods and services sold to final consumers.[4]

The 1967 specific energy intensity of almost 400 goods and services has been estimated [46]. These have been allocated according to whether they are goods (manufacturing and agriculture), commercial transportation activities, or services. A frequency distribution of the specific energy intensities for the production in each sector indicates that almost three-quarters of all goods and services produced fall within a range of 0.5 to 1.5 times the average specific energy intensity for the economy as a whole. But while three-fourths of the goods and transportation activities fell within this range, only half of the services provided are within it. The major difference between the sectors is at the extremes. Two-fifths of the services, and essentially none of the goods or transportation activities, have specific energy intensities that are less than half of the average. A fourth of the goods and transportation activities—but almost no services—have specific energy intensities that are over 1.5 times the average.

The direct and indirect energy content per dollar of the typical

4. This overall, or average, specific energy intensity differs from gross energy intensity because it does not include energy sold directly to final consumers. The average specific energy intensity focuses on production activities and excludes primarily the household purchase of energy for home and personal transportation purposes—what has been called the proceeds as opposed to the springboard of growth.

service delivered to final consumers is probably less than half of the energy typically embodied in goods that are purchased by final consumers. Because of these differentials, a shift of product mix from goods to services would result in substantial energy saving. Such saving shows up as a fall in gross energy intensity.

A fall in energy intensity, implying reduced pressure on the available energy supply, would offset the growth-depressing consequence of energy immobilities. However, if there are factors that intervene with a decline in gross energy intensity, this would increase the likelihood that energy immobilities will slow down growth in national output.

One of these intervening factors may be a relatively rapid increase in the direct consumption of energy by households for home and personal transportation purposes. A reduction in specific energy intensity because of product mix changes may be canceled by an increase in the direct energy consumption of final consumers. This would result in a rise, rather than fall, in gross energy intensity.

The change in product mix may also fail to lower gross energy intensity if the goods-producing sectors that are already energy-intensive become even more so, for the shift to less energy-intensive products may be outweighed by increases in the specific energy intensity of particular products. One reason for such increases is that more energy is needed for the production process to take advantage of scale economies in the production of these particular products. This is a case of resource mobility playing a creative role in improving productivity through increased energy usage. Such forces toward increased energy intensity are most likely to be present within the manufacturing sector. It may well be that the impact of increasingly unfavorable conditions of energy supply will ultimately be determined by whether intensity-increasing or intensity-decreasing factors dominate in manufacturing.

If intensity-decreasing factors prevail, the resulting energy savings can be significant. As an indicator of these savings, the amount of additional energy consumption has been calculated that would have been needed if the 1947 levels of energy intensity had not changed and the 1973 levels of output and productivity were still being achieved. Empirical Highlights 6-4 present these calculations, which suggest that changes in manufacturing energy intensity have the potential for significantly influencing the size of the increment to energy consumption. If manufacturing energy intensity increases while the conditions of energy supply become more unfavorable, future growth in national output is likely to be jeopardized. The potential importance to economic growth of energy consumption by

Empirical Highlight 6-4. Energy Savings and Losses Resulting from Changes in Energy Intensity

- Because of the decline in overall energy intensity from 1947 to 1973, energy consumption in the United States was one-fifth less than would have otherwise been required. However, all of these savings occurred before 1966. Each year between 1947 and 1966, an additional 1 percent of energy consumption was saved because of the overall decline in energy intensity.

- One-quarter of manufacturing energy consumption in 1966 was saved because of the declining energy intensity that had been going on since 1947; however, only one-sixth of the 1966 nonmanufacturing energy consumption was saved for similar reasons. As a result, almost half of the total energy savings occurred in the manufacturing sector, considerably higher than the actual manufacturing share of total energy consumption.

- After 1966, energy intensity rose, causing an energy consumption add-on equivalent to almost 5 percent of the energy actually consumed in 1973. Almost all of this addon could be attributed to the increase in manufacturing energy intensity. Manufacturing energy consumption in 1973 was about one-sixth higher than it would have been if manufacturing energy intensity had remained at its 1966 level. Thus the impact on energy consumption growth of an increasing manufacturing energy intensity was even greater than the effect that a declining manufacturing energy intensity had on energy consumption saving.

manufacturing is ample reason to look more closely at what has recently been happening within the manufacturing sector.

Since 1947, manufacturing has accounted for about 30 percent of gross energy consumption. In most postwar years, the manufacturing share has fluctuated within the narrow range of 29 to 32 percent, although in several years it was somewhat higher. It needs to be asked why the manufacturing share of energy consumption has remained relatively stable, even though there has been a shift of product mix to nongoods production, and even though industrial energy consumption has been declining relative to other energy-consuming sectors.

One reason is that until the mid-1960s the manufacturing share of the nation's employment and of its outputs has also been about 30 percent, although drifting slightly downward. The observed shift to nongoods production and employment since the war has been primarily at the expense of agriculture rather than manufacturing.

Since the relative position of manufacturing in the economy did not change by very much between 1947 and 1966, the relative position of manufacturing in total energy consumption also remained fairly stable. However, the sharp drop in the manufacturing share of employment that occurred after 1966 has not been matched by a drop in the manufacturing share of energy consumption. Empirical Highlight 6-5 shows how postwar trends until the mid-1960s differed from the trends that followed and indicate that during the early postwar interval the impact of the manufacturing sector on overall energy demands was not out of line with manufacturing's relative position in the economy as a whole. Since changes in manufacturing

Empirical Highlight 6-5. Postwar Trends in the Manufacturing and Nonmanufacturing Sectors

1947 to 1966 Interval	*1966 to 1973 Interval*
• Energy consumption in manufacturing increased faster than manufacturing employment, slower than output, and about the same as capital stock.	• Energy consumption in manufacturing increased at a more rapid rate than in the earlier period; the growth in manufacturing output and employment slowed down; and the rate of growth in capital stock remained the same.
• As a result there was: 1. A substantial increase in manufacturing labor productivity. 2. A substantial decline in manufacturing energy intensity. 3. A moderate increase in manufacturing energy depth. 4. An increase in manufacturing capital intensity.	• As a result there was: 1. Only a modest increase in manufacturing labor productivity. 2. Manufacturing energy intensity reversed its historic decline and showed a substantial increase. 3. A substantial increase in manufacturing energy depth. 4. A decline in manufacturing capital intensity.
• Energy consumption in nonmanufacturing (which includes direct energy consumption by households as well as the energy consumed by all nonmanufacturing business activities) increased faster than employment, but slower than output and capital stock.	• The increase in nonmanufacturing energy consumption was substantially faster than in the earlier postwar period. However, unlike manufacturing, the rates of growth in employment, output, and capital stock were faster in the later period than in the earlier period.

Empirical Highlight 6-5 (cont.)

- As a result there was:
  1. A substantial increase in non-manufacturing labor productivity at a somewhat slower pace than in manufacturing.

  2. A decline in nonmanufacturing energy intensity at a somewhat slower pace than in manufacturing.

  3. A moderate increase in non-manufacturing energy depth at the same pace as in manufacturing.

  4. An increase in nonmanufacturing capital intensity at a faster pace than in manufacturing.

- As a result:
  1. The rate of improvement in non-manufacturing labor productivity slowed down from the earlier period, but was substantially faster than for manufacturing.

  2. Nonmanufacturing energy intensity also reversed its historic decline, but its increase was substantially slower than for manufacturing.

  3. Nonmanufacturing energy depth increased at about the same pace as in the earlier period, and was substantially below the manufacturing increase in the later interval.

  4. Nonmanufacturing capital intensity increased, unlike the decline in manufacturing.

productivity and energy consumption were not substantially different from those in the nonmanufacturing sector, it is not likely that manufacturing trends were uniquely responsible for the rate of decline in gross energy intensity or the rate of increase in gross energy depth that occurred during this period.

During this early postwar interval, labor productivity in manufacturing increased at about the same rate as energy consumption, while energy depth also drifted upward. These trends are consistent with the hypothesis that increased energy consumption made some contribution to improved manufacturing productivity. During this interval, however, there was a considerable decline in manufacturing energy intensity, which implies that factors other than energy consumption have also contributed to manufacturing productivity improvements. These other factors were important enough to make improved labor productivity and energy savings (as reflected in the reduced energy intensity) go hand in hand.

Events after 1966 require a different interpretation. Decline in the rate of manufacturing productivity improvement contributed to the slowdown that took place in overall productivity improvement. In spite of the productivity slowdown, energy consumption in manufacturing rose rapidly. So either a considerable part of the increased energy consumption did not make its customary contribution to manufacturing productivity, or the effects of other productivity-improving factors were comparably dampened.

Given the available information, we cannot determine whether it was energy consumption or some other factor—or both—that accounted for the slowdown in manufacturing productivity. But since these same trends were not strongly manifested in the nonmanufacturing sector, we do know that essentially the entire increase in the economy's overall gross energy intensity that occurred between 1966 and 1973 can be attributed to developments within the manufacturing sector. From 1966 to 1973, forces that raised manufacturing energy intensity overbalanced those that reduced it. The reverse occurred between 1947 and 1966.[5]

Because manufacturing energy intensity has been shown to be a crucial factor in assessing whether unfavorable conditions of energy supply will slow down economic growth, a closer examination of the intensity-changing forces is in order. For this purpose the forces affecting manufacturing energy intensity have been grouped into four categories relating to capital intensity, labor productivity, energy resource characteristics, and product energy intensity. Although this classification is arbitrary and overlapping, it may help to clarify the separate forces that influence energy intensity and assist in speculation about the impacts of these forces.

Capital-Intensity Factors: Manufacturing plant and equipment can be energy-saving or energy-using. Energy-saving capital cuts down energy intensity, while energy-using capital raises it. Energy-saving capital includes those investments that lower energy consumption without reducing labor productivity. In this category are not only all the energy-saving devices needed to reduce energy waste, but also all the equipment and structures designed to lower energy consumption.

5. Gelb [104] has developed recent data that come to the opposite conclusion. Not only has manufacturing energy intensity not increased in recent years but, according to Gelb, the rate of decline in manufacturing energy intensity was faster from 1972 to 1976 than the decline between 1947 to 1972. He reports that the decline in manufacturing energy intensity between 1947 to 1972 was primarily attributable to the reduction in energy intensity for the specific products in the few highly intensive manufacturing industries which were also very large energy users. This occurred at the same time that demand was shifting to the products of the less intensive manufacturing industries whose intensities were declining only modestly. The trend from the early to mid-'70s, according to his data, shows that the major source of the manufacturing intensity decline was not found in the largest energy-using industries. Rather, the energy intensity of the more moderate energy-using industries declined most rapidly, assisted by a demand shift to the products of these industries. At the same time the demand increased and the intensity declined for the products of the least energy-intensive industries. The largest energy users experienced a slowdown in their energy-intensity decline accompanied by a large relative loss in demand.

Energy-using capital comprises investments that raise energy consumption proportionately more than labor productivity. In this category would be many of the safety, pollution-control, and worker-amenity devices that are installed in plants. In addition, capital purchases requiring complementary energy inputs to improve production processes would be included in this category.

Direct information about the energy-saving or energy-using characteristics of capital stock is not available. Yet trends in capital intensity—that is, the ratio of capital stock to energy consumed—suggest how these characteristics have been changing: an increase in capital intensity implies that the energy-saving characteristics of capital stock are dominating the energy-using ones. In the postwar interval, capital intensity for the economy as a whole has drifted slightly upward, but after the early sixties, there was a decline.

Capital intensity for manufacturing is less than for nonmanufacturing, indicating, as might be expected, that the manufacturing sector will be more inclined to seek energy-saving capital devices. In the postwar years, manufacturing's capital intensity tends to increase until the early sixties, and then to decline. As a consequence the current level of manufacturing capital intensity is not too different from what it was in the early postwar years. Our conclusion is that the energy-saving characteristics of manufacturing capital stock dominated the early postwar period, but the energy-using characteristics became increasingly important in the later years. But why did this shift occur?

What happened was that since the mid-sixties industrial sector productivity improved at only half the rate that was experienced during the interval from 1947 to 1960. In the earlier period rapid productivity improvement, partly influenced by the expansion in capital stock, contributed to a sizable expansion in output. This output exapsnion was at a faster rate than the growth in energy consumption resulting from the added energy-saving equipment so that the manufacturing energy intensity declined. In the later period, the modest productivity improvements resulted in such a slow output growth that energy intensity rose along with the expansion in energy-using equipment.

Labor-Productivity Factors: If productivity improves without commensurate increases in energy consumption, energy intensity will decline. For example, improvements in the health status of employees raises labor productivity. Changes in energy consumption would be unrelated to health improvements, so output could increase without a rise in energy input, and energy intensity would decline.

There are undoubtedly a number of factors unrelated to energy that could cause productivity to rise or fall. Apart from changes in the quantity of capital stock, the energy-related factors that might affect labor productivity include changes in the rate at which available capacity is used, changes in the size of plants, and changes in technology or production processes.

If capacity is underutilized, it tends to be "inefficient" in the sense that upping utilization would produce greater increments to output than to the noncapital inputs required. This is probably true for the energy input in most production processes. Therefore, one would expect increases in the capacity utilization rate to lower intensity, and decreases to raise intensity. Historic data support this hypothesis somewhat, showing that changes in energy are more sluggish than those in output as the economy moves in and out of recessions.

Increasing plant size could raise output more than it raises energy needs. The larger size may particularly lead to more efficiency in the energy used to move goods or to heat space in the factory. However, upping plant size may also raise energy consumption by more than output if new opportunities to substitute energy for labor become available. It is not possible, on an *a priori* basis, to determine which of these elements would dominate.

Independent of changes in the quantity of capital stock, changes in technology or production processes can be energy-saving or energy-using. In the latter case the new process would have a high energy requirement relative to productivity improvement; in the former, the energy requirement would be low. Both of these types of technological change have occurred in the past. When energy costs are not high, there is a tendency for management to be indifferent to the energy-using characteristics of technology. As the conditions of energy supply become more unfavorable, we can expect such indifference to shift to concern.

Energy Resource Characteristics. Various characteristics of the energy resource will directly affect energy intensity. Thermal efficiency is the most obvious of these. Thermal efficiency is an engineering concept that relates the energy actually doing useful work to the raw energy input. As thermal efficiency improves, energy intensity will be reduced. Improvements in thermal efficiency have occurred continually over the long term, but there is some indication that these improvements have slowed down or possibly even stabilized since the mid-sixties.

Another reason it can be anticipated that manufacturing energy intensity will fall relates to the particular way that it is usually measured. Conversion losses from the production of electricity have not been allocated to the consuming sectors. Therefore, as more electricity is used in the manufacturing sector, more and more of the primary energy consumption goes into conversion loss and is not credited to manufacturing. So part of the observed decline in manufacturing energy intensity is caused solely by this measurement convention, and the effects are not small. Conversion losses increased from about one-tenth to one-fifth of gross energy input over the postwar interval. If half the conversion loss is allocated to manufacturing, then manufacturing energy intensity would be 20 to 25 percent higher. If adjustments for the conversion loss are made, the 1947 to 1966 rate of decline in manufacturing energy intensity would be dampened by about a third, while the rate of increase between 1966 to 1973 would be raised by a quarter.

Some manufacturing establishments internally produce and consume their own energy; in this case, the thermal losses are attributed to manufacturing consumption of energy. Other companies will purchase their energy requirements from utilities, so their thermal losses are not attributed to manufacturing energy consumption. Therefore, if establishments have been shifting to purchased energy sources, energy intensity in the manufacturing sector will go down. It has been estimated [63, p. 18] that about 15 percent of manufacturing energy consumption is internally produced and that this share has declined somewhat over the postwar interval. As a result, the shift to purchased energy has also contributed to the decline in manufacturing energy intensity.

Product Energy-Intensity Factors.   There is a considerable variation in the energy intensity of specific manufactured products. The six most energy-intensive manufacturing industries are mostly "heavy" manufacturing, and accounted for three-fifths of energy consumption in the early 1970s. The average energy intensity of these industries was six times that of all other manufacturing, which tends to be light-fabricating industries. There was also considerable variation of energy intensity among the six major energy consuming industries—the highest intensity being seven times the size of the lowest. And the variation among specific products within each industry is even greater, some products having ten times the intensity of others within the same industry.

This variation emphasizes the potential importance that shifts in product mix within manufacturing could have for manufacturing energy intensity in the aggregate. Output for the energy-intensive industries has grown slower than for the remaining manufacturing industries, indicating that the shift of product mix toward the light-fabricating type industries has contributed to lowering intensity for manufacturing as a whole. But among the major energy-consuming industries, the least intensive ones have not necessarily been growing the most rapidly, which leaves uncertain the net effect of shifts in product mix on manufacturing energy intensity.

The factors affecting manufacturing energy intensity during the 1947 to 1973 period were identified in a thorough study of postwar developments in twenty-nine high energy-consuming manufacturing industries [63]. Consistent with the decline in overall manufacturing energy intensity during this period, two-thirds of the twenty-nine specific industries experienced a decline in energy intensity. There were both energy intensity-increasing and intensity-decreasing factors at work in most industries, but the intensity-decreasing factors dominated on balance. In those industries where intensity did not decline there were twice as many instances of intensity-increasing factors than intensity-reducing factors. In those industries where intensity did decline, there were three times as many intensity-reducing as intensity-increasing factors.

The most prevalent factor that raised intensity was the increase in energy-using capital. This investment occurred at least as much in intensity-declining industries as in intensity-increasing ones. In the latter, however, there was a marked shift to the production of more energy-intensive products. New technologies adopted by these industries tended to be energy-saving and, along with increases in energy-saving capital, they dominated developments in the intensity-declining industries. "The principal method by which energy per unit of output was reduced was a substitute of capital embodying new technology for energy" [63, p. 2].

It is conceivable that these substitutions slowed down in the later years. If so, it would help to explain the increase in manufacturing energy intensity that began in the mid-sixties. It is probable that the rate of increase in energy-using capital for pollution control and safety purposes picked up in the later period. These elements could have been sufficient to cause overall manufacturing energy intensity to rise, even as the shift in product mix toward less intensive manufacturing products continued. Yet there is some evidence that the increased energy costs since 1973 have fostered investment in energy-saving processes and capital. If this trend continues, manufacturing will be playing an important role in the future conservation of energy.

Resources Shifts among Types of Innovators

The relative mobility or immobility of energy in transferring from one producing sector to another is one channel through which energy may influence economic development. A second channel relates to the effect that energy consumption has on the forces bringing about improvements in productivity.

If energy is substituted for labor, labor productivity (output per unit of labor) will probably improve. However, overall productivity in the economy (that is, total factor productivity as measured by output per weighted unit of all inputs, including labor, capital, and energy) will not necessarily rise as well. Similarly, a substitution of energy for capital may reduce the capital requirements per unit of output, but need not raise productivity as a whole.

Improvements in the economy's overall productivity depend on advances in knowledge and the organization of production. So to evaluate the effect that adverse conditions of energy supply would have on overall productivity, we would need to know how they influence the advance of knowledge and the organization of production. Unfortunately there is very little empirical investigation of these relationships, although there are some suggestive theoretical analyses. These analyses throw light on two issues: (1) how adverse conditions of energy supply affect advances in knowledge and their diffusion; and (2) how the form of energy supply affects the organization of production and other features of society.

Advances in Knowledge. From an industrial perspective, the growth of knowledge is implemented through the dynamic or innovating sectors of the economy. Output in these sectors usually grows rapidly, since new knowledge tends to expand markets and lower costs. Because of this the rate at which advances in knowledge occur will be influenced by the amount of resources that are made available to these sectors. There are limits, however, to the amount of resources that society is willing to devote to the dynamic economic sectors [57].

These limits are set by society's perceived need for the output of the nondynamic sectors or for putting to work the particular resources going to these sectors. Since, by definition, productivity improvement in the nondynamic sectors is relatively slow, the greater the share of resources they obtain, the slower will be the overall rate of economic growth.

What happens if the real costs of energy increase in this kind of economic environment? Activity in the nondynamic sectors, which are often energy-intensive, will still need to be maintained. Therefore, an increased share of the nation's total resources will probably go to the nondynamic sectors to pay for their added energy costs,[6]

---

6. If the elasticity of substitution between energy and other resource inputs is less than 1.0, rising energy costs will mean that the dollar value share of energy in gross output will go up. Considering energy as an input in the production of

lowering the rate of overall productivity improvement for two reasons. First, by shifting the weight of resource uses to the slower productivity-improving sectors, the aggregate productivity improvement is reduced. Second, it subtracts resources from the dynamic sectors, reducing the growth of knowledge and therefore slowing down the pace of productivity improvement in the dynamic sectors themselves.

Thus the effects of increased energy costs on productivity-improving advances in knowledge are initially less dependent on the energy requirements of the dynamic sectors than on the energy needs of the nondynamic ones. Furthermore, even if energy comprises only a small part of the total costs of the nondynamic sectors, the productivity consequences of increased energy costs can be significant. This is because the proportion of economic resources destined for the dynamic sectors is much smaller than the share going to the nondynamic sectors. So even if the increased cost of energy is only a small burden to the nondynamic sectors, it may nevertheless lead to a proportionately large reduction in the resources earmarked for the dynamic sectors.[7]

Under these circumstances—that is, maintenance in the demand for energy by the nondynamic sectors, with fewer resources going to the dynamic ones—the slowdown in overall productivity improvement is likely to be accompanied by a relatively unchanged level of energy consumption, and energy intensity will increase as a result. This outcome can be contrasted with the view that energy and capital complement each other so that the response to increased energy costs is a reduction in energy-using capital investments. The resulting slowdown in overall productivity improvements could drop output by less than the decline in energy consumption. As a result there would be a decline, rather than increase, in energy intensity.

The early stages of any particular advance in knowledge have little immediate effect on total output, productivity, or resource use because the new knowledge has not had time to spread through the economy. As this diffusion occurs, the activities it spawns grow larger, and their impact on the economy becomes more pronounced. If these activities consume energy, their diffusion not only raises real output, this means that the nation's total resources will decline. Since we have assumed that output of the nondynamic sectors is less flexible than that of the dynamic ones, the nondynamic sector will increase its share of total resources as a result of rising energy costs. This result depends on the assumption that the elasticity of substitution is less than 1.0, which all evidence suggests to be the case.

7. It is sometimes argued that relatively small increases in energy costs will not cause relatively large reductions in national output because total energy costs are less than 5 percent of GNP. Such an argument ignores the possible long-run effects of changes in the quantity and use of innovating resources.

overall productivity but also adds to the demands for energy. So the dynamic sectors then compete with the nondynamic ones for the available energy.

If the supply of available energy is limited and the demand for the nondynamic sector output stays high, the pace of diffusion will slow down. This, in turn, will retard the rates of productivity improvement and output growth.

Thus it can be seen that adverse conditions of energy supply may have a double impact on overall productivity improvement. First, higher energy costs may reduce the resources available for the creation of new, productivity-improving knowledge; second, limits to the availability of energy may slow down the dissemination of productivity-improving processes and equipment.

One way to mitigate the adverse consequences of rising energy costs would be to lower the share of available energy going to those types of energy consumption contributing least to productivity improvement. As a crude approximation, the amenity activities that do not relate directly to productivity improvement include the energy used in the home and for personal transportation or travel. The productivity-enhancing activities would then include the uses of energy for producing finished fuels, for producing industrial goods, and for providing commercial services (including commercial activities and nonpersonal transportation).

When all energy consumption is separated into these two categories—the amenity activities and the productivity-enhancing activities—it can be seen that there has been a long-term trend toward increasing the productivity-enhancing share of energy uses. For example, a century ago over three-fourths of the energy used produced heat for physical comfort [92]. With the development of the steam engine, electric drives, and other energy-using innovations, the share of energy devoted to productivity-enhancing activities has increased until the present, when the proportions that prevailed in the middle of the nineteenth century have been reversed. Currently about three-fourths of energy consumption goes to purposes directly associated with overall productivity in the economy, while only one-quarter of the energy used is associated with household amenities produced directly by energy consumption.

Interpretation of the trend toward productivity-improving energy consumption activities probably would not change even if finer distinctions could be made between what is and what is not productivity-improving. The part of household energy consumption that is productivity-enhancing is probably smaller than the part of industrial and commercial energy consumption that is amenity-creating. As a result, productivity-enhancing energy consumption might now be less than three-quarters of total energy consumption, but it is surely higher than the share that occurred a hundred years ago.

One reason for this trend is that the products created through innovation in the dynamic sectors have tended to require a large energy input for their production. If such innovations continue under conditions of adverse energy supply, then the pace of the relative energy shift to productivity-enhancing activities will probably pick up. This is because some of the energy used for amenity purposes will need to be diverted to productivity purposes.

Suppose, however, that energy-saving innovations become a desirable target to pursue. Adverse conditions of energy supply would then be mitigated in two ways: (1) the overall levels of energy consumption would be lowered by the energy-conservation technologies; and (2) the rising trend in the share of energy earmarked for productivity-enhancing activities would be slowed down.

Technology opens the door to energy conservation through three categories of innovation: energy consumption technologies, task realignment technologies, and materials recycling technologies. Any task actually performed uses up more energy than the theoretical minimum energy requirements dictated by physical laws. Energy-consumption technologies can be developed that would permit those tasks to be performed with less energy than they currently require. These technologies can be applied in the production of energy (which is itself an important energy consumer), as well as in the production of industrial goods, commercial services, and household amenities, all of which are energy users.

The production of goods, services, and amenities can be thought of as an intermediate step in providing utilities or well-being to people. This well-being can be achieved through different combinations of work tasks. For example, a home can be more efficiently heated through better insulation or by simply turning up the furnace—to achieve the same utility one task uses considerable energy; the other does not. Task realignment technologies can be developed that would select a combination of tasks that would consume less rather than more energy to provide some particular utility.

There is considerable energy embodied in the stock of equipment, goods, and materials produced. Obtaining utility from this physical stock does not require using up that energy. Materials recycling technologies can be developed that would capture that energy and allow materials to become a significant supplement to primary fuels as an energy source.

Energy conservation technologies will save energy. But in the process they may require more labor or more capital, which would raise the economic costs and lower the economic productivity of these processes. Therefore it can be said that while it is the physical conditions that determine the potential for energy conservation technologies, it is the economic conditions—including but not limited to the relative cost of energy—that will largely determine which of these potentials will be pursued and the extent to which they will be achieved.

If resources to advance knowledge are limited, they will need to be shared between the development of energy-using processes that create overall productivity improvements and the development of energy-saving ones that may or may not enhance overall productivity. In both cases, advances in knowledge would mitigate the depressing effect on output that would result from higher energy costs and reduced energy availability. The development of energy-saving processes would constrain output reductions by raising the elasticity of substitution between energy and other inputs. The development of energy-using processes would achieve the same constraint by upping the productivity of the labor and capital used jointly with the energy input.

Suppose that under the current methods of large-scale industrial production, the potential for substitution between energy and other inputs is low, that advances in knowledge are not capable of raising the elasticity of substitution, and that overall productivity can be improved only through substantial increases in energy uses. Under these circumstances, if energy costs increase the inevitable result will be a reduction in national output. As energy costs continue to rise, furthermore, the national output, or at least per capita output, will drop lower and lower. One way that society might respond to this would be to abandon the value it attaches to material well-being, the work ethic, and the pursuit of technologically-oriented sciences.

In another possible response, as suggested by Schumacher, society could abandon the large-scale production and the mass consumption associated with industrialization. By going "smaller" rather than staying with industrialized society, advances in knowledge may raise the elasticity of substitution between energy and other inputs, and thereby prevent a continued output decline. There are, however, stiff conditions that need to be satisfied if industrial society's predicted output declines are to be prevented by a shift to small-scale production: elasticity of substitution in an industrial society must be low; advances in knowledge must be incapable of raising an industrial society's elasticity of substitution but can do so in a nonindustrial society; and overall productivity enhancement, in an industrial society, must be dependent on increased energy consumption. There is little evidence to support any of these conditions.

Organization of Production. A focus on knowledge advance has led us to consider how energy costs and availability relate to the economy's overall productivity and to the efficiency with which energy itself is employed. But a focus on organization of production leads to considerations not of the costs of energy but the form in which it is supplied. Ignoring the consequences of the form in which energy is provided may well overlook the most important channel through which the conditions of energy supply have affected the economic and social characteristics of modern society. It was not the costs or quantity of energy available but rather the shifts from one type of energy to another that prompted the observation by Schurr that "many of the fundamental features of contemporary Western societies have had their origins, at least in part, in development in the field of energy supply technology" [85, p. 27].

In the past 100 years, there have been three major shifts in energy form: from wood to coal, from coal to liquid fuels, and from direct consumption of raw energy to converted energy (such as electric power and diesel fuel). These shifts did not coincidentally accompany the newly created opportunities for economic and social development. Rather, they have been a major factor in making these opportunities possible. The connection between changing energy form and economic development takes on added importance in view of the almost universal expectation that oil and gas must give way to some other energy source in the future.

Neither the widespread adoption of new energy forms in the past nor their impact on economic and social developments are adequately explained by the relative abundance or low cost of particular energy forms. Indeed, in most instances the new fuels were neither more abundant nor cheaper than those being replaced. Rather, the new forms of energy were capable of doing things that were essentially not feasible with the earlier forms, because the new kinds of energy possessed particular attributes that the older ones did not have. And it was these attributes (rather than price or quantity of energy) that had major impacts on future developments. The relevant attributes can be characterized in terms of the technical properties, the complementary technologies, and the inherent characteristics of the different energy forms.

Technical properties refer to the ability of fuel to produce heat or to do mechanical work. The most important thermodynamic property of a fuel is the temperature difference it can produce, which is a measure of the quality of energy available from that fuel. Electricity can produce extremely high temperature and is of the highest quality, which in part explains why electricity had replaced direct primary fuel consumption in many end-use applications and why it is becoming more popular. Similarly, it was the superior combustible properties of oil and gas—a property not possessed by other fuels—that to a large extent accounted for the rapid rise in their consumption and, in the process, enabled the internal combustion engine to triumph over the steam and electric forms of power for moving vehicles. Conversely, the replacement of wood by coal cannot be explained by the superior quality of energy in coal—its BTU content is the same as wood [84, p. 52]—but was related to other attributes. And, as another illustration, solar energy is of low quality [95, p. 260], which partly explains its slow pace of adoption for uses other than those requiring low-quality heat.

The widespread adoption of new energy forms is almost always linked to the development of *complementary technologies* that use the fuels. Starr reminds us that "the early industrial revolution was based on the use of the water wheel and the windmill as prime movers" [92, p. 4]. The development of the steam engine not only signalled a pickup in the pace of mechanization, but also the adoption of wood as the major industrial fuel. The advent of the stove helped coal to replace wood-burning for heat in the home. Rapid growth of the iron and steel industry depended upon the development of the Bessemer process, which caused coal to dominate industrial fuel uses. The electric motor, in turn, heralded the demise of coal in industry, while the internal combustion and the diesel engines marked the end of coal in transportation. And just imagine the number of horses or mules—and the resources required to sustain them—that would have been needed by the agriculture sector if mechanical forms of power had not been developed.

When a new technology is joined with a new fuel form, economic and social trends tend to be dramatically redirected. The flavor of this drama is captured in the following (preenvironmental) tribute to the automobile:

> However, the thermal efficiency of the automobile is a matter of small significance compared with the changes that automotive vehicles have wrought in the American way of life, and, through these, on national productivity and the economic efficiency of energy use.
> It is obvious that the rise of the automobile has brought about a new era of mobility, with increasing flexibility in the location of industry and population which must have had an important influence on the over-all

productivity of the national economy. On the farm, too, the spreading use of internal combustion engines has served to multiply the productivity of U.S. agriculture. Automobiles have also tended to equalize urban and rural ways of life in important respects: to cite one example, in making possible consolidated schools, to which children travel by bus, and which offer a higher quality of instruction than the one-room rural schoolhouse of an earlier day. In some ways similar to the introduction of adequate artificial illumination in the nineteenth century, the automobile has added useful hours to the day by reducing the time needed to overcome the increasing distances between home, place of work, of shopping, education, and recreation. This greater mobility, however, has encouraged the growth of suburbanization and the dispersion of the population of metropolitan areas and increased the distances which must be covered in the routine of everyday living. In view of the complexity of the interrelationship between the growth of automotive transportation and national output, it would be quite unrealistic to evaluate the substantial increase in consumption of internal combustion fuels for automotive purposes in terms of thermal efficiencies alone. The net influence of automotive transportation on the acceleration in national productivity following World War I would, by itself, be the subject for another book. [84, p. 179.]

Three economic consequences resulted from the advent of the automobile, and these are the same consequences that have tended to follow each of the major fuel and technological shifts of the past. There has been an increase in the *mobility* of families and industry, making activities less bound to specific locations. There has been an upswing in *productivity*, creating rising living standards. And there has been a proliferation in the variety of goods and amenities available, permitting the adoption of new *living and work styles* by major segments of the population.

Advances in mobility, productivity, and living styles tend to interact with each other. For example, when industry becomes more mobile, productivity rises, just as productivity improvements tend to create opportunities for new living styles. Therefore, if a change in energy form initially contributes to enhancing mobility, productivity, or living styles, there will be multiplier effects that eventually advance all three. But it is the *inherent characteristics* of a new energy form that determine whether or not it will set off this process by enhancing any one of the consequences of economic development. These characteristics are the attributes of energy forms (other than their cost, availability, technical properties, and complementary technologies) that facilitate the expansion of mobility, productivity, and living styles.

The ideal energy form would possess the following inherent characteristics to an optimal degree [76, p. 70]:

- It would be versatile—that is, capable of being produced from a variety of primary energy sources.
- It would be transportable—that is, large amounts could be economically moved over long distances.
- It would be storable—that is, both large and small amounts of energy could be stored economically.
- It would be flexible—that is, capable of being utilized economically for a variety of purposes.
- It would be clean—that is, capable of doing all these other things without excessive damage to the environment.

We have not yet found the ideal energy form, although advances in the technology of energy supply have tended to affect the versatility transportability, storability, flexibility, and cleanliness characteristics of particular energy forms; and new forms have possessed these inherent characteristics in different degrees from those they have replaced. For this reason the dynamic economic consequences of mobility, productivity, and living styles can be linked to changing energy form. The following review of some past changes in energy form illustrates this relationship.

A major difference between wood as a source of industrial power and the wind and water sources it replaced was that wood was more transportable. Consequently it increased the mobility of charcoal and wood-burning iron and textile factories so they could locate away from both fixed sources of power and their agricultural markets. The development of urbanized clusters with a manufacturing economic base thereby was encouraged, since the transportation system needed to support such clusters could depend on wood-burning locomotives and steamboats. In alluding to this process, Starr says,

> The steam engine was the first mechanical prime mover to provide basic mobility, unlike the water wheel or the windmill. However, it was some time before this mobility was used . . . It was the geographic limitation on the expansion of water power which gave the steam engine an opportunity to continue the growth of manufacturing centers. [92, p. 4.]

Coal replaced fuel wood because it was more transportable, more storable, and cleaner. For purposes of home-heating in the cities, increased cleanliness counted. According to Schurr, "In the first decade of the nineteenth century, it was demonstrated that anthracite could be burned in a grate in a fireplace without an artificial draft, and being comparatively clean and smokeless, it gradually became the preferred domestic coal in the cities" [84, p. 63]. Its smaller bulk made coal easier to move and store than wood, which was particularly important to the industrial users of energy. For growing demands for iron and steel were imposing severe strains on the timber supplies in the factory areas, resulting in the costly practice of abandoning furnaces as timber was exhausted and moving closer to the timber source. By transporting coal this practice could be eliminated and productivity improved. The ability to move coal to the factories also enabled urbanization to continue. The fact that coal can be stored was important to the transportation industry. In the 1880s, for example, when coal became the major fuel, locomotives accounted for almost half the bituminous consumption [84, p. 68]. Since railroad transportation was at the core of the rising mobility of industry and families, the fact that coal took up less space than wood was a matter of some importance.

Electric power production began to grow rapidly after 1900 and has not yet stopped. As compared with coal, it is more flexible, versatile, and cleaner in its end uses—almost the "ideal" energy form except that it is costly to transport, difficult to store, and is polluting at the point of production. On balance the positive attributes of electric power have been more important than the negative, and account not only for the increasing use of electric power but also for its contributions to mobility, productivity, and living styles.

Because electric power is versatile (that is, it can be produced by converting a variety of primary energy agents), its further growth is not dependent on the continued availability of a particular fuel. In fact its versatility is a major reason for expecting electricity to displace other energy forms in the future. "The phrase 'new energy sources' is fast becoming synonomous with 'new sources of electricity' " [42, p. 97]. Versatility enhances mobility and productivity by providing options to choose a low-cost fuel source. Thus, as relative fuel costs change, the production of electricity can adapt to the cheaper fuel. And even more important, since there are regional differences in fuel costs, electric power production in particular locations can adapt to local fuel-supply conditions.

The versatility of electric power offsets, to some extent, the difficulties in its transportation, for electric power can be produced closer to the point of consumption by using the fuels available to local areas. So its versatility gives electric power production a ubiquitous character, which means that the locational options and mobility of people and industry are enhanced.

Overall productivity in the economy has been promoted by electric power's flexibility. Although energy is produced in large units, it tends to be consumed in small, noncontinuous ones [76, p.

76]. Electric power is flexible because it can make the transition efficiently from large to small and thereby provide new ways for achieving particular results. Consequently, the result is more than some savings in energy costs. According to Schurr, "The unique characteristics of electricity as an energy form have permitted the performance of tasks in altogether different ways than if fuel had to be used directly as a source of energy" [85, p. 6]. For example, before the introduction of the individual electric motor, all mechanical power in the factory was provided by a prime mover, producing enough power to satisfy the maximum needs and involving continuous idling of shaft and belting. Under these circumstances it was efficient to locate large energy-using operations close to the prime mover rather than adopting a plant design permitting a "sequence and layout of production more in keeping with the logic of the production process" [85, p. 6]. The individual electric motor made possible this kind of plant reorganization, and at the same time it permitted the power to be shut off when it was not being used. Thus flexibility of energy form does inside the factory what transportability does outside: it provides a greater number of locational options and thereby more mobility to important activities.

Electric power increases these locational opportunities not only within the factory but also within the office, both through the provision of climate control and a more logical design for the sequence of office activities. In this way electric power has contributed not only to improving the productivity of goods but also to providing services and office support activities. "The release from the restrictions of internal mechanical energy transmission systems opened up wholly new possibilities for applying modern techniques of industrial and business management" [84, p. 189].

The flexibility of electric power, that is, the variety of end uses in which it can be efficiently employed, has led directly to increased opportunities for improved living styles. These opportunities have been enhanced by the relatively low environmental cost of electricity's end uses. Electricity's flexibility is most apparent from the multitude of devices, made possible through electrification, that have lightened the burden of household tasks and "fundamentally altered the comfort and convenience of living for the mass of the population" [85, p. 28]. Furthermore, this flexibility has been uniquely important in developing communication devices and automatic control equipment that have not only enhanced living styles and quality of the work environment but have also made major contributions to the economy's overall productivity.

The main drawbacks of electricity—its relatively poor transportability and storability, and polluting effects at the point of generation—all impede advances in productivity and mobility. Electricity demand is variable both in seasonal and daily contexts. Since it is difficult to store, the peak-load demands are met by having generating facilities available when they are needed, which ordinarily means that the peak-load needs are met through less efficient, underutilized, and more polluting power stations, all of which lower productivity.

The costs of transmitting electricity are higher than for transporting coal or liquid fuels [42, p. 99]. These transmission costs not only lower productivity directly but tie up tremendous amounts of capital in the transmission system that might otherwise be used to develop productivity-enhancing innovations. And the high costs of transmission heighten the difficulties of finding environmentally suitable sites for power stations, which in turn lowers industrial mobility.

Where electricity is weak, the liquid fuels are strong; in other words, they rank high on ease of transportation and storage and have been fundamentally important to the nation's increasing mobility. "One of the main reasons for the importance that hydrocarbons have now acquired is their many advantages as energy carriers from the production, transport and storage aspects" [76, p. 77]. Petroleum, with its capacity for being transported and stored, was eminently suited for truck and automobile traffic. Besides being stored in vehicles carrying their own fuel, gasoline can be transported and stored compactly enough to establish a fuel distribution system that enables any vehicle to be in virtually continuous contact with an available fuel supply.

Unlike oil, natural gas was not always easily transportable, which was a major reason why it was not used in earlier periods, despite its wide availability. "The technological advances, which made possible long distance interstate pipelines, became the foundation for the spectacular increase in the use of natural gas" [84, p. 127].

Liquid and gaseous fuels are also flexible in the same sense as is electric power: they have provided an opportunity to change the way goods and services are produced. Agriculture particularly benefitted from this flexibility. What the motor powered by electricity did for the factory, the internal combustion engine powered by liquid fuels did for agriculture. It permitted new ways to farm through mechanization, which made agriculture more productive, which in turn affected overall productivity throughout the economy. Similarly, the diesel engine, powered by diesel fuel, expanded productivity in railroads, while trucks, powered by gasoline, revolutionized the movement of freight; and boilers, fueled by natural gas, heightened productivity in the chemical, petroleum, and paper industries.

Oil and gas are more flexible than coal in their end uses, but less so than electric power. The direct end use of natural gas relates primarily to the heating process—space, water, and industrial heating, as well as process steam. Over half the nation's oil is consumed as a transportation fuel, with heating accounting for about a quarter of the end-use consumption. What makes oil relatively versatile, and therefore a factor in living style changes, is the one-tenth going into feedstocks. Out of these uses, and particularly petrochemicals, a variety of new consumer products are being provided.

It is tempting to speculate about the future from the perspective of the inherent characteristics of energy form. The United States now seems less intent than in earlier years on expanding productivity and with it the variety of goods and services that contribute to our living styles. As a result the inherent characteristic of flexibility is likely to become less important to us. The major characteristics for the future are transportability, storability, cleanliness, and versatility. It is these qualities that will permit continued mobility of industry and people, a better environment, and a hedge against energy supply disruptions. Over the long run we can expect research to be directed toward developing energy forms embodying these characteristics, and we can also anticipate considerable investment in devices that will provide these characteristics.

Chapter Seven

The Energy Future

The preceding chapters have described alternative views about the desirability of economic growth and the role of energy in that growth. Convincing arguments, theoretical as well as empirical, can be made to support contending and even conflicting views. Consensus is difficult to reach in light of historic trends that can be variously interpreted, a future that is even more uncertain, value systems that clash, and interests that compete. It has been my intent to present, not reconcile, the alternative views. It is appropriate, however, that I now indicate where I stand.

I am a reluctant alpha expansionist. I am an alpha expansionist because I favor policies that will expand the supply and use of fossil and nuclear fuels. I favor such policies because I believe that although energy conversion and use can be disabling and destructive, they are much more likely to be enabling and constructive in the progress of civilization; that substantial economic growth, in the United States and in the world, is, on balance, a desirable rather than undesirable social objective; and that although continued economic growth is not in lock-step with the increased use of fossil and nuclear fuels, it is, at present, dependent on their expansion.

I am reluctant because I wish the world were different from what it is. I wish that the energy production and use cycle could be environmentally pure. I wish that the energy sector would require less of the nation's resources. I wish that low-cost energy conservation could completely substitute for energy expansion. I wish that benign, but still economically efficient, energy technologies could satisfy a major part of the future energy needs. Perhaps some day these wishes will be realized. But, in my view, these are still wishes and not yet facts.

As an alpha expansionist I do not deprecate the importance of what the beta expanionists and beta conservationists are saying. Developing the nondisabling soft technologies and stimulating energy conservation are compatible with expanding the proven energy sources. It would be folly to ignore the contributions that conservation and new technology can make toward easing the burden of the transitional years and speeding up the race into the more distant future. But it would be worse than folly to intensify the transitional burden and to risk the future through actions or inactions that foster an unnecessary energy gap.

I believe we are running out of economically available oil and gas, and possibly even coal over the longer run. However, I do not find that sufficient reason to artificially curtail their use. It is a mistake to believe that by slowing the growth in our living standards we can assure the comfort of still later generations. Our legacy to the future is not what we leave deposited under the ground but what we put into the minds of people.

I believe that all forms of energy production and use degrade the environment and some may threaten the human as well as other species. Furthermore, the currently dominant energy sources and technologies are among the worst of the culprits. However, the solution is not to be found in premature scrapping of technologies but in the promise of economic growth to make resources available for repairing the damage, protecting the environment, and developing the benign processes.

I believe that substantial energy conservation is feasible and in many cases less expensive than equivalent energy expansion. Not only will rising energy costs result in conservation, but paramarket inducements and policies will also make their contribution. Yet there is a danger of overestimating the conservation potential. The conservation lead time is long because it takes time to change energy-using devices and user attitudes. The conservation process is complex because it ordinarily involves more than some single, independent procedure; rather, it requires interrelating a variety of market, technical, and managerial actions.

I believe that in their present state the soft technologies and the alternative fuels can add relatively little to the energy supply. Over the years this will change. But I would expect the changeover to be slow rather than rapid, and costly rather than cheap.

I believe that concerns about the future availability of energy are legitimate and serious. However, some of these concerns can reasonably be diminished because an expected slowdown in population growth and a decline in energy intensity—the energy-to-GNP ratio—will lower the rate of growth in U.S. energy consumption.

I believe that energy intensity will decline because of the demand-depressing effects of energy price increases and conservation, a shift away from the use of energy-intensive goods, services, and materials, and a relatively rapid improvement in the economy's productivity.

I believe that productivity improvement is to a perceptible extent dependent on the availability of energy. When this energy feedback is ignored, as it often is, the seeming importance of energy to the economy is diminished. In my view when energy becomes less available and more costly, it lowers the potential for investment in productivity-improving energy-using capital, particularly in manufacturing and agriculture; it restricts the locational opportunities for plants, offices, and homes; and it diverts resources away from the dynamic sectors that raise productivity through expanding capacity and enhancing technology. If this does happen then it is the challenge for society to develop new techniques to make productivity advance less dependent on energy use.

Finally, I believe that as new energy forms emerge they will embody characteristics of flexibility, storability, transportability, and cleanliness that will provide new opportunities for the reorganization of production and the adoption of new styles of living and work. Because of this I expect the future to be different from the present, not only in the types of energy it consumes but also in the economic and social structure it supports.

Appendix
Sources and Derivation of
Data

TABLE 1: ECONOMIC INDICATORS

Column 1
Refers to total national output produced.
    1850-1910 [52].
    1920 [97].
    1929-1973 [3].
    1975-1977 [96].

Column 2
    1850-1940 [97].
    1947-1977 [96].

Column 3
Refers to "full-time equivalent employees," i.e., part-time employees
are converted to a full-time basis.
    1850-1860: Based on proportionate increase in "gainful workers"
                 as shown in [97] indexed against 1929 estimate of
                  full time equivalent employees.
    1870-1920: Based on indexes of man-hours worked as shown in
                  [52], indexed against 1929 estimate.
    1929-1973 [3].
    1975-1977: Based on rate of growth in index of hours worked by
                  all persons engaged in private production as shown in
                  [96].

Basic data sources are identified by reference number in brackets.

Column 4

Refers to fixed nonresidential business equipment plus structures for all industries.

1890-1920: Real Capital Stock as shown in [52] p. 320, indexed against 1929 estimate.

1929-1973 [98].

1975-1977: Private Communication from U.S. Dep't. of Commerce.

Column 5

1890-1920: Col. 6 times Col. 1

1929-1973 [3].

1973-1977 [96].

Column 6

1890-1920 [52].

1929-1977: Col. 5 ÷ Col. 1.

Column 7

Col. 1 ÷ Col. 2.

Column 8

Col. 1 ÷ Col. 3.

Column 9

Col. 4 ÷ Col. 3.

Column 10

Col. 3 ÷ Col. 2.

Column 11

Col. 1 ÷ Col. 4.

TABLE 2: ENERGY INDICATORS

Column 1

Refers to all energy consumption including wood.

1850-1940 [84, Table VII]. Interpolated estimates for wood where necessary.

1947-1973 [31].

1975-1977 [103].

Column 2
Refers to all energy consumption less conversion losses. This also equals the end-use consumption of direct fuels plus purchased electricity.
   1880-1940: Table 2, Col. 1, less Table 4, Col. 8.
   1947-1973 [31].
   1975-1977 [103].

Column 3
Refers to ratio of net to gross energy.
   1880-1940: Col. 2 ÷ Col. 1.
   1947-1973 [96].
   1975-1977 [103].

Columns 4-8
Refers to energy consumption of separate fuel sources. Sum of these sources equals Col. 1. This is only approximately correct for the years 1947-1975 since the specific fuel-source data exclude nonfuel uses, included in Col. 1 and shown separately in Table 5.
   1850-1940 [84].
   1947-1973 [99].
   1975-1977 [103].

Columns 9-14
Refers to domestic production by fuel source.
   1850-1940 [84].
   1947-1975 [99].

TABLE 3: ENERGY ECONOMIC RELATOINSHIPS

Column 1
   Table 2, Col. 1 ÷ Table 1, Col. 2.

Column 2
   Table 2, Col. 1 ÷ Table 1, Col. 1.

Column 3
   Table 2, Col. 1 ÷ Table 1, Col. 4.

Column 4
   Table 2, Col. 1 ÷ Table 1, Col. 3.

Column 5
Table 2, Col. 1 ÷ Table 1, Col. 2.

Column 6
Table 1, Col. 4 ÷ Table 2, Col. 1.

Column 7
Table 2, Col. 2 ÷ Table 1, Col. 1.

TABLE 4: SECTOR PURCHASES BY FUEL SOURCE

Columns 1-4
Refers to end-use sector consumption of each primary fuel.
   1880-1940: The estimates for 1880-1940 required piecing to-
              gether primary fuel consumption for specific purposes
              as found in [84 pp. 64, 68, 76, 79, 106, 122, 133,
              160; and 87, p. 159], and relating these to total
              end-user consumption for the indicated years.
   1947-1970 [99].
   1973-1977 [103].

Column 5
Sum of Cols. 1-4.

Column 6
Refers to electric utility consumption by each end use sector. This
consumption is implicit in the energy consumption by fuel source
shown in Table 2.
   1880-1940: Estimated from data in [87, 84].
   1947-1970 [99].
   1973-1977 [103].

Column 7
Refers to total of primary fuel consumption plus electricity purchased.
   1880-1940: Col. 5 plus Col. 6
   1947-1970 [99].
   1973-1977 [103].

Column 8
Conversion losses are shown in the electric utility purchase panel
since the conversion loss represents an energy input in the electric
utility sector. It is derived from Table 2, Col. 1 less Col. 2 for

1947-1977, and is independently estimated for 1880-1940 as based on data in [87, 84].

TABLE 5: NONFUEL USES OF ENERGY

Column 1
1947-1975: Refers to total energy and nonenergy through fossil fuel sources. Equals total energy in Table 2, Col. 1 less the consumption of hydro and nuclear sources in Table 2, Col. 8.

Column 2
1947-1975: Refers to that part of fossil fuel used for energy purposes. Equals Col. 1 less Col. 3.

Columns 3-8
1947-1975: Refers to the nonenergy uses of fossil fuels. Distributed first according to the nonenergy uses by end-use sectors, and then according to the fossil fuel sources of the nonenergy uses. Data in [99].

TABLE 6: FOREIGN TRADE IN ENERGY

Columns 1-5
Refers to U.S. imports by fuel source [99].

Columns 6-10
Refers to U.S. exports by fuel source [99].

Columns 11-15
Refers to U.S. net trade, that is, the excess of imports over exports by fuel source [99].

Columns 16-19
Refers to the share of U.S. energy consumption that is imported. Derived from Cols. 1-5 and energy consumption data in Table 2.

Columns 20-23
Refers to the share of U.S. energy production that is exported. Derived from Cols. 6-10 and energy production data in Table 2.

Columns 24-27
Refers to the ratio of U.S. energy production to consumption. Derived from data in Table 2.

TABLE 7: SELECTED DATA FOR ECONOMIC SECTORS

Personal Consumption Expenditures
Refers to household expenditures as defined in the national income accounts.
    1880-1920: Based on personal expenditure indexes in [52].
    1929-1966 [97, Series F-27].
    1973-1975 [98].

National Income Produced
Refers to the national income originating in each producing sector as defined in the national income accounts: the sum of the sector estimates equals the total U.S. national income.
    1880-1920: Based on indexes of national income by sector in [52].
    1929-1970 [97, Series F226-237, adjusted by implicit GNP deflator].
    1973-1975 [98].

Persons Employed
Refers to the number of persons employed in the nation. Differs from the full-time equivalent employment shown in Table 1 because no adjustment for part-time employment is made.
    1880-1890: Data on "Persons Engaged" in [52, p. 308], indexed against 1920 data in [97].
    1910-1970 [97, Series D16, D127].
    1973-1975: *Employment and Training Report of the President.*

Income Produced Per Employee
Refers to the national income produced divided by persons employed, on a sector-by-sector basis. Derived from other data in Table 7.

Energy Intensities
Refers to a variety of relationships between types of energy consumption and types of economic activity. The national income and personal expenditures data are shown in Table 7. The GNP data are shown in Table 1. Gross energy consumption data are shown in Table 2, Col. 1. Industrial energy consumption is shown in Table 4, Col. 7. Nonindustrial energy consumption is the sum of household-, commercial-, and transportation-sector energy consumption as shown in Table 4, Col. 7. Conversion loss is shown in Table 4, Col. 8.

National Income Produced Per GNP
Refers to the share of national income in the GNP. Derived from data in Table 7 and Table 1, Col. 1.

Full-Time Equivalent Employees Per Person Employed
Derived from data in Table 7 and Table 1, Col. 3.

Income Produced Per Person Employed ÷ GNP
Per Full Time Equivalent Employee
Derived from data in Table 7 and Table 1, Col. 8

TABLE 8: MANUFACTURING SECTOR

Column 1
Refers to energy consumed by industrial sector, including allocated electric power. Derived from Table 4.

Column 2
Refers to energy consumed in manufacturing activities (Col. 1 times Col. 3).

Column 3
Refers to manufacturing share of industrial energy consumption. Estimates of manufacturing energy consumption for years 1947, 1954, 1962, 1967, 1971 available in [63]. Ratio of manufacturing to industrial energy consumption calculated for these years. Other years interpolated.

Columns 4, 5
See Source to Table 7, "Persons Employed."

Column 6
Col. 5 ÷ Col. 4.

Columns 7, 8
See Source to Table 7, "National Income Produced."

Column 9
Col. 8 ÷ Col. 7

Column 10
Refers to industrial energy intensity (Col. 1 ÷ Col. 7).

Column 11
Refers to industrial energy intensity for manufacturing (Col. 1 ÷ Col. 8).

Column 12
Refers to manufacturing energy intensity (Col. 2 ÷ Col. 8).

Column 13
Refers to industrial energy depth (Col. 1 ÷ Table 1, Col. 3).

Column 14
Refers to industrial energy depth on a persons employed basis (Col. 1 ÷ Col. 4).

Column 15
Refers to industrial energy depth for manufacturing employees (Col. 1 ÷ Col. 5).

Column 16
Refers to manufacturing energy depth (Col. 2 ÷ Col. 5).

Column 17
Refers to manufacturing capital stock (Col. 18 ÷ Table 1, Col. 4).

Column 18
Refers to share of manufacturing in total capital stock. Derived from [98], which shows total and manufacturing capital stock data in constant 1972 dollars.

Column 19
Refers to industrial capital intensity (Table 1, Col. 4 ÷ Col. 1).

Column 20
Refers to manufacturing capital intensity (Col. 17 ÷ Col. 2).

TABLE 9: FUEL COSTS AND PRICES

Columns 1-5
Refers to current dollar costs of production at well head or mine head.
　1880-1955 [84, Table XXXIII].
　1960-1975 [99, p. 89].

Columns 6-10
Refers to current dollar production costs for each year in relation to their costs in 1973. Derived from data in Columns 1-5.

Column 11
Refers to overall current dollar production-cost index for all fuels. Derived by weighting each fuel production-cost index by its share of total fuel production.

Columns 12-14
Refers to wholesale price index: 1973 = 100 [97].

Columns 15-20
Refers to index of real (constant dollar) fuel-production costs. Derived by dividing Columns 6-11 by Column 12.

Columns 21-22
Refers to index of real (constant dollar) energy prices. Derived by dividing Cols. 13-14 by Col. 12.

Columns 23-24
Refers to a weighted composite of fossil-fuel costs at point of production in current-year energy prices and in 1958 prices [99].

Column 25
Refers to the total U.S. expenditure on fossil fuels in 1958 prices.
    1880-1940: Col. 4 times Table 1, Col. 1.
    1950-1975: Col. 2 times gross energy consumption as shown in
            Table 2, Col. 1. (Note: this implicitly includes hydro
            and nuclear power at the composite fossil fuel price.)

Column 26
Refers to the proportion of national output spent on fossil fuels.
    1880-1949 [84, Table XIX].
    1950-1975: Col. 3 divided by Table 1, Col. 1.

TABLE 10: SOURCES OF ENERGY CONSUMPTION

Annual Growth Rates:
Growth rates for each variable except end-use energy intensity were derived from the basic data in Tables 1, 2, 3.
    The aggregate energy-intensity growth rate is obtained from the

change in the ratio of overall energy consumption to national output. Therefore, the energy-intensity growth rates for each end-use sector need to be weighted by the sector's share of total energy consumption if the sum of the sector intensity growth rates is to equal the overall intensity growth. The residential plus commercial energy intensity is derived as the ratio of energy consumption in that sector to personal expenditures; the transportation sector energy intensity is the ratio of transportation energy use to personal expenditures; the industrial sector energy intensity is the ratio of industrial energy consumption to income produced by the industrial sector.

If the growth rates of these sector energy intensities are weighted by their shares of energy consumption they will not total to the overall energy-intensity growth rate. This is because, in addition to the within sector intensity changes, there is a product-mix shift between sectors. Thus, if the shift is from more to less energy-intensive goods and services the overall energy-intensity decline will be greater than the decline registered by adding the sector-weighted energy intensities. Our approximation of this product-mix shift is the difference between the overall intensity growth and the sum of the sectors growth. This arbitrary procedure, therefore, would allocate all errors in the estimates of the specific energy intensities to the product mix shift.

Percent of Energy Consumption Growth Rate:
These data show the relative contribution to changes in energy consumption that were made by each variable. They are derived by taking the ratio of the rate of growth for each variable to the rate of growth in energy consumption.

Table 1. Economic Indicators ($1972)

	GNP	Popula-tion	Employ-ment	Capital Stock	Business Invest.	Investment Share of GNP	GNP per Capita	GNP per Employee	Capital Stock per Employee	Employ-ment per Capita	GNP per Capital Stock
	Billion	Millions	Millions	Billion	Billion	%	$	$	$	%	%
	1	2	3	4	5	6	7	8	9	10	11
1850	14.4	23.3	5.9	n.a.	n.a.	n.a.	618	2441	n.a.	.253	n.a.
1860	23.0	31.5	8.1	n.a.	n.a.	n.a.	729	2834	n.a.	.251	n.a.
1870	27.9	39.9	9.9	n.a.	n.a.	n.a.	699	2817	n.a.	.248	n.a.
1880	56.5	50.3	12.8	84.8	n.a.	n.a.	1123	4414	6625	.255	.666
1890	77.4	63.1	18.6	134.7	18.3	.237	1226	4161	7242	.295	.575
1900	112.8	76.1	22.5	234.5	20.1	.178	1482	5013	10422	.296	.481
1910	166.8	92.4	28.8	354.3	29.2	.175	1805	5792	12302	.312	.471
1920	216.5	106.5	31.9	477.8	24.9	.115	2033	6786	14978	.300	.453
1929	308.2	121.8	35.9	623.8	40.1	.130	2530	8585	17376	.295	.495
1930	277.8	123.2	33.8	633.2	32.8	.118	2255	8219	18733	.274	.439
1940	343.9	132.1	38.3	576.5	28.5	.083	2603	8979	15052	.290	.597
1947	468.3	144.1	47.5	618.1	48.9	.117	3250	9858	13012	.330	.758
1950	533.5	152.3	49.1	693.6	50.0	.094	3503	10865	14126	.322	.769
1955	654.8	165.9	54.9	830.2	61.2	.100	3947	11927	15122	.331	.789
1960	736.8	180.7	57.1	963.9	66.0	.097	4077	12904	16881	.316	.764
1966	981.0	196.6	66.1	1193.1	106.1	.109	4990	14841	18050	.336	.822
1970	1093.7	204.9	71.6	1421.6	117.0	.107	5337	15275	19855	.349	.769
1973	1233.4	210.4	75.9	1594.3	131.3	.112	5862	16250	21005	.361	.774
1975	1202.1	213.4	73.6	1701.7	111.4	.095	5633	16332	23121	.345	.706
1977	1337.5	216.8	78.2	1800.1			6169	17104	23019	.361	.743

Table 2.   Energy Indicators (Quads BTU)

	Gross Energy Input	Net Energy Input	Conversion Efficiency	Gross Energy Consumption of:					Domestic Production of:					
				Wood	Coal	Oil	Gas	Hydro and Nuclear	Total	Wood	Coal	Oil	Gas	Hydro plus Nuclear
	1	2	3	4	5	6	7	8	9	10	11	12	13	14
1850	2.4	2.4	100.0	2.1	.2	—	—	—	2.4	2.1	0.2	—	—	—
1860	3.2	n.a.	n.a.	2.6	.5	—	—	—	3.2	2.6	.6	—	—	—
1870	4.0	n.a.	n.a.	2.9	1.1	—	—	—	4.0	2.9	1.0	—	—	—
1880	5.0	5.0	n.a.	2.9	2.1	—	—	—	5.1	2.9	2.1	0.2	—	—
1890	7.0	6.8	97.1	2.5	4.0	0.1	0.3	0.1	7.1	2.5	4.1	.3	0.3	—
1900	9.6	n.a.	n.a.	2.0	6.8	.2	.3	.2	9.9	2.0	7.0	.4	.3	0.3
1910	16.6	15.9	95.8	1.8	12.7	1.0	.5	.5	17.1	1.8	13.1	1.2	.5	.5
1920	21.4	20.0	93.5	1.6	15.5	2.6	.8	.8	23.0	1.6	17.2	2.6	.8	.7
1929	25.1	23.4	93.2	1.5	15.4	5.3	2.1	.9	26.2	1.5	15.9	5.8	2.1	.8
1930	23.7	22.1	93.2	1.5	13.6	5.7	2.2	.8	23.6	1.5	14.0	5.2	2.1	.8
1940	25.2	23.3	92.5	1.4	12.5	7.5	3.0	.9	26.5	1.4	13.4	7.8	3.0	.9
1947	33.0	29.2	88.5	—	15.5	10.8	5.0	1.5	35.1	—	18.0	10.8	5.0	1.3
1950	34.0	29.7	87.3	—	12.9	12.7	6.7	1.6	30.4	—	14.6	11.5	6.8	1.4
1955	39.7	34.3	86.4	—	11.7	16.3	10.2	1.5	39.1	—	12.8	14.5	10.5	1.4
1960	44.6	38.2	85.7	—	10.1	20.1	12.7	1.7	41.6	—	11.2	14.7	14.1	1.6
1966	56.4	47.6	84.7	—	12.5	24.4	17.4	2.1	51.9	—	13.8	16.9	19.0	2.1
1970	67.1	56.0	83.0	—	12.9	29.5	22.0	2.9	62.0	—	15.2	19.8	24.2	2.8
1973	74.6	61.2	82.0	—	13.3	34.9	22.5	3.9	61.7	—	14.4	18.8	24.8	3.2
1975	70.6	56.4	79.9	—	12.8	32.7	19.9	5.0	61.3	—	14.7	18.6	23.7	3.5
1977	75.9	60.0	79.1	—	14.3	37.0	19.6	5.1	n.a.	n.a.	n.a.	n.a.	n.a.	n.a.

Table 3. Energy/Economy Relationships

	Gross Energy Consumption Per:				Net Energy Per Capita	Capital Stock Per Energy	Net Energy Per GNP
	Capita	GNP	Capital Stock	Employee			
	(Million BTU Per Person)	*(Thous. BTU Per 1972 Dollar)*	*(Thous. BTU Per 1972 Dollar)*	*(Million BTU Per Employee)*	*(Million BTU Per Person)*	*($1972 Per Million BTU)*	*(Thous. BTU Per $1972)*
	1	*2*	*3*	*4*	*5*	*6*	*7*
1850	103.0	166.7	n.a.	406.8	n.a.	n.a.	167.1
1860	101.5	138.1	n.a.	395.1	n.a.	n.a.	n.a.
1870	100.3	142.0	n.a.	404.0	n.a.	n.a.	n.a.
1880	99.4	88.5	59.0	390.6	99.4	17.0	88.5
1890	111.0	90.4	52.0	376.3	n.a.	19.2	87.9
1900	126.1	85.2	38.6	426.7	n.a.	25.9	n.a.
1910	179.6	99.5	46.9	576.4	n.a.	21.3	95.3
1920	200.9	98.8	44.8	670.8	187.8	22.3	92.5
1929	206.1	81.4	40.2	699.2	192.1	24.9	75.9
1930	192.3	85.3	37.4	701.2	179.4	26.7	79.5
1940	190.7	73.3	43.7	658.0	176.4	22.9	67.8
1947	229.0	70.5	53.4	694.7	202.8	18.7	62.2
1950	223.2	63.2	46.7	692.5	194.8	21.3	55.2
1955	239.3	60.6	47.8	723.1	206.7	20.9	51.7
1960	246.8	60.5	46.3	781.1	211.5	21.6	51.7
1966	286.9	57.5	47.3	853.3	242.1	21.2	48.0
1970	327.5	61.4	45.5	937.2	273.3	21.2	50.9
1973	355.0	60.5	46.8	984.2	290.9	21.4	48.2
1975	330.8	58.7	41.5	959.2	264.5	24.1	46.9
1977	350.1	56.7	42.2	970.6	276.9	23.7	44.8

Table 4.   Sector Purchases by Fuel Source (Quad BTU)

	Household and Commercial Purchases							Industry Purchases						
	Coal	Gas	Petro-leum	Wood	Primary Fuel Consumption	Electricity Purchased	Total Energy Inputs	Coal	Gas	Petro-leum	Wood	Primary Fuel Consumption	Electricity Purchased	Total Energy Inputs
	1	2	3	4	5	6	7	1	2	3	4	5	6	7
1880	0.4	—	—	2.8	3.2	—	3.2	1.2	—	—	0.1	1.3	—	1.3
1920	3.6	0.3	0.2	1.6	5.7	0.2	5.9	7.4	0.5	1.0	—	8.9	0.1	9.0
1930	3.8	.4	1.0	1.5	6.7	.2	6.8	6.1	1.8	.7	—	8.6	.2	8.8
1940	3.4	.7	1.4	1.4	6.9	.3	7.2	5.5	2.3	1.6	—	9.4	.2	9.6
1947	3.4	1.1	2.3	—	6.8	.4	7.1	7.3	3.0	2.5	—	12.8	.5	13.3
1950	2.9	1.6	3.0	—	7.7	.5	8.1	6.0	3.7	2.7	—	12.4	.6	12.9
1955	1.7	2.8	4.0	—	8.8	.9	9.4	5.7	4.9	3.4	—	14.1	1.0	15.1
1960	1.0	4.3	4.9	—	10.2	1.3	11.4	4.6	6.3	3.7	—	14.6	1.3	15.9
1966	0.6	5.9	5.8	—	12.4	2.1	14.5	5.4	8.2	4.4	—	18.0	1.8	19.8
1970	0.4	7.1	6.5	—	14.0	3.0	17.0	4.9	10.2	5.2	—	20.4	2.2	22.6
1973	0.3	7.6	7.1	—	15.0	3.5	18.5	4.4	10.5	6.4	—	21.3	2.3	23.8
1975	0.3	7.7	6.1	—	14.1	3.5	17.6	3.8	8.4	6.0	—	18.2	2.3	20.5
1977	0.3	7.5	7.1	—	14.9	3.9	18.8	3.7	8.3	6.9	—	18.9	2.6	21.5

	Transportation Purchases				Total Energy Inputs	Miscellaneous Primary Fuel Consumption	Electric Utility Purchases					
	Coal	Gas	Petroleum	Primary Fuel Consumption			Coal	Gas	Petroleum	Hydro and Nuclear	Primary Fuel Consumption	Conversion Loss
	1	2	3	5	7	5	1	2	3	4	5	8
1880	0.5	—	—	—	0.5	—	0.5	—	—	—	—	—
1920	3.9	—	1.2	5.1	5.1	—	.8	—	0.1	0.8	1.7	1.4
1930	2.7	—	3.8	6.5	6.5	—	1.0	—	.2	.8	2.0	1.6
1940	2.3	—	4.3	6.6	6.6	0.4	1.3	—	.2	.9	2.4	1.9
1947	3.0	—	5.8	8.8	8.8	.5	2.1	.4	.5	1.3	4.3	3.8
1950	1.7	0.1	6.8	8.6	8.6	.6	2.2	.6	.7	1.4	5.0	4.3
1955	.5	.3	9.1	9.8	9.8	.7	3.5	1.2	.5	1.4	6.6	5.4
1960	—	.4	10.4	10.8	10.8	.6	4.2	1.8	.6	1.7	8.3	6.4
1966	—	.6	12.8	13.3	13.3	.2	6.3	2.7	.9	2.1	12.1	8.8
1970	—	.7	15.6	16.3	16.3	.2	7.2	4.0	2.1	2.7	16.2	11.1
1973	—	.7	17.9	18.6	18.7	.2	8.6	3.7	3.7	3.9	19.6	13.7
1975	—	.6	17.5	18.1	18.2	.3	8.7	3.2	3.2	5.0	20.0	14.2
1977	—	.5	19.1	19.7	19.8	.3	10.1	4.0	3.3	5.1	22.5	15.9

Table 5.   Nonfuel Uses of Energy (Quads BTU)

	Fossil Fuels			Nonenergy Uses, by:		Nonenergy Uses, from:		
	Total	For Energy	For Non-energy	H.H. Comm.	Industry	Coal	Oil	Gas
	1	2	3	4	5	6	7	8
1947	31.7	30.3	1.4	0.3	1.1	0.1	0.8	0.5
1950	32.6	31.2	1.4	.4	1.0	.1	.9	.4
1955	38.3	36.5	1.8	.6	1.2	.1	1.3	.4
1960	42.9	40.7	2.2	.7	1.5	.1	1.7	.4
1966	54.3	51.5	2.8	.9	1.9	.1	2.4	.3
1970	64.2	60.3	4.0	1.1	2.9	.2	3.1	.7
1973	70.7	66.2	4.5	1.3	3.2	.1	3.7	.7
1974	68.2	63.6	4.4	1.2	3.2	.1	3.6	.7
1975	65.6	61.2	4.2	1.1	3.1	.1	3.4	.7

Table 6. Foreign Trade in Energy

	Imports (Quads BTU)					Exports (Quads BTU)					Net Trade: Imports less Exports				
	Total	Crude	Petroleum Products	Gas	Coal	Total	Crude	Petroleum Products	Gas	Coal	Total	Crude	Petroleum Products	Gas	Coal
	1	2	3	4	5	6	7	8	9	10	11	12	13	14	15
1947	1.0	0.6	0.4	—	—	3.0	0.3	0.7	—	2.0	−2.0	0.3	−0.3	—	−2.0
1950	1.8	1.0	.8	—	—	1.4	.2	.4	—	.8	.4	.8	.4	—	−.8
1955	2.8	1.7	1.1	—	—	2.3	.1	.7	—	1.5	.5	1.6	.4	—	−1.5
1960	4.1	2.1	1.8	0.2	—	1.5	—	.4	—	1.0	2.6	2.1	1.4	0.1	−1.0
1966	6.1	2.5	3.1	.5	—	1.8	—	.4	—	1.4	4.3	2.5	2.7	.5	−1.4
1970	8.2	2.7	4.7	.8	—	2.6	—	.5	0.1	2.0	5.6	2.7	4.2	.8	−2.0
1973	14.6		13.5	1.1	—	2.1	—	.5	.1	1.5	12.5		13.0	1.0	−1.5
1974	14.2		13.1	1.0	0.1	2.2	—	.5	.1	1.7	11.9		12.6	.9	−1.5
1975	13.8		12.7	1.0	.1	2.1	—	.5	.1	1.9	11.4		12.3	.9	−1.8

Table 6. (cont.)

| | Import Percent of Consumption | | | Export Percent of Domestic Production | | | | Production as Percent of Consumption | | | |
	Total Imports	Crude Plus Petroleum Products	Gas	Coal	Total Exports	Crude Plus Petroleum Products	Gas	Coal	Total	Crude Plus Petroleum Products	Gas	Coal
	16	17	18	19	20	21	22	23	24	25	26	27
1947	3.0	9.3	–	–	9	9	–	11	106	100	100	116
1948	3.5	10.1	–	–	6	7	–	8	106	98	102	115
1949	4.4	12.2	–	–	5	7	–	7	97	93	104	100
1950	5.3	14.2	–	–	5	5	–	5	89	91	101	113
1955	7.1	17.2	–	–	6	6	–	12	98	89	103	109
1960	9.2	19.4	1.6	–	4	3	–	9	93	73	111	111
1966	10.8	23.0	2.9	–	3	2	–	10	92	69	109	110
1970	12.2	25.1	3.6	–	4	3	0.04	15	92	67	110	120
1973	19.5	38.7	4.8	–	3	2	.04	10	89	63	109	111
1974	19.5	39.1	4.6	0.8	4	3	.04	12	83	53	110	111
1975	19.5	38.8	5.0	.8	–	–	–	–	–	–	–	–

Table 7.   Selected Data for Economic Sectors (monetary data in constant $1958)

	1880	1890	1910	1920	1929	1930	1940	1947	1955	1960	1966	1973	1975
Personal Consumption Expenditures													
Total (Billion $1958)	21.2	31.7	74.2	93.1	139.6	130.4	155.7	206.3	274.2	316.1	418.1	546.4	546.6
Durables	n.a.	n.a.	n.a.	n.a.	16.3	12.9	16.7	24.7	43.2	44.9	71.7	109.6	99.1
Nondurables	n.a.	n.a.	n.a.	n.a.	69.3	65.9	84.6	108.3	131.7	149.6	87.0	226.6	224.7
Services	n.a.	n.a.	n.a.	n.a.	54.0	51.5	54.4	73.4	99.3	121.6	159.4	212.6	221.8
National Income Produced													
Total (Billion $1958)	28.1	41.0	92.1	122.7	171.5	152.9	186.0	266.7	363.2	402.1	546.1	683.0	659.4
Goods	14.6	21.9	41.0	48.2	71.8	60.0	75.1	122.0	158.0	164.1	222.2	256.2	233.2
Manufacturing	4.3	7.9	18.7	26.2	43.3	37.1	50.8	79.8	115.0	122.0	168.5	182.0	166.7
Agriculture, Fisheries	8.5	10.6	14.2	15.1	16.8	13.0	14.1	25.3	17.7	16.4	20.0	30.2	23.9
Mining, Construction	1.8	3.4	8.1	6.9	11.7	9.9	10.2	16.9	25.3	25.7	33.7	44.0	42.6
Nongoods	13.5	19.1	51.1	74.5	99.6	92.9	110.9	144.8	205.2	238.0	323.9	426.8	426.2
Transportation & Utilities	1.1	2.8	8.4	13.2	13.0	11.4	11.4	15.5	17.4	17.7	21.9	26.6	24.1
Services & other nongoods	12.4	16.3	42.7	61.3	86.6	81.5	119.5	129.3	187.8	220.3	302.0	400.2	402.1
Services	2.6	3.1	9.7	12.5	17.4	17.0	20.3	24.3	37.1	43.2	62.6	87.8	88.8
Other nongoods	9.8	13.2	33.0	48.8	69.2	64.5	79.2	105.0	150.7	177.1	239.4	312.4	313.3
Persons Employed													
Total (Millions)	17.2	21.5	33.0	37.9	41.8	39.8	42.0	51.8	57.0	59.8	68.0	80.3	80.4
Goods	13.2	15.5	21.5	23.2	23.8	22.3	22.8	26.4	26.9	25.9	27.1	28.2	25.9
Manufacturing	2.9	4.2	7.8	10.7	10.7	9.6	11.0	15.5	16.9	16.8	19.2	20.1	18.3
Agriculture, Fisheries	9.4	10.1	11.3	10.4	10.5	10.3	9.6	7.9	6.4	5.5	4.0	3.5	3.4
Mining, Construction	0.9	1.2	2.4	2.1	2.6	2.4	2.2	3.0	3.6	3.6	3.9	4.6	4.2
Nongoods	4.0	6.0	11.5	14.7	18.0	17.5	19.2	25.5	30.1	33.9	40.9	52.1	54.5

Table 7. (cont.)

Transportation & Utilities	1.0	1.7	3.4	4.3	3.9	3.7	3.0	4.2	4.1	4.0	4.2	4.6	4.5
Services & other nongoods	3.0	4.3	8.1	10.4	14.1	13.8	16.2	21.3	26.0	29.9	36.7	47.5	50.0
Services	0.8	1.3	2.4	3.1	3.4	3.4	3.7	5.1	6.3	2.4	9.5	13.0	14.0
Other nongoods	2.2	3.0	5.7	7.3	10.7	10.4	12.5	16.2	19.7	22.5	27.2	34.5	36.0
Income Produced Per Employee													
Total ($1958)	1634	1907	2791	3237	4103	3842	4428	5149	6372	6724	8031	8505	8201
Goods	1106	1413	1907	2078	3017	2691	3293	4621	5874	6335	8200	9085	9004
Manufacturing	1483	1881	2397	2449	4047	3864	4618	5148	6805	7262	8726	9055	9110
Agriculture, Fisheries	904	1050	1256	1452	1600	1262	1469	3203	2765	2987	5000	8629	7029
Mining, Construction	2000	2833	3375	3281	4500	4125	4636	5633	7028	7139	8641	9565	10143
Nongoods	3375	3183	4443	5068	5533	5308	5776	5678	6817	7021	7919	8192	7820
Transportation & Utilities	1100	1647	2471	3070	3333	3081	3800	3690	4243	4425	5214	5783	5355
Services & other nongoods	4133	3791	5272	5894	6142	5905	5486	6070	5889	5838	6589	6754	6343
Services	3250	2385	4042	4032	5117	5000	6336	4765	7650	7871	8801	9055	8703
Other nongoods	4455	4400	5789	6685	6467	6202	6142	6481	7223	7368	8229	8425	8042
Energy Intensities (000 BTU Per $1958)													
Gross Energy Consumption Per GNP	134.0	137.0	150.6	149.7	123.2	129.2	110.9	106.4	90.6	91.4	85.7	89.0	87.6
Gross Energy Consumption Per Nat. Income	177.9	170.7	180.2	174.4	146.3	155.0	135.5	123.7	109.3	110.9	103.3	109.2	107.1
Nonindustrial Energy Consumption ÷ Personal Expenditure	174.5	138.8	113.2	118.1	94.5	87.6	88.6	77.1	70.0	70.2	66.5	68.1	66.2
Industrial Energy Consumption ÷ National Income	46.3	58.5	81.4	73.3	59.5	57.5	51.6	49.9	41.6	39.5	36.8	34.6	31.1
Energy Conversion Loss ÷ National Income	—	4.9	7.6	11.4	9.9	10.5	10.2	14.2	14.9	15.9	16.1	19.6	20.8
Industrial Energy Consumption ÷ Manufacturing National Income	302.3	303.8	401.1	343.5	235.6	237.2	189.0	166.6	131.3	130.3	119.3	129.7	123.0

National Income Produced ÷ GNP (%)	75	80	84	86	84	83	82	86	83	82	83	81	82
Full-Time Equivalent Employees ÷ Persons Employed (%)	74	87	87	84	86	85	91	92	96	95	97	94	91
Income Produced Per Persons Employed ÷ GNP Per Full-Time Equivalent Employees (%)	56	69	73	72	72	71	75	79	80	79	81	77	75

Table 8. Manufacturing Sector (monetary data in constant $1958)

	Energy Consumption			Persons Employed			National Income			Energy Intensity		
										Industrial Energy Consumption Per		Mfg. Energy Consumption Per Mfg. Nat. Income
	Industrial	Manufacturing	Mfg. ÷ Industrial	Total	Manufacturing	Mfg. ÷ Total	Total	Manufacturing	Mfg. ÷ Total	Total Nat. Income	Mfg. Nat. Income	
	(Quads BTU %)			(Millions)		(%)	(Billion $1958)		(%)	(000 BTU Per $1958)		
	1	2	3	4	5	6	7	8	9	10	11	12
1880	1.3	n.a.	n.a.	17.2	2.9	16.9	28.1	4.3	15.3	46.3	302.3	n.a.
1890	2.4	n.a.	n.a.	21.5	4.2	19.5	41.0	7.9	19.3	58.5	303.8	n.a.
1910	7.5	n.a.	n.a.	33.0	7.8	23.6	92.1	18.7	20.3	81.4	401.1	n.a.
1920	9.0	n.a.	n.a.	37.9	10.7	28.2	122.7	26.2	21.4	73.3	343.5	n.a.
1929	10.2	n.a.	n.a.	41.8	10.7	25.6	171.5	43.3	25.2	59.5	235.6	n.a.
1930	8.8	n.a.	n.a.	39.8	9.6	24.1	152.9	37.1	24.3	57.5	237.2	n.a.
1940	9.6	n.a	n.a	42.0	11.0	26.2	186.0	50.8	27.3	51.6	189.0	n.a.
1947	13.3	10.5	78.9	51.8	15.5	29.9	266.8	79.8	29.9	49.9	166.7	131.6
1950	12.9	10.8	83.4	52.4	15.2	29.0	301.1	95.0	31.6	42.8	135.8	108.5
1955	15.1	13.5	89.5	57.0	16.9	29.6	363.2	115.0	31.7	41.6	131.3	117.4
1960	15.9	13.9	87.7	59.8	16.8	28.1	402.1	122.0	30.3	39.5	130.3	113.9
1966	20.1	17.2	85.8	68.0	19.2	28.2	546.1	168.5	30.9	36.8	119.3	102.1
1970	22.4	20.3	90.5	74.1	19.4	26.2	592.1	160.9	27.2	37.8	139.2	126.2
1973	23.6	21.7	92.1	80.3	20.1	25.0	683.0	182.0	26.6	34.6	129.7	119.2
1974	22.8	n.a.	n.a.	81.9	20.0	24.4	666.1	171.7	25.8	34.2	132.8	n.a.
1975	20.5	n.a.	n.a.	80.4	18.3	22.8	659.4	166.7	25.3	31.1	123.0	n.a.

	Energy Depth				Capital Stock		Capital Intensity	
	Industrial Energy Consumption Per			Mfg. Energy Consumption Per Mfg. Employ.		Manufacturing + Total	Total Capital Stock Per Industrial Energy Consumption	Mfg. Capital Stock Per Mfg. Energy Consumption
	FTE Employ.	Total Persons Employ.	Mfg. Persons Employ.		Manufacturing			
	13	14	15	16	17	18	19	20
	(Million BTU Per Employee)				Billion $1958	(%)	($1958 Per Million BTU)	
1880	102	76	448	n.a.	n.a.	n.a.	n.a.	n.a.
1890	129	112	571	n.a.	n.a.	n.a.	n.a.	n.a.
1910	260	227	962	n.a.	n.a.	n.a.	n.a.	n.a.
1920	282	237	841	n.a.	n.a.	n.a.	n.a.	n.a.
1929	284	244	953	n.a.	n.a.	n.a.	n.a.	n.a.
1930	260	221	917	n.a.	n.a.	n.a.	n.a.	n.a.
1940	251	229	873	n.a.	n.a.	n.a.	n.a.	n.a.
1947	280	257	858	677	113.8	26.6	407	10.8
1950	263	246	849	711	128.9	26.8	445	11.9
1955	275	265	893	799	155.2	27.1	424	11.5
1960	278	266	946	827	175.2	26.4	477	12.6
1966	300	296	1047	896	202.0	24.7	475	11.7
1970	316	302	1155	1046	233.6	24.0	480	11.5
1973	311	294	1174	1080	248.6	22.8	502	11.5
1974	299	278	1140	n.a.	256.2	22.6	n.a.	n.a.
1975	280	255	1120	n.a.	262.5	22.5	n.a.	n.a.

Table 9. Fuel Costs and Prices

	Fuel Production Costs: Current $					Current $ Production-Cost Indexes: 1973 = 100						Nominal Price Indexes: 1973 = 100		
	Bituminous Coal ($ Per Net Ton)	Anthracite Coal ($ Per Net Ton)	Crude Oil ($ Per Barrel)	Natural Gas (Cents Per Cubic Foot)	Natural Gas Liquids (Cents Per Gallon)	Bituminous Coal	Anthracite Coal	Crude Oil	Natural Gas	Natural Gas Liquids	Composite Fuels	All Commodities	Fuels and Power	Electric Power Only
	1	2	3	4	5	6	7	8	9	10	11	12	13	14
1880	1.25	1.47	0.94	–	–	.13	.11	.24	–	–	.14	.26	.25	–
1890	0.99	1.43	0.77	7.0	–	.11	.11	.20	.31	–	.12	.22	.20	–
1910	1.12	1.90	0.61	5.3	–	.12	.14	.16	.24	–	.13	.27	.25	–
1921	2.89	5.00	1.73	10.1	13.7	.31	.38	.44	.45	.87	.34	.39	.52	1.36
1929	1.78	5.22	1.27	8.2	7.1	.19	.40	.33	.37	.97	.24	.37	.44	1.27
1930	1.70	5.11	1.19	7.6	5.8	.18	.39	.31	.34	.79	.23	.33	.42	1.32
1940	1.91	3.99	1.02	4.5	2.9	.21	.30	.26	.20	.40	.23	.30	.38	1.02
1947	4.16	7.22	1.93	6.0	5.3	.45	.55	.50	.27	.73	.44	.57	.57	.88
1955	4.50	7.86	2.77	10.4	5.2	.48	.60	.71	.47	.71	.55	.65	.68	.83
1960	4.69	7.82	2.88	14.4	5.7	.50	.59	.74	.65	.78	.64	.70	.72	.78
1966	4.53	8.08	2.88	16.1	5.3	.49	.61	.74	.72	.73	.63	.74	.73	.77
1973	9.30	13.21	3.89	22.3	7.3	1.00	1.00	1.00	1.00	1.00	1.00	1.00	1.00	1.00
1974	17.18	21.87	6.74	31.3	12.4	1.85	1.66	1.73	1.40	1.70	1.61	1.19	1.55	1.26
1975	20.46	24.99	8.00	44.9	15.6	2.20	1.89	2.06	2.01	2.14	2.07	1.30	1.83	1.50

	Real Production Cost Indexes: 1973 = 100						Real Energy Price Indexes		Fossil Fuels & (Cents Per Million BTU)		Total Fuel Cost	Fuel Cost Share of GNP (%)
	Bitu-minous	Anthra-cite	Crude Oil	Natural Gas	Natural Gas Liquids	Compo-site Fuels	Fuels and Power	Elec-tric Power Only	Current Prices	1958 Prices	Billion $1958	
	15	16	17	18	19	20	21	22	23	24	25	26
1880	.50	.42	.92	—	—	.53	.96	—	n.a.	n.a.	0.4	1.1
1890	.51	.51	.93	1.44	—	.55	.94	—	n.a.	n.a.	0.8	1.6
1910	.44	.52	.59	.89	—	.48	.93	—	n.a.	n.a.	2.4	2.2
1921	.84	1.03	1.19	1.22	5.05	.92	1.41	3.67	n.a.	n.a.	4.2	3.3
1929	.52	1.10	.90	1.01	2.66	.68	1.20	3.43	n.a.	n.a.	5.3	2.6
1930	.54	1.18	.94	1.03	2.39	.69	1.27	4.00	n.a.	n.a.	5.1	2.8
1940	.70	1.00	.86	.66	1.33	.76	1.06	3.40	n.a.	n.a.	5.7	2.5
1947	.79	.97	.88	.48	1.29	.77	1.00	1.54	n.a.	n.a.	9.0	2.9
1955	.74	.92	1.09	.72	1.09	.85	1.04	1.28	28.5	30.7	12.3	2.8
1960	.71	.84	1.05	.92	1.11	.91	1.02	1.11	29.8	28.7	12.8	2.6
1966	.66	.82	1.00	.97	.98	.85	.98	1.04	29.1	25.0	14.1	2.1
1973	1.00	1.00	1.00	1.00	1.00	1.00	1.00	1.00	41.9	26.2	19.5	2.3
1974	1.56	1.40	1.46	1.18	1.43	1.36	1.30	1.06	75.7	42.9	31.2	3.8
1975	1.70	1.46	1.59	1.55	1.65	1.60	1.41	1.15	87.9	46.0	32.5	4.0

Table 10. Sources of Energy Consumption in the Major Eras

	Average Annual Growth Rate (%)				
	The Century 1880 to 1977	The Wood/Home Heating Period 1850 to 1880	The Coal/Mechanizing Period 1880 to 1920	The Liquid Fuel/Industrializing Period 1920 to 1955	The Power/Servicing Period 1955 to 1977
Population	1.52	2.60	1.89	1.27	1.22
Employment Participation	0.36	0.03	0.41	0.28	0.40
Capital Productivity	0.11	2.10	-0.95	1.60	-0.27
Capital Intensity	0.34		0.68	-0.19	0.57
Energy Depth	0.94	-0.14	1.36	0.21	1.35
Energy Intensity	-0.46	-2.09	0.28	-1.39	-0.30
Residential plus commercial	-0.56	n.a.	-0.81	-0.45	0.15
Industrial	0.06	n.a.	0.70	-0.68	-0.11
Transportation	0.07	n.a.	0.38	-0.28	-0.08
Product Mix Shift	-0.03	n.a.	0.01	0.03	-0.26
Energy Consumption	2.84	2.48	3.70	1.78	3.00
Per Capita Energy Consumption	1.31	-0.12	1.77	0.50	1.75
Labor Productivity	1.41	1.99	1.08	1.62	1.65
GNP	3.32	4.66	3.42	3.21	3.30
Capital Stock	3.20	n.a.	4.42	1.59	3.58
Employment	1.88	2.61	2.31	1.56	1.62

Percent of Energy Consumption Growth Rate

	55%	105%	50%	70%	40%
Population	10	1	10	15	15
Employment Participation	5	⎫	−25	90	−10
Capital Productivity	10	⎬ 85	20	−10	20
Capital Intensity	10	−5	20	−10	20
Energy Depth	35	−85	40	15	45
Energy Intensity	−15		5	−80	−10
Residential plus commercial	−20	n.a.	−25	−25	5
Industrial	2	n.a.	20	−40	−5
Transportation	3	n.a.	10	−15	−3
Product Mix Shift	1	n.a.	0	0	−10
Energy Consumption	100	100	100	100	100

References

1. Abromovitz, Moses. "Economics of Growth." In *A Survey of Contemporary Economics*, ed. Bernard Haley. New York: Irwin, 1952.

2. Academy Forum. *Energy: Future Alternatives and Risks.* Cambridge, Mass.: Ballinger, 1974.

3. Allen, Edward, et al. *U.S. Energy and Economic Growth.* Oak Ridge: Institute for Energy Analysis, 1976.

4. Anderson, C., et al. *An Assessment of U.S. Energy Options for Project Independence.* Lawrence Livermore Laboratory. Springfield, Va.: National Technology Information Service, 1974.

5. Armstrong, Joe E., and Willis W. Harmon. *Plausibility of a Restricted Energy Use Scenario.* Stanford, Ca.: Stanford Research Institute, Center for the Study of Social Policy, 1975.

6. Aron, Raymond. *The Industrial Society.* New York: Praeger, 1967.

7. Barnett, Harold J. *Energy, Resources, and Growth.* St. Louis, Mo.: Department of Economics, Washington University, 1973.

8. Behling, David J., Jr., Robert Dullien, and Edward Hudson. *The Relationship of Energy Growth to Economic Growth under Alternative Energy Policies.* Upton, N.Y.: Brookhaven National Laboratory, 1976.

9. Bell, Daniel. *The Coming of Post-Industrial Society: A Venture in Social Forecasting.* New York: Basic Books, 1973.

10. Berndt, E.R., and D.O. Wood. "Technology Prices and the Derived Demand for Energy." *Review of Economics and Statistics*, August 1975, pp. 259-68.

11. Brubaker, Sterling. *In Command of Tomorrow: Resource and Environmental Strategies for Americans.* Baltimore: Johns Hopkins Press, 1975.

12. *Business Week.* "How OPEC's High Prices Strangle World Growth," December 20, 1976.

13. *Business Week.* "Will Energy Conservation Throttle Economic Growth?" April 25, 1977.

14. Carter, Anne P. "Energy, Environment, and Economic Growth." *Bell Journal of Economics*, Autumn 1974.
15. Chapman, Duane. "Energy Conservation, Employment and Income." Cornell University, February 1977 (draft, mimeo).
16. Chatterji, M., and P. Van Rompny, eds. *Energy, Regional Science and Public Policy*. International Conference on Regional Science, Energy and Environment, Louvain, 1975.
17. Chenery, Hollis, and Moises Syrquin. *Patterns of Development, 1950-1970*. New York: Oxford, 1975.
18. Clark, Colin. *Conditions of Economic Progress*. London: Macmillan, 1940.
19. Commoner, Barry, Howard Boksenbaum, and Michael Corr. *Energy and Human Welfare: A Critical Analysis*. 3 vols. New York: Macmillan, 1974.
20. Commoner, Barry. *The Poverty of Power*. New York: Knopf, 1976.
21. Crump, Lulie H. *Historical Fuels and Energy Consumption Data, 1960-1972: United States by States and Census Districts*. 2 vols. Washington, D.C.: Bureau of Mines, 1976.
22. *Daedelus*. "The Oil Crisis in Perspective." Fall 1975.
23. Daly, H.E. *Toward a Steady-State Economy*. San Francisco: W.H. Freeman, 1973.
24. Darmstadter, Joel, Joy Dunkerly, and Jack Alterman. *How Industrial Societies Use Energy*. Washington, D.C.: Resources for the Future, 1977.
25. Darmstadter, Joel, and Hans H. Landsberg. *The Economic Background of the Oil Crisis*. Reprint No. 123. Washington, D.C.: Resources for the Future, 1975.
26. David, Paul A., and Melvin W. Reder. *Nations and Households in Economic Growth: Essays in Honor of Moses Abramovitz*. New York: Academic Press, 1974.
27. Denison, Edward. *Why Growth Rates Differ: Postwar Experience in Nine Western Countries*. Washington, D.C.: Brookings Institution, 1974.
28. _____. *Accounting for United States Economic Growth, 1929-1969*. Washington, D.C.: Brookings Institution, 1974.
29. _____. "Classification of Sources of Growth." *Review of Income & Wealth*, Series 18, No. 1 (March 1972).
30. Dubin, Fred S. "Energy Management for Commercial Buildings." In *Proceedings* of the 1976 Summer Workshop, Lawrence Berkeley Lab., Univ. of California, May 1977.
31. Dupree, Walter, Jr., and John S. Corsentiono. *U.S. Energy Through the Year 2000*. Washington, D.C.: Bureau of Mines, 1975.
32. Ehrlich, Paul, and Anne Ehrlich. *The End of Affluence*. New York: Ballantine Books, 1975.
33. Energy Modeling Forum. *Energy and the Economy*. Vol. 1 and 2. Institute for Energy Studies, Stanford Univ., 1977.
34. Fisher, Anthony C. and Frederick M. Peterson. "The Environment in Economics: A Survey." *Journal of Economic Literature* 14 (March 1976).
35. Ford Foundation Energy Policy Project. *Time to Choose*. Cambridge, Mass.: Ballinger, 1974.

36. Foster Associates. *Energy Prices: 1960-73*. Cambridge, Mass.: Ballinger, 1975.

37. Fried, Edward, and Charles Schultze. *Higher Oil Prices and the World Economy*. Washington, D.C.: Brookings Institution, 1975.

38. Georgescu-Roegen, Nicholas. *The Entropy Law and the Economic Process*. Cambridge, Mass.: Harvard University Press, 1971 and 1973.

39. Gould, John Dennis. *Economic Growth in History*. New York: Barnes & Noble, 1972.

40. Goen, Richard, and Ronald White. *A Comparison of Energy Consumption between West Germany and the United States*. A Report for the U.S. Federal Energy Administration. Stanford: Stanford Research Institute, 1975.

41. Hahn, F.H. and P.C.O. Mathews. "The Theory of Economic Growth." *Economic Journal* 74 (Dec. 1964).

42. Hammond, Allen, William Metz, and Thomas Mauigh. *Energy and the Future*. Washington, D.C.: American Association for Advancement of Science, 1973.

43. Heilbroner, Robert. *An Inquiry into the Human Prospect*. New York: W.W. Norton, 1975.

44. Heller, Walter, ed. *Perspectives on Economic Growth*. New York: Random House, 1968.

45. Herendeen, R., and J. Tanaka. *Energy Cost of Living*. CAC Doc. No. 171. Urbana: Center for Advanced Computation, University of Illinois, 1975.

46. Herendeen, R., and Clark W. Bullard. *Energy Cost of Goods and Services, 1963 and 1967*. CAC Doc. No. 140. Urbana: Center for Advanced Computation, University of Illinois, 1974.

47. Hirschman, J. *Strategy of Economic Development*. New Haven: Yale University Press, 1960.

48. Hogan, William W., and Alan S. Manne. "Energy Economy Interactions: The Fable of the Elephant and the Rabbit." Stanford: Stanford University, January 1977 (draft mimeo).

49. Hollander, Jack, and Melvin K. Simmons. *Annual Review of Energy*. Vol. 1. Palo Alto: Annual Review, Inc., 1976.

50. Hudson, E.A., and D.W. Jorgenson. "U.S. Energy Policy and Economic Growth, 1975-2000," *Bell Journal of Economics* 5 (Autumn, 1974).

51. LaForce, V.C. ed. *No Time to Confuse*. San Francisco: Institute for Contemporary Studies, 1975.

52. Kendrick, John W. *Productivity Trends in the United States*. Princeton: Princeton University Press, 1961.

53. Khazzoom, J. Daniel. "A Perspective on Energy Modeling." Paper delivered at the Joint Energy Seminar of the Electric Power Research Institute and the Institute for the Energy Studies. Stanford: Stanford University, Institute for Energy Studies, March 1976.

54. King, M.A. "Economic Growth and Social Development—A Statistical Investigation." *Review of Income and Wealth* 20 (Sept. 1974):251-72 [St. John's College, Cambridge, England].

55. Knecht, R., and C. Bullard. *Direct Use of Energy in the U.S. Economy*. Tech. Memo No. 43. Urbana: University of Illinois, Center for Advanced Computation, 1975.

56. Kneese, Allen V., and Charles L. Schultze. *Pollution, Prices, and Public Policy*. Washington, D.C.: Brookings Institution, 1975.

57. Kuznets, Simon. *Economic Growth of Nations: Total Output and Production Structure*. Cambridge, Mass.: Harvard University Press, 1971.

58. Lovins, Amory B. "Energy Strategy: The Road Not Taken," *Foreign Affairs* (Fall 1976).

59. _____. *World Energy Strategies*. Cambridge, Mass.: Ballinger, 1975.

60. Macrakis, Michael S., ed. *Energy: Demand Conservation and Institutional Problems*. Cambridge, Mass.: M.I.T. Press, 1974.

61. Meadows, Dennis, et al. *Limits to Growth*. New York: Universe Books, 1972.

62. Mesarovic, Mihajlo, and Eduard Pestel. *Mankind at the Turning Point*. Second Report of the Club of Rome. New York: Dutton, 1974.

63. Meyers, John G., et al. *Energy Consumption in Manufacturing*. Cambridge, Mass.: Ballinger, 1974.

64. Miller, G. Tyler, Jr. *Energy and Environment: The Four Energy Crises*. Belmont, Calif.: Wadsworth, 1975.

65. Mishan, Edward J. *Technology and Growth*. New York: Praeger, 1970.

66. Mitchell, Edward J. *U.S. Energy Policy: A Primer*. National Energy Project. Washington, D.C.: American Institute for Public Policy Research, 1974.

67. Mobile Oil Corp. *Toward a National Energy Policy*. New York, 1974.

68. Moss, Milton, ed. *The Measurement of Economic and Social Performance*. New York: National Bureau of Economic Research, 1973.

69. Myrdal, Gunnar. *Rich Lands and Poor*. New York, Harper, 1958.

70. _____. "Growth and Social Justice." *World Development* 1 (Mar.-Apr. 1973):119-20.

71. Nadiri, M., Ishaq. "International Studies of Factor Inputs and Total Factor Productivity, A Brief Survey." *Review of Income and Wealth*, Series 18, no. 2 (June 1972).

72. Nadiri, Ishaq, "Theory and Measurement of Total Factor Productivity." *Journal of Economic Literature* 8, no. 4 (Dec. 1970), pp. 1137-1177.

73. National Academy of Science. *Energy Consumption Measurement: Data Needs for Public Policy*. Washington, D.C., 1977.

74. Nef, John V. "An Early Energy Crisis and its Consequences." *Scientific American*, Nov., 1977.

75. Newcombe, K. *A Brief History of Concepts of Energy and the Use of Energy by Humankind*. Human Ecology Group Wkg. Paper. Canberra, Australia: Australian National Univ., Centre for Resource and Environmental Studies, n.d.

76. OECD *Energy R&D*, Paris: OECD, 1975.

77. Olsen, Marvin E. *Conserving Energy by Changing Societal Goals*. Seattle: Battelle Human Affairs Research Centers, 1976.

78. Olson, Mancur. *The No Growth Society*. New York: Norton, 1974.

79. Paley Commission. *Resources for Freedom*. Vol. III: *Outlook for Energy Resources*. Washington, D.C.: USGPO, 1952.

80. Ross, M.H., and R.H. Williams. *Energy and Economic Growth*. Prepared for U.S. Congress Joint Economic Committee, June 7, 1976.

81. Searl, Milton. *Energy Modeling: Art Science and Practice.* Washington, D.C.: Resources for Future, 1976.

82. Schipper, Lee, and A.J. Lichtenberg. *Efficient Energy Use and Well-being: The Swedish Experience.* Rpt. Nos. LBL-4430 and ERG-76-89. Berkeley: University of California, Lawrence Berkeley Laboratory, 1976.

83. Schumacher, E.F. *Small Is Beautiful: Economics as if People Mattered.* New York: Harper, 1973.

84. Schurr, Netschert, et al. *Energy in the American Economy, 1850-1975.* Baltimore: Johns Hopkins Press, 1960.

85. Schurr, Sam, and Joel Darmstadter. "Some Observations on Energy and Economic Growth." Prepared for Oak Ridge Associated Universities Conference on Future Strategies for Energy Development, 1976.

86. Schurr, Sam, and Jacob Marschak. *Economic Aspects of Atomic Power: An Exploratory Study.* Published for the Cowles Commission. Princeton, N.J.: Princeton University Press, 1950.

87. Schurr, Sam. *Energy Economic Growth and the Environment.* Washington, D.C.: Resource for the Future, 1972.

88. Simmons, Henry. *The Economics of America's Energy Future.* Washington, D.C.: U.S. Energy Research and Development Admin., 1975.

89. Solow, Robert. "Economic Resources or Resources of Economics." *American Economic Review* 64 (March 1974):1-14.

90. _____. *Growth Theory An Exposition.* Oxford: Oxford University Press, 1970.

91. Starr, Chauncey. "Electricity Needs to the Year 2000 as Related to Employment, Income and Conservation." Testimony to Subcommittee on Energy Research, Development and Demonstration, House Committee on Science and Technology, Wash., D.C., Feb. 1976.

92. _____. "Energy, Power and Society." *Scientific American*, Sept. 1971.

93. Taylor, L.D. "The Demand for Electricity: A Survey." *Bell Journal of Economics* 6 (Spring 1975).

94. U.S. Congress, Joint Economic Committee. *U.S. Economic Growth from 1976 to 1986,*, Vol. 4: *Resources and Energy.* Washington, D.C.: USGPO, 1976.

95. U.S. Congress, House, Committee on Interstate & Foreign Commerce, Subcomm. on Energy & Power. *Energy Choices Facing the Nation and Their Long-Range Implications*, Pt. 1: *Middle- and Long-Term Energy Policies and Alternatives.* Serial No. 94-63. Washington, D.C.: USGPO, 1976.

96. U.S. Council of Economic Advisors. *Economic Report of the President, 1978.* Washington, D.C.: USGPO, 1978.

97. U.S. Department of Commerce. *Historical Statistics of the United States, Colonial Times to 1970.* Washington, D.C.: USGPO, 1975.

98. _____. *Survey of Current Business* 56 (April 1976).

99. U.S. Department of the Interior. *Energy Perspectives, 2.* Washington, D.C., USGPO, 1976.

100. U.S. ERDA. Report to Congress, 1976: *National Plan for Energy Research.* Vols. 1 and 2. Washington, D.C.: USGPO, 1976.

101. U.S. Federal Energy Administration. *The Nation's Energy Outlook.* Washington, D.C.: USGPO, 1976.

102. Williams, Robert. *Energy Conservation Papers.* Cambridge, Mass.: Ballinger, 1975.

103. U.S. Department of Energy. *Monthly Energy Review*, April 1978.

104. Gelb, Bernard A. *U.S. Energy Price and Consumption Changes in the Mid-1970's*, Information Bulletin No. 38, The Conference Board, 1978.

Index

About the Author

Sidney Sonenblum was research professor at UCLA when the basic research for this book was being done. His particular research interests relate to economic development, urban policy, government finance, information systems, and energy and the economy. He has pursued these interests in government agencies, at universities, and in the private sector. He is now an economic research consultant and lecturer at USC. His most recent publications include *Local Government Program Budgeting; Governing Urban America in the 1970's; Selecting Regional Information for Government Planning and Decisionmaking;* and *How Cities Provide Services.*